This book is presented to:

On: _____

By: _____

THE
PURPOSE
DRIVEN LIFE

DEVOTIONAL FOR KIDS

RICK WARREN

ZONDERKIDZ

The Purpose Driven Life Devotional for Kids
Copyright © 2015 by Rick Warren

ISBN 978-0-310-75046-8

This title is also available as a Zondervan ebook. Visit www.zondervan.com/ebooks.

Requests for information should be addressed to:

Zonderkidz, *3900 Sparks Drive SE, Grand Rapids, Michigan 49546*

The Scripture versions cited in this book are identified on pages 382-383, which hereby become part of this copyright page.

Cover design: Brand Navigation
Interior design: Denise Froehlich
Contributors: Andrea Vinley Jewell, Crystal Kupper, Elsa Kok Colopy, Greg Asimakoupoulos

Printed in China

15 16 17 18 19 20 21 22 23 24 /DHC/15 14 13 12 11 10 9 8 7 6 5 4 3 2 1

Table of Contents

The Purpose Driven Life
Devotional for Kids Introduction
7

⸱⸱⸱

PURPOSE 1:
The Reason for Everything
11–72

PURPOSE 2:
Faith and Friendship with God
74–150

PURPOSE 3:
Your Part in God's Family
152–194

PURPOSE 4:
Becoming Like Christ
196–283

PURPOSE 5:
Serving God, Serving Others
286–338

PURPOSE 6:
You Were Made for a Mission
340–381

⸱⸱⸱

Why So Many Translations?
382

INTRODUCTION

Purpose-Driven Life Devotional for Kids

Rick Warren

This is more than a book! It is a guide about God, your life, your purpose, and your mission. Over the next year, I want you to read one page a day. By the time you finish this book, you will have a better understanding of God's plan for you and how you can make a difference in the world. When you see how all the pieces of your life fit together, it'll be easier to make decisions, be happy with what you have and who you are, and prepare for eternal life with God.

Don't just read this devotional. Interact with it. Underline it. Write notes in the margins. Make it your book.

Your life is worth taking the time to think about. And God is worth knowing, because he's the only one who can give your life real meaning.

I get excited when I think about kids discovering their life purpose, because when you understand why you are here on Earth, God will do great things in your life and use you—no matter how young you are—to make a difference in the world. He did those things for me, and I have never been the same. Neither will you!

The Reason for Everything

The Big Question

It is God who directs the lives of his creatures; everyone's life is in his power.

(JOB 12:10 TEV)

Do you ever wonder:

What do I want to be when I grow up?
What should I do with my life?
What are my dreams?

The search for the meaning of life has puzzled people for thousands of years. People want to know why they are here on Earth and if they matter. But the truth is, focusing on yourself will not reveal the answers.

You didn't create yourself. So how could you know what you were created for? If I handed you an invention you had never seen before, you wouldn't know what it was supposed to do. And the invention itself wouldn't be able to tell you either. Only the creator or the owner's manual could tell you the answers.

God is our Creator, and the Bible is his manual. He put us here on Earth for a reason—to love him and love others. If we ask God and read his Word, we'll find out exactly how we should do that.

Prayer

God, show me how I can love you better and love others around me. Show me who you want me to be.

Singled Out

These are the clans of the Levites listed according to their fathers.

(1 CHRONICLES 6:19B)

If you've ever auditioned for a play or tried out for a team, you probably looked for your name and any of your friends on the list of kids who made it as soon as it was posted. Or if you entered a writing contest at school, you read the list of winners to find out if you or anyone you know won.

However, reading a bunch of names of people you don't know is not on anyone's list of favorite things to do. So it may seem strange that God had the author of Chronicles write down name after name after name. We don't know anything about them, except who their fathers or mothers were and maybe where they lived. But this list of names in the book of Chronicles shows how important recognition is. God recognized the people who were a part of Israel's history and accomplishments. He knew them by name and took the time to point them out.

God knows your name too. He knows who you are, and you matter to him. Even if your name never makes it on a winners' list or try-out roster, God will recognize you as his child. That's reward enough.

Prayer

Lord, it's easy to feel overlooked or unimportant, especially when others get so much attention and recognition. I need to remember that you love me and value me. I need to remember that I'm yours.

Meaning of a Name

God also said to Abraham, "As for Sarai your wife, you are no longer to call her Sarai; her name will be Sarah. I will bless her and will surely give you a son by her. I will bless her so that she will be the mother of nations; kings of peoples will come from her."

(GENESIS 17:15–16)

Sarai was married to a well-known man, so for most of her life, she was known simply as Abraham's wife. Imagine if everyone always called you by another name rather than your own—Mary's kid, Susan's sister, Andrew's friend.

Then at ninety years old, Sarai became well known herself. She had a baby! That got her recognized. But this new fame was all from God. God blessed her husband for his faith, and he blessed Sarai too. To show how pleased he was, God gave them new names. Names were important in Bible times. Names indicated personality, standing, or family. Sarai's new name, Sarah, meant princess.

Ask your parents how they came up with your name. Did you know God has names for you too? He calls you beloved, royalty, and his child. He also calls you names that fit with his plans for your life. Perhaps God's name for you will be doctor, Olympian, mechanic, or artist. When God gives you a name, he's telling you who he created you to be. As you grow up, he may even give you a new name, just like he did with Sarai.

Prayer

God, what names have you given me? Show me who you have created me to be and what plans you have for my life.

Show Stopper

Where were you when I laid the earth's foundation? . . . Who shut up the sea behind doors when it burst forth from the womb, when I made the clouds its garment and wrapped it in thick darkness?

(JOB 38:4A, 8–9)

What is the most amazing thing you've ever seen or read? Astronauts going into space? An athlete breaking a world record? A triple rainbow? Those things can blow you away. But God has done more amazing, mind-blowing stuff. He created boundaries for the seas, so they don't flood countries under water. He set the sky in place around the earth and made gravity that keeps us on the ground, not floating off into space. God makes the sun rise in the morning so we can see to work and play, and he makes it set at night so we can sleep and rest. Psalm 104 also describes a few of the mind-boggling things God does.

When you read a little bit of God's awesome, huge, magnificent, power, it's hard to wrap your brain around it. Hey, even your brain, with its hundred-billion neurons and sixty-thousand miles of bloods vessels, is one of his miraculous works. God is unstoppable, unmatchable, and unbeatable. He is worthy of your praise!

Prayer

Lord, you are awesome and amazing. I don't even realize everything you are capable of doing. But you have my praise and honor.

Beyond Magic

By the word of the LORD the heavens were made, their starry host by the breath of his mouth. He gathers the waters of the seas into jars; he puts the deep into storehouses.

(PSALM 33:6–7)

What's the best magic trick you've ever seen? A woman being "sawed" in half? A bird appearing out of nowhere? Sometimes we read about magic, like in a story where someone finds a magic shoe or lamp? Fairy tales are made up, and magic is just illusions that trick your eyes. But God doesn't need magic or illusions—he is divine power.

God uses his supernatural power. When he breathes, he can actually create stars, rivers, and planets. His hands can pick up the oceans (the Atlantic Ocean alone is over forty-one million square miles—that's twenty percent of the earth). Those are some pretty big hands that can save you from anything. God's power is better than a story of magic or a disappearing act. He can save or change anything he wants. He can even rescue you from your worst enemy.

Now that's a super power that every story needs.

Prayer

God, it's not easy to understand how powerful you are because I've never seen you create things or change the earth. Help me believe in you and trust your power.

Anything Is Possible

The sun stopped in the middle of the sky and delayed going down about a full day. There has never been a day like it before or since, a day when the LORD listened to a human being. Surely the LORD was fighting for Israel!

(JOSHUA 10:13–14)

Every day the sun rises. Every day the sun sets. Even if it's cloudy, Earth still revolves through day and night. If Earth stopped spinning, one side of the world would be night all the time, and the other side would always be daytime. Can you imagine playing in the dark all the time? Or going to bed with the sun still shining through your windows?

Joshua got to see the earth stand still. God stopped it, so Joshua had plenty of sunlight to defeat his enemies. The people on the other side of the world must have wondered what happened!

The Bible is full of miraculous stories. God can do anything anytime. The Old Testament may seem like a book of fiction, but everything written in it is true. God can stop planets, part seas, make animals talk, and change the heart of any person. He does miraculous things for his glory, which means to show who he is and his power. With God, anything is possible.

Prayer

God, I've never seen a miracle or an amazing work like you did for people in Old Testament times. But I believe you are a powerful God, and I want to be on your side always.

Start Here

For in him all things were created: things in heaven and on earth, visible and invisible . . . all things have been created through him and for him.

(COLOSSIANS 1:16)

I once got lost in the mountains. When I stopped to ask for directions to the campsite, someone told me, "You can't get there from here. You must start from the other side of the mountain!" It's kind of the same with trying to figure out who you were made to be. You cannot find your life's purpose by starting with yourself. That would be like wandering around on the wrong side of the mountain. You must begin with God, your Creator.

You were made by God and for God, so your purpose is not about you. The meaning of your life is far greater than your own happiness, your family, or even your wildest dreams. If you want to know why you were placed on this planet, you must begin with God.

In God, you can find your identity, your meaning, and your destiny. Every other path leads to a dead end.

Prayer

I want to know why you created me, God, and I know I can only find that through you. Keep my focus on you rather than on myself.

Bodies and Brains

In his hand are the depths of the earth, and the mountain peaks belong to him. The sea is his, for he made it, and his hands formed the dry land.

(PSALM 95:4–5)

History has seen its share of geniuses. Albert Einstein, the crazy-haired scientist, developed the theory of relativity. Wolfgang Mozart was a musical child prodigy who began composing masterpieces at age five. Marie Curie, famous for pioneering research on radioactivity, became the first person to win two Nobel prizes.

Talents don't stop with book-smarts. Human beings can make their bodies do amazing things too: dunk a basketball, flip backwards across a four-inch balance beam, play prestissimo (lightning speed!) on the piano, and run for a hundred miles straight.

Our bodies and brains are incredible. Think about this for a moment: If men and women are capable of such genius, how much smarter and beyond our limited comprehension is the One who made us?

Did you catch today's verses? The Lord hasn't just climbed a tall mountain, trekked across a continent, or journeyed to the deepest ocean trench. He hasn't merely memorized DNA sequences or solved the world's toughest math problems. They came out of his amazing power and genius. So if God has more than enough intelligence, artistic ability, creativity, and power to make our jaw-dropping world, why not trust him with your life?

Prayer

Lord, I don't know even a fraction of what you do. Your brilliance blows my mind. I can't believe you want a relationship with me. But I want that too, so my heart and life are yours.

The Perfect Guide

It's in Christ that we find out who we are and what we are living for. Long before we first heard of Christ and got our hopes up, he had his eye on us, had designs on us for glorious living, part of the overall purpose he is working out in everything and everyone.

(EPHESIANS 1:11, MSG)

God has not left us in the dark to wonder and guess about our lives. He has given us the Bible. It is our guidebook. It explains why we are alive, how life works, what to avoid, and what to expect in the future.

To discover the meaning and goal for your life, turn to God's Word. Then build your life on eternal truths, not on what other people say. Ephesians 1:11 gives three clues about your purpose:

1. God was thinking of you long before you ever thought about him. He planned your life before you existed, without your input! You may choose your friends, activities, hobbies, and other parts of your life, but not your purpose.
2. The meaning of your life fits into God's plans for the world and eternity.
3. You discover your identity and purpose through a relationship with Jesus Christ. If you don't have a relationship with him, turn to Day 26, where I explain how to begin one.

Prayer

Lord, I want to know you and the meaning of my life. Keep revealing to me through your Scripture who you want me to be.

He's Got Love for That

As a father has compassion on his children, so the LORD has compassion on those who fear him; for he knows how we are formed, he remembers that we are dust.

(PSALM 103:13–14)

God knows you inside and out—from your guts to the hairs in your eyebrows. He doesn't shake his head and wonder, "What happened with this one? I thought I did a better job with him." He doesn't slap his forehead and say, "Wow. I didn't think she would make that mistake today. I'm shocked!"

God knows that you won't always make the right decision. He knows the world is corrupted, and sometimes you will slip up. He also knows that people can be mean and hurt our feelings. But God is always there for you. His heart is big, and his love is strong. It doesn't change based on what you do or what happens to you.

He knows all the decisions you make over your lifetime. He has already planned out how he will shape you and change you based on everything that happens over the years. He even knows how long you will live. And every day, he shows his compassion and grace to you.

Prayer

God, I need you. I need you when I mess up, and I need you when I'm hurt. Thank you for being a good dad.

Born Right on Time

You know me inside and out, you know every bone in my body; You know exactly how I was made, bit by bit, how I was sculpted from nothing into something.

(PSALM 139:15, MSG)

You are not an accident. Your birth was no mistake. Your parents may not have planned you, but God was not at all surprised by your birth. In fact, he knew all about you before your mom was pregnant. It is not fate, chance, luck, or coincidence that you are breathing at this very moment. You are alive because God wanted to create you!

God chose every single detail of your body: the color of your skin, your hair, your eyes. He chose your height and the sound of your voice. He made your body just the way he wanted it. He also gave you natural talents and a unique personality. No one else is exactly like you.

God made you for a reason. He also decided when you would be born and how long you would live. He planned the days of your life. And you are exactly the way you are supposed to be.

Prayer

Thank you, God, for taking such care in creating me. When I forget how special I am to you, remind me that I am wonderfully made by you.

Worth a Lot

Yet you, LORD, are our Father. We are the clay, you are the potter; we are all the work of your hand.

(ISAIAH 64:8)

Would you consider a backpack a work of art? Probably not, but guys from a few centuries ago might disagree. Back then, people couldn't easily purchase a bag from the nearest department store. Someone had to make fabric or skin an animal, cut it into a bag shape, and bind it together by hand. Even the simplest items were made by hand, requiring skill, technique, and many hours of hard work.

Today, many of those "boring" items from long ago, such as bowls and utensils, are worth boatloads of money. Because there were no big, mass-producing factories, each piece was a one-of-a-kind, true work of art.

Did you know that you are an artistic masterpiece too? Even with over seven billion people on Earth, there's not one other kid out there made exactly like you. God made you one of a kind. And because God is perfect, he has never messed up. Our Father, the master potter, sculpted every detail about you into something unique and lovable.

You are worth far more than any centuries-old cowhide backpack. Just ask God, the Creator who thought you were worth making for his pleasure.

Prayer

Lord, I'm your valuable creation, but sometimes I'm not sure. I want to get rid of that doubt. Let the truth that I am your awesome creation fill my heart.

You-nique

You saw me before I was born and scheduled each day of my life before I began to breathe. Every day was recorded in your book!

(PSALM 139:16, TLB)

No matter the circumstances of your birth, God had a plan in creating you. It doesn't matter whether your parents were good or bad or you've ever met them. God knew that your mom and dad had exactly the right genetic makeup to create the "you" he had in mind.

While there are illegitimate parents, there are no illegitimate children. Many children are unplanned by their parents, but they are not unplanned by God. God's purpose took into account human error and even sin. And he never makes mistakes.

God also planned where you'd be born and where you'd live for his purpose. Your race and nationality are no accident. God left no detail to chance. He planned it all for his purpose.

Prayer

God, you are a creator who loves his creation and doesn't make mistakes. Thank you for including me as part of your purpose.

Just the Way You Are

*The boys grew up, and Esau became a skillful hunter,
a man of the open country, while Jacob was content
to stay at home among the tents.*

(GENESIS 25:27)

Esau and Jacob were twins. But they didn't look alike. They didn't act alike. They didn't even smell alike—their dad could smell the difference between them when they leaned in close!

Boys don't have to do the same things as other boys. Neither do girls have to like what other girls like. You might like to play chess and compete in speech or spelling competitions. Your sister or mom might prefer to play basketball or watch movies. God created you as a unique person. No one else will be like you! God wants you to enjoy being the boy or girl he created you to be and discover the interests and skills that he gave you. It might be hard when other boys or girls tease you for not being like them. But God didn't make you to be like anyone else. If you act like a bunch of other kids just to try to fit in, you're ignoring how God made you.

Confidence comes from believing God made you just the way you are for a reason. When you are confident, other kids will like being around you. And if you accept other kids for being different, you'll help them find confidence.

Prayer

God, it can be hard to be different from the other kids, even in small things. Will you build my confidence in how you made me to be?

On His Mind

Before I formed you in the womb I knew you, before you were born I set you apart; I appointed you as a prophet to the nations.

(JEREMIAH 1:5)

Long before you were born, God knew you would exist. He decided that you would be a part of the human race. It's true—your arrival on planet Earth was no surprise to him.

Have you ever wondered what came to God's mind when he first thought of you? The picture of you that he saw probably brought a smile to his face. He saw your unique abilities and potential. He saw your opportunities to make a difference in his world.

Like everyone who has ever lived, the prophet Jeremiah struggled with self-worth. That's why God spoke to Jeremiah and assured him that his life was not an accident. God had a plan for his life before he was born.

The same is true for you. You don't have to be a prophet or a pastor or a missionary for God to know your name. He not only knows your name, but he also knows your strengths and weaknesses. He knows what makes you afraid. And he knows your future. It's a future that will allow you to use your abilities and potential to do great things for God.

Prayer

Lord, it's amazing to me that you have known me since before I was born. I want to live as the person you saw when you first thought of me.

Out of This World

Long before he laid down earth's foundations, he had us in mind, had settled on us as the focus of his love, to be made whole and holy by his love.

(EPHESIANS 1:4, MSG)

God had a reason for everything he created. He made every redwood tree and every tough rhinoceros. He formed every sea, lagoon, and coral reef. He placed every cliff, iceberg, and desert. God designed everything with great precision.

He planned every person with a purpose in mind. We are the focus of his love and the most valuable of all his creation. God was thinking of us even before he made the world. In fact, that's why he created it! God designed the atmosphere, the environment, and the weather just so people could live here on Earth. The more physicists, biologists, and other scientists learn about the universe, the better we understand how perfect it is for us, custom-made to make human life possible. No other planet that we know of can support human life. Earth was made for us. And we were made for God. This is how much God loves and values us!

Prayer

God, you crafted a beautiful world for me to live in. Help me remember to notice each detail of your creation and that it was custom-made by you.

What's Your Plan?

In their hearts humans plan their course, but the Lord establishes their steps.

(PROVERBS 16:9)

For thousands of years, people have kept calendars. Ancient men and women didn't plan their time with computers or smart phones like we do, though. Instead, they counted hours by tracking shadows around an early kind of clock called a sundial. Then, they counted days between full moons and watched the stars to determine the time of year.

Just like our ancestors, we still want to know what's coming. And for good reason! Without calendars, we would be late for try-outs and art classes.

It's great to think ahead of time. That's called wise preparation. And it's fun to dream about your future. Yet all the planning in the world can't change one thing: You don't have the final say in how your days, months, and years go.

As the Ruler of the universe, God is the ultimate calendar. God knows exactly what's going to happen to you today, next month, and even fifty years from now. Sometimes that doesn't match up exactly with your plans.

Thankfully, God is more powerful than anything we could plan, and his love is *always* on time. Will you trust your days and months to your all-knowing Creator?

Prayer

Thanks, Lord, for "establishing my steps." Remind me to pray and talk about my plans and dreams with you from now on, instead of trying to do it all myself.

Guarded

Keep me as the apple of your eye; hide me in the shadow of your wings.

(PSALM 17:8)

What would be your first reaction if a ball or tree branch came flying toward your face? Arms up. Dive for cover. Protect your face. You wouldn't even have to think about covering your eyes. Your arms would automatically go up over your head. You'd probably duck or try to jump out of the way. Maybe you'd scream—all because your brain knows to protect your body.

God sees you like an important body part. He even calls his children the apple of his eye. That's the very center of the eye, meaning the most precious part—not a tasty snack. As his child, you are one of his most valued possessions. You are more important than a bank with a billion dollars. Because you are so precious, God is quick to protect you, just like you would protect your eyes or any part of your body from getting hurt. God will stand up for you and guard your life. He will care for you. He automatically puts his arms out for you. He doesn't have to think twice.

Prayer

Wow, God! I didn't realize I was so special to you. Thank you for taking care of me.

Awesome Love

He who created the heavens, he is God . . . he did not create it to be empty, but formed it to be inhabited.

(ISAIAH 45:18A)

Why did God go to all the trouble of creating a universe for us? Because he is a God of love. This kind of love is difficult to understand, but it's for real. The Bible tells us, "God is love" (1 John 4:8). It doesn't say God has love. He *is* love!

God didn't need to create you. He wasn't lonely. But he wanted to make you so he could express his love. God says, "I have carried you since you were born; I have taken care of you from your birth. Even when you are old, I will be the same. Even when your hair has turned gray, I will take care of you. I made you and will take care of you" (Isaiah 46:3b-4a, NCV). Wow. You were created as a special object of God's love! God made you just so he could love you. Nothing is more wonderful than that truth. You can bet your life on it.

Prayer

God, thank you for showing me your awesome love and for promising me that you'll love me forever.

Size Does Not Matter

Four things on earth are small, yet they are extremely wise . . . A lizard can be caught with the hand, yet it is found in kings' palaces.

(PROVERBS 30:24, 28)

Do friends or family tease you because of your size? Maybe you are short or look young for your age. Maybe you are bigger than all the other kids in your grade and feel like you always stand out—but not in a good way. Every girl and boy grows up at a different speed. Your height or weight doesn't make you any more or less valuable.

Size doesn't matter to God. Think about the lizard. If you are quick enough, you can catch one sunning on a rock and grab it before it gets away. It doesn't seem very stealthy or powerful. But that same lizard can find its way into the most heavily guarded and highly secure king's palace.

God can use something as small as a lizard to teach about wisdom and something as big as a lion (v. 30) to teach about strength.

God created you just the way you are. He will use you no matter your size and ability. Just turn to him for wisdom, and he'll get you in and out of the most unlikely places.

Prayer

Jesus, I don't like being teased. Will you help me not to worry about it or wish I were different than how you made me?

Totally Significant

But you, Bethlehem Ephrathah, though you are small among the clans of Judah, out of you will come for me one who will be ruler over Israel, whose origins are from of old, from ancient times.

(MICAH 5:2)

"O Little Town of Bethlehem" is a carol sung every Christmas. You might know the words, but do you notice the amazing fact it celebrates?

Jesus Christ was born in that little town eight miles outside of Jerusalem. Most everybody knows that. But not everybody knows it was the same little town where King David was born.

The prophet Micah predicted that Israel's Messiah would be born in Bethlehem. He wrote his prediction several hundred years after David was born and several hundred years before Jesus was.

But what really puts that little town on the map is this: Bethlehem was a nothing town. The people there weren't wealthy, famous, or highly educated. Yet God chose to use this very ordinary, insignificant town to bring about his amazing plan for our planet.

Do you ever question your significance? Do you ever wonder if God will use you? On days like that, start singing the words to "O Little Town of Bethlehem." Don't worry if it isn't Christmas. It's a hymn with truth that's sing-able all year long.

Prayer

Lord, I'm amazed that Jesus would be born in Bethlehem. I'm grateful that you use unknown places and people for your big plans.

Spark Your Creativity

In the beginning God created the heavens and the earth.

(GENESIS 1:1)

God has big ideas—so big in fact that his creativity started the whole world. He created thousands of animals, ginormous and tiny, fast like the cheetah and slow like the two-toed sloth. He designed tall lodgepole pine trees and massive redwoods too big to climb. His hands carved mountains and rivers and poured the whitewater rapids. Every time you eat tasty pancakes or a juicy burger, you're feasting on God's creativity.

When God got around to creating people, he decided to make them with many of his own characteristics. That means he designed you to be creative. When you think of how to build a fort in the woods, draw a picture of another planet, or dream up a new version of your favorite game, that's because of God's creativity in you. So build, draw, write, design. See how creative you can be with your hands, your body, your stories, and more. God's creativity has no limits. What ideas has he put into your head?

Prayer

God, thank you for the creativity you gave me. I want to create cool things for you.

No Comparisons

To one he gave five bags of gold, to another two bags, and to another one bag, each according to his ability. Then he went on his journey.

(MATTHEW 25:15)

Fast feet. Clever comebacks. Strong arms. Charming smile. Ever see other kids with these characteristics and wish you had what they did? If everyone had the same brains, the same speed, the same wit, the same strength, the world would be boring. Everyone would be exactly the same. Can you imagine that? Every time you played a game with your friend, you'd tie. You'd get tired of that pretty fast.

No one else has the combination of family, friends, personality, and abilities you do. That's how God wants it. Don't waste your time looking at what someone else has.

What has God given you? You may wish your family had more money so you could live in a bigger house. But God put you right where you are so you could serve the people in your neighborhood. Or, you may wish you were better at sports, but God may want you to reach out to someone else who's sitting on the sidelines so that person can know about God's love.

Whatever God has given you is exactly what he wants you to have. Wishing you had what someone else does is like telling God that he didn't make you good enough.

Prayer

God, sometimes I wish I were smarter or better looking. Sometimes it's hard to accept how you made me. Will you remind me how special I am to you?

All In

*For all have sinned and fall short of the glory of God,
and all are justified freely by his grace through the
redemption that came by Christ Jesus.*

(ROMANS 3:23–24)

Know anyone who is the teacher's pet or the coach's favorite player? Maybe you've been in a place of honor like that before. The teacher asks you to be the helper or the coach lets you be captain of the team. It feels good to be favored.

Did you know that God doesn't have favorites? Though he chooses people for different jobs and gives people different blessings, he loves everyone the same. Everyone has the opportunity to know God and believe in his son Jesus Christ.

Jesus died on the cross to pay the price for everyone's sins. No one is left out. And no one gets more grace than anyone else. God's gifts are free to whoever asks and acknowledges God as Lord. There are no special qualifications or requirements for certain people. It's all the same: turn to God for forgiveness of sins and the gift of eternal life. No favorites.

Prayer

Jesus, thank you for the gift of salvation and grace. You give freely to me, and I pray for [name your friends or family who don't know Christ] to receive these gifts from you too.

Who Jesus Is

Once when Jesus was praying in private and his disciples were with him, he asked them, "Who do the crowds say I am?" They replied, "Some say John the Baptist; others say Elijah; and still others, that one of the prophets of long ago has come back to life." "But what about you?" he asked. "Who do you say I am?"

(LUKE 9:18–20)

Jesus still asks each person the same question: "Who do you say I am?" And people still argue about who Jesus is. Some say he was just a really nice guy who wandered around like a hippie, talking about love, joy, and happiness. Others think Jesus was a great teacher who taught people good lessons about how to do what's right and make friends. Still others say Jesus wasn't even real, that he was just a character in a story—like the star of a good movie.

The truth is that Jesus is the Son of God, and he came to Earth to change people's lives and put them in a relationship with God. If we get to know Jesus as Savior and friend, we will be with him in Heaven forever. We'll also be able to share his love and power with others. He's the Jesus that changes everything.

Who do you say he is?

Prayer

Jesus, I believe you are the Son of God. Because of love, you came to Earth to give your life away, to give us a way to join you in eternity. Thank you!

Real Life

To all who did receive him, to those who believed in his name, he gave the right to become children of God.

(JOHN 1:12)

Your real purpose begins when you pledge your life to Jesus Christ. All you need to do is believe and receive. Will you accept God's offer?

First, believe. Believe God loves you and made you for a reason. Believe you're not an accident. Believe you were made to last forever. Believe Jesus died on the cross for you, to forgive your sins no matter what you've done. Believe God chose you as part of his plans.

Second, receive. Receive Jesus into your life as your Lord and Savior. Receive his forgiveness for your sins. Receive his Spirit, who will give you the power to do what God created you to do. You can bow your head right now and say the prayer that will change your life forever: "Jesus, I believe in you, and I receive you." Go ahead.

If you sincerely meant that prayer, congratulations! Welcome to the family of God! You are now ready to discover and start living God's purpose for your life.

Prayer

I believe I am loved and made for a purpose. Jesus, I invite you to come into my life. Help me live out your purpose for me every day.

Sins Erased

If anyone sins and does what is forbidden in any of the Lord's commands, even though they do not know it, they are guilty and will be held responsible.

(LEVITICUS 5:17)

How does it feel when somebody hurts you? Maybe a friend tells a lie about you or a sibling blames you for breaking a glass in the kitchen. It feels bad.

Do you know that we do that to God? God created everything, and he is perfect and good all the time. Sadly, because of Adam and Eve's choices in the Garden of Eden, people turn on God and hurt him. This is called sin. Sin is when we do wrong or make choices against God's perfect goodness. And it's like calling God, who loves us, a very bad name.

The fantastic news is that God doesn't hold our sins against us. In the Old Testament, he gave the Israelites a way to make things right. They could bring offerings as a way of admitting their wrong and saying they were sorry. These offerings were to be sacrifices and would be payment for their sins. In the New Testament, Jesus came along to make things right for everyone. And nowadays, we can do the same thing through sincere prayer.

Prayer

God, I know that sin happens every day, but I didn't realize it hurt you. Please forgive me for betraying you.

Taking the Blame

The man who releases the goat as a scapegoat must wash his clothes and bathe himself with water; afterward he may come into the camp.

(LEVITICUS 16:26)

Ever heard of a scapegoat? You may have been one yourself. Your older brother breaks a glass. Before your mom starts yelling, he blames you because he tripped on your sneakers in the middle of the floor. You just became the scapegoat. Here's another scenario: You're playing first base in a kickball game. When the pitcher retrieves the ball and tries to throw out the runner at first base, she hesitates a moment too long because you are not yet at the base to catch the ball. The runner is safe, and you blame the pitcher for not being fast enough, even though you weren't quite fast enough either. The pitcher became the scapegoat.

Nobody wants to be the scapegoat—the one who gets blamed for a problem. But it sure is easy to blame someone else when we get in trouble.

The Israelites had a real scapegoat—an actual goat. They presented the goat to God as a sacrifice. The goat took the blame for the Israelites' sin. Then they sent the goat off into the wilderness. Thankfully, we don't need scapegoats for our sin anymore. Jesus, God's Son, became the final scapegoat. He took care of paying for our sin, so we don't have to take the full blame.

Prayer

Jesus, thank you for being my scapegoat—not so that I can blame you but so that I don't have to pay for my own sins.

Treasure Worth Finding

Again, the kingdom of heaven is like a merchant looking for fine pearls. When he found one of great value, he went away and sold everything he had and bought it.

(MATTHEW 13:45–46)

If you found a box of diamonds in a field, your life would change. You'd run home right away to tell your mom or dad. Then you'd do everything to keep those jewels safe. Did you know Jesus says his truth and his ways are more awesome than finding jewels? If we only knew how incredible it is to live for Jesus, we would live it with all our hearts. Loving Jesus changes everything, but it can be hard to really believe that.

If you found a bucket of oysters on the beach, you might think they were a bunch of smelly slimy sea creatures. You might not believe that they could have valuable pearls inside. So deep inside you may wonder, "Where is this treasure everyone keeps talking about?"

But don't give up. The treasure of following Jesus is more beautiful than any other treasure this world has to offer. Everything else is worthless in comparison—even a box full of diamonds and pearls.

Prayer

Lord, will you show me how wonderful it is to follow you? It's hard to understand when I can't see you. But I want to find your treasure.

Heaven Ready

*For we will all stand before God's judgment seat. . . .
So then, each of us will give an account of ourselves
to God.*

(ROMANS 14:10B, 12)

Knowing your purpose prepares you for life after you die. Yes, you read that right. Life after death. One day you will stand before God, and he will examine your life before you enter eternity. Fortunately, God wants you to pass this test, so he has given you the questions ahead of time.

First, "What did you do with my Son, Jesus Christ?" The answer will determine where you spend eternity. The only thing that will matter is if you accepted what Jesus did for you and learned to love and trust him. Jesus said, "I am the way and the truth and the life. No one comes to the Father except through me" (John 14:6).

Second, "What did you do with what I gave you?" What did you do with your life—all the gifts, talents, energy, and relationships? Did you spend them on yourself, or did you use them for the purposes God made you for? The answer will determine what you do in eternity.

Following God's ways will prepare you to give the best answers.

Prayer

I spend a lot of time focusing on myself, Lord. Help me to use what you gave me for your purposes and not for my own gain.

Worth the Time

During those days another large crowd gathered. Since they had nothing to eat, Jesus called his disciples to him and said, "I have compassion for these people; they have already been with me three days and have nothing to eat."

(MARK 8:1–2)

How far would you go to see your favorite sports team play a big game? How long would you go without eating because you were so engrossed in an exciting adventure novel? If you heard your favorite action hero was going to be at an event in a nearby city, would you try everything to get your parents to take you there? How much allowance would you save to buy a new bike or game that you really, really wanted?

People will give up a lot to get something they really want. You've probably even heard about people who camp out overnight just to get a good place in line for a blockbuster movie's opening weekend.

When Jesus was coming to town, people gave up a lot to hear him speak. They would leave home, camp out, and go without meals for a few days just so they could be around him. People didn't have cars or bikes. They had to walk miles and miles to hear him speak. They may as well have hiked a mountain without food. That's how excited and curious they were about him. That says a lot about Jesus. He was so awesome that people gave up a lot to be near him.

Prayer

Wow, Jesus! You are so amazing that people gave up so much to learn from you. I don't want to miss out on who you are. Help me to do whatever it takes to know you better.

A Dad's Love

And the Holy Spirit descended on him in bodily form like a dove. And a voice came from heaven: "You are my Son, whom I love; with you I am well pleased."

(LUKE 3:22)

"I love you." Those three words are probably the most important three words you will ever hear. You may hear them from your mom or dad. You may hear them from your grandparents. One day you may hear them from a certain young man or woman when you marry him or her.

When you know someone loves you, it boosts your confidence to reach for your dreams. That's why dads and moms tell their kids they love them so much.

Even Jesus needed to hear those three words. When Jesus was about to go around the country teaching and healing people, he had a big assignment. God the Father understood how Jesus felt. So there at the Jordan River, as Jesus was baptized, God spoke from Heaven: "I love you. I am proud of you."

The same words Jesus heard the Father speak are the words God also says to you. God loves you more than you can possibly understand. There is nothing you could ever do—no matter how wonderful—that would cause him to love you any more. And there is nothing you could ever do—no matter how bad—that would make him love you any less.

Prayer

Lord, it blows my mind to think you love me as much as the Bible says you do. Please give me the faith to believe it and never doubt it.

Secret Plans

On coming to the house, they saw the child with his mother Mary, and they bowed down and worshiped him. Then they opened their treasures and presented him with gifts of gold, frankincense and myrrh.

(MATTHEW 2:11)

Many years ago, God sent his son, Jesus, to Earth to tell people about God. God let some people know right away. The Magi, who were known as very wise men, looked for a sign in the sky from God. Then they took a long journey from their country just to meet Jesus and his parents, Mary and Joseph. It was like God had whispered a big secret to the Magi. Well, he did, actually! He led them to see Jesus first. As soon as the Magi saw the baby Jesus, they knew he was God's Son. They were so honored and thrilled that they bowed down on the ground. Then they loaded him up with presents. For many years, only a few people knew about Jesus and what he was going to do for God one day. Everyone else was in the dark. When Jesus grew up, he did supernatural miracles and healed sick people. The Magi knew he would do all that years before anyone else knew.

God doesn't always reveal his secrets and plans to people. Sometimes that's because people aren't ready for what God is doing. When God lets you in on his plans, you'll get to see some big surprises and find out just how amazing he is.

Prayer

God, thank you for sending Jesus to tell us about you. Thank you also for letting me be a part of your plans.

What Just Happened?

*The angel said to the women, "Do not be afraid,
for I know that you are looking for Jesus, who was
crucified. He is not here; he has risen, just as he said.
Come and see the place where he lay."*

(MATTHEW 28:5–6)

The followers of Jesus had just faced the worst day of their lives. Soldiers and angry crowds had killed Jesus. The disciples were scared for their own lives. They had no idea how this mess would turn out.

Just three days later, it was all turned upside down.

Jesus had risen from the dead! His death was part of God's plan to pay the price for people's sin. The disciples thought his death was the end, but God had planned a grand finale: resurrection! Defeating death with life. God showed people and the devil who is really in charge. The death and Resurrection of Jesus Christ was the most awesome event ever. Even angels were involved in the plan.

Jesus' Resurrection was for everyone, including you and your family and your friends. Before any of you were even born, Jesus paid the price for everyone's sins and then came back to life so that everyone could see God's power, favor, and forgiveness. Would you thank God for Jesus' death and life and ask him to forgive your sins? When you do that, you accept this amazing gift from God and become a Christian, a Christ follower.

Prayer

Thank you, God, for Jesus' life and death and life again. Please forgive my sins. I want to accept your gift of grace and forgiveness and follow the ways of Jesus.

Light the Darkness

In him [Jesus] was life, and that life was the light of all mankind. The light shines in the darkness, and the darkness has not overcome it.

(JOHN 1:4–5)

Ask your mom or dad to do an experiment with you. Grab a flashlight. Head to a room that you can make completely dark. Shut the curtains and doors, and put pillows or towels in front of any cracks. It has to be absolutely black. After a few minutes, turn on the flashlight. Ask everyone in the room what they see once the flashlight is on. Light, even the smallest one, always shows up more than the darkness. But if you shut off the flashlight or hide it under something, the darkness will be all you see.

Did you know Jesus called himself the light of the world? He outshines sin and darkness—neither can put out Jesus. He exposes the truth of good and evil. Wherever Jesus goes, he shines a light. The sad thing is that many people don't want to see Jesus' light, so they run away from him. Like shoving towels and pillows into cracks in a room, they shut out the light.

If you've told Jesus that you want to follow him, everywhere you go you take his light—just like a flashlight in a pitch-black room.

Prayer

Jesus, light is powerful. It helps me see my clothes, what's on my plate at dinner, and where to walk. Your light is even more powerful. Let me take your light to dark places and help people discover your truth.

Laser Sharp

Therefore do not be foolish, but understand what the Lord's will is.

(EPHESIANS 5:17)

The power of focusing can be seen in light. Diffused light that shines in all directions—like a big fluorescent light bulb—doesn't do anything except light up a room. But you can concentrate the energy of a light. With a magnifying glass, the rays of the sun can be focused to set grass or paper on fire. When light is focused even more, like a laser beam, it can cut through steel.

Nothing is quite as powerful as someone with a focused life. The men and women who have made the greatest difference in history were the most focused. For example, the apostle Paul almost single-handedly spread Christianity throughout the Roman Empire. His secret was a focused life. He said, "I focus on this one thing: Forgetting the past and looking forward to what lies ahead" (Philippians 3:13, NLT).

If you want your life to have power, focus it on God's purpose for you. You can be busy without a purpose, but what's the point? Do only activities that matter most.

Prayer

Lord, help me live my life with your focus in mind. I want to make a difference for your Kingdom here on Earth.

Wired to Last

He has also set eternity in the human heart.
(ECCLESIASTES 3:11B)

This life is not all there is.

Life on Earth is like a dress rehearsal before a play or concert.

You will spend far more time on the other side of death—in eternity—than you will here. Earth is like the preschool or the try-out for your life after death. It is the practice workout before the actual game or the warm-up jog before the race begins. This life is preparation for the next.

At most, you will live a hundred years on Earth, but you will spend forever in eternity. You were made to last forever.

Even though we know everyone eventually dies on Earth, death always seems unnatural and unfair. The reason we feel we should live forever is that God wired our brains with that desire. You have a natural instinct that longs to live forever. This is because God designed you in his image.

Prayer

Lord, thank you that you created me to live forever. Help me to remember that when my problems on Earth feel too big or scary. There is so much more to life than what I can see now.

Listen and Obey

[Jesus] said to Simon [Peter], "Put out into deep water, and let down the nets for a catch." Simon answered, "Master, we've worked hard all night and haven't caught anything. But because you say so, I will let down the nets."

(LUKE 5:4–5)

Jesus told the disciples where to fish, when to fish, and how to fish. Simon Peter followed his instructions.

Simon Peter's reaction to Christ was perfect. First, he didn't argue. He didn't say, "Wait a minute, Jesus! I'm the best fisherman on this lake. Who are you to tell me how to fish?" He didn't ask, "Lord, are you sure?" He also didn't hesitate.

Second, he didn't listen to his feelings. I'm sure he was dog-tired from working all night, but he didn't ask, "What's the use? Why should I keep on going?" Peter was eager to cooperate with God's plan. When he did, God poured out blessing. Simon Peter caught so many fish that his nets started to break.

Are you ready to obey as you listen to God's instructions? When God is guiding your life, you cannot fail.

Prayer

God, it is not always easy to listen to your instructions, but you know what is best for me. Help me to obey and be eager to follow your plans.

In an Instant

Listen, I tell you a mystery: We will not all sleep, but we will all be changed—in a flash, in the twinkling of an eye, at the last trumpet. For the trumpet will sound, the dead will be raised imperishable, and we will be changed.

(1 CORINTHIANS 15:51–52)

You won't need a secret decoder ring or night vision glasses. You don't have to hire a private detective to figure out this mystery. The apostle Paul, whom God included on the case, tells us plainly how God will change the world—and us—one day.

Someday, God is going to send Jesus Christ back to Earth. This time when he comes, he will raise the dead and create a new Heaven and earth. *Bam! Flash! Wink!* Our bodies will be changed. With real supernatural power, God will transform our skin and bones, organs and muscles. He will upgrade our form to the heavenly version—the version that will never need another upgrade. The version that will live eternally with him. The version that has no death or pain or physical glitches. No more graveyards. No more hospitals. No more separation from God. We will live with him, happy, free, and joyful in perfect bodies in a perfect world.

Prayer

God, what a wonderful day it will be when we get to live with you forever! It seems unbelievable, but I am so thankful that you have planned for me an eternity of life and joy with you.

Eyes on God

But the LORD was with Joseph and extended kindness to him, and gave him favor in the sight of the chief jailer.

(GENESIS 39:21, NASB)

How should we respond when other people cause us trouble? When family hurts us? When a good friend double-crosses us? A good example of suffering because of other people is Joseph of the Old Testament (Genesis 37–50).

After being sold by his brothers into slavery, Joseph found himself in a foreign country, alone and hurting. He had every right to ask, "Why me?"

How was Joseph able to hang in there?

First, Joseph recognized that God has given everyone free choice. No one is a puppet or a robot. We can choose to ignore what is right, and God does not force his will on us.

Second, Joseph knew that God saw everything he went through. He never doubted that God cared about him. There is an important phrase that is found five times in the story of Joseph, each time after a major crisis or defeat: "But the Lord was with Joseph." Even when everything was going wrong, the Lord was still with Joseph.

Remembering these truths allowed Joseph to survive the pain and forgive his brothers in the end—because he kept his eyes on God.

Prayer

Lord, I need to remember that you are with me through sadness and joy, just as you were with Joseph. Thank you for caring for me and caring about me.

Count on Him

Your word, LORD, is eternal; it stands firm in the heavens. Your faithfulness continues through all generations; you established the earth, and it endures.

(PSALM 119:89–90)

Forever is a long time. Have you ever tried to think about how long forever is? It will make your brain hurt! God is forever. He's been around longer than your parents, your grandparents, or the oldest person you know. He was around before the earth was even made. That's old!

The Bible tells us that God has been faithful for as long as he has been around. Faithful is just part of who he is. That means you can count on him to be trustworthy, loving, and just. You can be sure that he will answer prayers, honor his word, and protect those who follow him.

Every time you need him, God will be the same God who has been with your parents, your grandparents, and Adam and Eve. When things don't make sense and you don't understand why bad things happen, you can count on God to be there with you and use those hardships for good in your life. Thank God.

Prayer

Thank you, Lord, that you are dependable and trustworthy. Please help me trust in your faithfulness. Thank you for always being there.

Peek into Heaven

These were the living creatures I had seen beneath the God of Israel by the Kebar River, and I realized that they were cherubim. Each had four faces and four wings, and under their wings was what looked like human hands.

(EZEKIEL 10:20–21)

Wouldn't you love a glimpse into Heaven? A few special prophets, including Ezekiel, have been allowed to see what's going on up there.

Heaven, God's throne room, is unlike anything here on Earth. So imagine trying to describe creatures you've never seen. Ezekiel watched a few scenes unfolding in Heaven, including the work of cherubim. So he tried to describe them—sort of human, sort of animal, sort of angelic. Otherworldly for sure!

Cherubim are God's attendants, part of the angelic forces. They move his chariot. They sing in his choir. They guard his throne. Though we can't see them, Heaven is full of creatures who serve and love God. He is not up there alone with his Son and Holy Spirit, just the three of them hanging out. There's a whole community of beings working for God. We'll be added to that otherworldly crowd one day and join the celebration going on up there with the rest of the believers.

Prayer

I can't even imagine what Heaven is like, God. I know it must be more beautiful and awesome than any place down here. Thank you for my salvation and for preparing a place for me with you and the crowds of Heaven.

Oh, Wow!

So the Word became human and made his home among us . . . And we have seen his glory, the glory of the Father's one and only Son.

(JOHN 1:14, NLT)

Glory isn't a word you hear people use very much. Glory means all that shows off how amazing someone is. For instance, a baseball player's batting average is his "glory"—in terms of how good a player he is. Or a ballerina's pirouettes are her "glory".

The Bible talks a lot about glory. God's glory is his beauty and power and majesty. God possesses glory because he is God. It is his nature. Jesus Christ is the best example of it. As the Light of the World, he reflects God's nature. Because of Jesus, we are no longer in the dark about what God is really like. The Bible says, "The Son is the radiance of God's glory" (Hebrews 1:3; see also 2 Corinthians 4:6b). Jesus came to Earth so we could fully understand God's glory.

We cannot add anything to this glory, just like we can't do anything to make the sun shine brighter. But we are told to recognize, honor, declare, praise, reflect, and live for his glory. Why? Because God is awesome, amazing, and powerful. We owe him every honor we can possibly give. Since God made all things, he deserves all the glory.

Prayer

God, your glory is so amazing! I want to live my life seeing and praising you for how glorious and awesome you are.

Forget the Past

Jephthah the Gileadite was a mighty warrior. His father was Gilead; his mother was a prostitute. . . . So Jephthah fled from his brothers and settled in the land of Tob, where a gang of scoundrels gathered around him and followed him.

(JUDGES 11:1, 3)

Jephthah was unlucky. His father got a woman pregnant who was not his wife, and Jephthah was the baby. This was bad news for Jephthah because everyone knew about the sin of his father. His own brothers hated him because he had a different mother. They didn't care that Jephthah was strong and mighty or that he could protect them. The only people who would hang out with Jephthah were scoundrels.

Guess what, though. God didn't care about Jephthah's parents' mistakes. God cared about Jephthah. God grew him into a mighty fighter and leader who saved his country and his family from death.

Do you ever feel like other people look down on you or your family? Maybe you stand out from other kids because you are different or because your parents have made some poor choices. God doesn't care. He loves you. He has a plan for your life. He loves to take people who are different or broken or hurt and use them to do wonderful things. Don't let others get you down. God is on your side. That's all that matters.

Prayer

God, it's hard when others look down on me, especially people I want to be friends with. Are you really on my side? Please show me how much you love me and the plan you have for my life.

Imagine

Never again will they hunger; never again will they thirst. The sun will not beat down on them, nor any scorching heat. For the Lamb at the center of the throne will be their shepherd; he will lead them to springs of living water. And God will wipe away every tear from their eyes.

(REVELATION 7:16–17)

Half a century ago, a hit song invited listeners to imagine what it would be like if Heaven didn't exist. But it does exist. So imagine what Heaven will be like with a little help from the apostle John, who got to see some of it.

Heaven is an awesome place. For one thing, those who are there are in the presence of Jesus Christ. The same person we read about in the Bible will be there in all his power and glory—the one who loved children and healed their parents and told fascinating stories. But there is more. In Heaven people never get hungry, never get thirsty, and never get sad. Doesn't a place like that sound awesome? Imagine feeling good all the time.

Heaven is something to look forward to. Especially when you think about all the hunger and sadness in our world, it gives us hope to know that life won't always be this way. The fact that Heaven exists gives us something to live for.

Prayer

Lord, I can't fully imagine what Heaven is going to be like. But I am so amazed by Jesus that I can't wait to see him face-to-face and ask him questions I've been thinking about for a long time.

Supporting Role

Pharaoh's daughter said to her, "Take this baby and nurse him for me, and I will pay you." So the woman took the baby and nursed him. When the child grew older, she took him to Pharaoh's daughter and he became her son. She named him Moses, saying, "I drew him out of the water."

(EXODUS 2:9–10)

A lot of people were involved in God's plan for Moses. But they didn't know it! Moses' sister saved him from death. Pharaoh's daughter raised Moses in the Egyptian palaces. Pharaoh even considered Moses his own son. Each person in Moses' story didn't know Moses was going to be one of the greatest men in Israel's history. They didn't know God would use Moses to perform miracles, such as turning loose thousands of frogs and locusts and rolling back the Red Sea. But each person had a part in God's plan.

From the day you were born, God had a plan for you. He knows what choices you'll make in school and at home. He knows who your friends will be. God uses those details to fit into his gigantic scheme and send his love and truth to everyone in the world. Sometimes God may tell you why your part is so important. Other times, you may never know. But your life matters to God. You might be like Moses one day, or you may be the brother or sister who protects a sibling who becomes like Moses. Everyone is part of God's plan, so take your part seriously.

Prayer

Lord, I'm glad to be part of your big plans. Please help me know how to play my part well.

The Beginning after the End

No eye has seen, no ear has heard, and no mind has imagined what God has prepared for those who love him.

(1 CORINTHIANS 2:9, NLT)

Would you be able to describe the Internet to an ant? No way! That'd be impossible.

In the same way, it's almost impossible to describe or imagine Heaven. Words have not been invented that could fully explain eternity with God. Our brains cannot handle the wonder and greatness of Heaven.

God's purpose for your life doesn't end on Earth. His plan involves far more than the few years you will spend on this planet. It's an opportunity beyond your lifetime.

God is preparing a heavenly home for us, and he gives glimpses of eternity in the Bible. In Heaven, we will be reunited with loved ones who believe in Jesus. There will be no pain and suffering. God will reward us for our faithfulness on Earth and assign us to do work that we will enjoy. We won't lie around on clouds with halos playing harps! We will enjoy perfect friendship with God.

Prayer

God, thank you for preparing a place for me in Heaven, with work that I will enjoy. I look forward to seeing people I love there and having a perfect friendship with you.

Careful, That's Not Yours

God blessed them and said, ". . . Fill the earth and be its master. Rule over the fish in the sea and over the birds in the sky and over every living thing that moves on the earth."

(GENESIS 1:28, NCV)

Some friends let me use their beautiful home on the beach in Hawaii for a vacation. They told me, "Use it just like it's yours." So I did! I swam in the pool, ate the food in the refrigerator, used the towels and dishes. I even jumped on the beds for fun! But I took good care of everything because it all belonged to someone else.

When God created Adam and Eve, he told them to take care of his creation. This was the first job God gave to humans—manage God's "stuff" on Earth. It is still part of our job today. God trusts us to treat his property well—animals, plants, our bodies, and other people. God has placed all this in our hands. The Bible says, "What do you have that God hasn't given you? And if everything you have is from God, why boast as though it were not a gift?" (1 Corinthians 4:7b, NLT)

Since God owns everything, let's take care of it the best that we can.

Prayer

I realize you gave us the job of taking care of your creation, God. Your creation is so beautiful and detailed, and I thank you that we can enjoy it too while we manage it.

Home Away from Home

LORD, remind me how brief my time on earth will be. Remind me that my days are numbered—how fleeting my life is.

(PSALM 39:4, NLT)

In California, where I live, many people have moved from other parts of the world to work here. They are still citizens of their home country, so they carry a visitor card here in the United States (called a "green card"). This card allows them to stay here and work.

Christians should carry spiritual "green cards" to remind us that our citizenship is really in Heaven. Although God made the earth for us to enjoy, we will not live here forever.

The Bible describes life as a mist, a fast runner, a breath, and a wisp of smoke. Life on Earth is short. Your real homeland is Heaven. God says his children are to think differently about life: There is far more than the few years we live on this planet. We will live forever with him in Heaven. When you believe this, you will worry less about life on Earth and look forward to the forever home that is waiting for you.

Prayer

Lord, when I worry about life here on Earth, help me remember my forever home is with you in Heaven. Help me enjoy my time here on Earth in your creation too.

The Way to Life

There is a way that appears to be right, but in the end it leads to death.

(PROVERBS 14:12)

Appearances can be deceiving. Just because something seems right doesn't mean it is. Many movie stars and sports celebrities with a lot of money and fame appear to be happy. But if you could see them at home, you'd understand how unhappy life is for some of them because of drug or alcohol abuse, unhealthy relationships and broken families, and angry hearts. It's so sad, but it's so common. The road they chose didn't get them where they wanted to go. What seems right often ends in a kind of death.

The same applies to going to Heaven. The Bible is clear that only one way leads to everlasting life. Jesus said, "I am the way and the truth and the life. No one comes to the Father except through me." But not everybody believes that. They are deceived by possessions, fame, money, or paths that sound easier to take.

For those who are following a false god or creating their own path to eternal life, it doesn't look like the wrong way from a distance. But unless they accept Jesus as the one way to God, eternal death will be their destination. That's why it's important to talk to God about friends and family who don't believe in his one true way.

Prayer

Lord, I don't want the special people in my life to miss out on Heaven. Help me to tell them how much you love them.

Ever After

After this I looked, and I saw in heaven the temple—that is, the tabernacle of the covenant law—and it was opened . . . [The angels] were dressed in clean, shining linen and wore golden sashes around their chests.

(REVELATION 15:5–6)

This is not all there is—thank God! Sometimes it can be tough to hear about all the bad things that happen. Just walking down the hall at school, you might hear kids talking badly about one another, or you might hear about parents divorcing or fighting. It's painful!

Thankfully, we have all of Heaven ahead of us. If we compare the time here on Earth (seventy to eighty years) to the time we will spend with Jesus (eternity), it makes the hard things a lot easier to deal with.

Jesus walked through hard times too. He was accused of all kinds of things, betrayed by his friends, and eventually killed. We will face hard times just like he did. But that means we will get to experience all the good that comes with following Jesus too. We'll get to go to Heaven, see Jesus face-to-face, and spend forever with our friends and family.

So, even though it's hard here, remember this is not all there is!

Prayer

Thank you, God, for the wonderful gift of Heaven. Remind me of that gift when my life gets tough.

What's Distracting You?

What we see will last only a short time, but what we cannot see will last forever.

(2 CORINTHIANS 4:18B, NCV)

Compared with other countries, life is much easier for those of us who live in the United States. Most of us don't have to worry about our next meal. We can entertain ourselves with music and movies. If we need something, our parents can just go to a store to buy it.

With all the fun attractions, amusing shows and books, and enjoyable experiences, it's easy to think that life is all about happiness. But all those things are distractions from what's most important. It is a mistake to think that God's goal for your life is lots of possessions or popularity or fun.

Even though God made the world for us and wants us to enjoy it, he doesn't want us to get too attached to anything in it. He is preparing us for something even better. One day this world will come to an end, and God will create a new one that lasts forever.

Prayer

God, thank you for all the fun things we can enjoy here on Earth. Although I get distracted by those things I know you are preparing a world even better than I can imagine.

Overstuffed

Don't store up treasures here on earth, where moths eat them and rust destroys them, and where thieves break in and steal. Store your treasures in heaven . . . Wherever your treasure is, there the desires of your heart will also be.

(MATTHEW 6:19–20, NLT)

When you watch TV or videos or surf websites, what do all the ads tell you? You need more, more, more—more games, more clothes, more gadgets, more shoes. It's easy to get sucked in. The word for this is "materialism."

Materialism drives you to be unhappy and dissatisfied with what you already have. Having more may seem like it will make you happier or more important, but it's a trap. Possessions only provide short-term happiness. We eventually become bored with them and then want newer, bigger, better versions.

It's also a myth that if you get more, you will be more important. Your value is not determined by what you own or what you wear. God says the most valuable things in life are not *things*!

Real value can only be found in what can never be taken from you—your relationship with God. He is the only thing you need more of.

Prayer

Lord, it feels like all I want is more new things. Keep me focused on the part of me that has true and forever value—my relationship with you!

Next Chapter

All these people were still living by faith when they died. They did not receive the things promised; they only saw them and welcomed them from a distance . . . They were longing for a better country—a heavenly one. Therefore God is not ashamed to be called their God, for he has prepared a city for them.

(HEBREWS 11:13, 16)

The apostle Paul was faithful, yet he ended up in prison. John the Baptist was faithful, but he was beheaded. Millions of faithful people have faced a similar fate, losing everything or being killed. But the end of life is not the end!

I heard an old story about a missionary coming home to America on the same boat as the president of the United States. Cheering crowds, a military band, a red carpet, banners, and the media welcomed the president home. But nobody noticed the missionary get off the ship. Feeling let down, he began complaining to God. Then God gently reminded him, "But my child, you're not home yet."

Your time on Earth is not the complete picture of your life. You must wait until Heaven for the rest of the chapters. It'll be a wonderful story.

Prayer

It is hard to see bad things happen to those who are faithful followers of Christ. Give me patience, Lord, as I wait to see the rest of my story unfold.

Timeless

*With the Lord a day is like a thousand years, and a
thousand years are like a day. The Lord is not slow in
keeping his promise, as some understand slowness.
Instead he is patient with you, not wanting anyone to
perish, but everyone to come to repentance.*

(2 PETER 3:8–9)

Can you solve this riddle? Every person on Earth has it. You can't buy it from a store, and you can't store it. It can't be traded or upgraded, but you can run out of it.

Think you know "it"? It's time. No matter how rich, poor, young, old, short, or tall, we all have twenty-four hours in a day. And unfortunately for recess-loving boys and girls everywhere, you can't speed them up.

Keeping track of time is uniquely human. We track seasons, growth, and deadlines. But of course, God isn't human. He doesn't need any heavenly wristwatches, calendars, or alarm clocks. He doesn't need those things because God exists outside of time.

So when you pray for something to happen, it might not come immediately. That doesn't mean God is forgetful or not listening. He sees exactly when he should answer your prayers. It may seem like he keeps you waiting, but everything happens in his time—on his agenda—at the very best time for you.

The next time you feel like you've been waiting forever, remember that God knows when and what is best for you.

Prayer

God, I'm sorry for being so impatient. I want to see time like you do, so I choose to trust your master plan for my life.

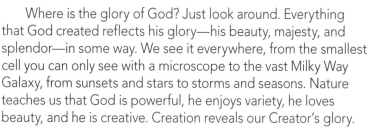

Glimpses of Glory

The heavens declare the glory of God; the skies proclaim the work of his hands.

(PSALM 19:1)

Where is the glory of God? Just look around. Everything that God created reflects his glory—his beauty, majesty, and splendor—in some way. We see it everywhere, from the smallest cell you can only see with a microscope to the vast Milky Way Galaxy, from sunsets and stars to storms and seasons. Nature teaches us that God is powerful, he enjoys variety, he loves beauty, and he is creative. Creation reveals our Creator's glory.

Throughout history, God has revealed his glory to people in different settings. The Bible portrays it as a consuming fire, a cloud, thunder, smoke, and a brilliant light (Exodus 24:17, 40:34; Psalm 29:3; Isaiah 6:3–4, 60:1; Luke 2:9). God revealed his glory in the Garden of Eden, to Moses, in the tabernacle and the temple, through Jesus and through the Church on Earth. In Heaven, God's glory provides all the light needed. Someday those who love and follow God will see his glory face to face.

Prayer

Wow, God—you put so much care into creating this world! While I can see your glory here on Earth, I look forward to seeing you face-to-face one day.

Pitch In

You are worthy, our Lord and God, to receive glory and honor and power.

(REVELATION 4:11A)

Birds bring glory to God by flying, chirping, and nesting—bird-like activities that God intended. Even ants bring glory to God when they fulfill the purpose they were created for. God made ants to be ants, and he made you to be you.

How can you bring glory to God? Here are five ways that you reveal God's creation and purpose in you:

1. You bring God glory by worshiping him.
2. You bring God glory by loving other Christians. When you accept Jesus' gift of salvation, you become a part of God's family.
3. You bring God glory when you think, feel, and act like Christ.
4. You bring God glory by helping others through your talents, gifts, skills, and abilities.
5. You bring God glory by telling others about him. God doesn't want his love and purposes kept a secret. Once you know the truth, he expects you to share the Good News with others.

Prayer

God, I know I don't always recognize or praise you for how glorious you are. I want my life to reflect your glory.

Searching and Searching

*He who forms the mountains, who creates the wind,
and who reveals his thoughts to mankind, who turns
dawn to darkness, and treads on the heights of the
earth—the LORD God Almighty is his name.*

(AMOS 4:13)

When you are playing hide-and-seek, how long do you search before you give up? Five minutes? Ten minutes? You'd be very persistent if you searched for fifteen minutes or more.

But did you know that it wouldn't be fair to play hide-and-seek with God because he always knows where we are! And he will stop at nothing to capture our hearts. He whispers our name. He shows us truth through people and his written Word. He shows us mercy and miracles. He sacrificed his perfect Son. And sometimes he gives us tough love.

That's what he was doing for Israel in the book of Amos. His chosen people had wandered away from his love and stubbornly refused to return. Five times he urged them to come back. "I did this, but you didn't return to me," he says. "So I did that, but you didn't return to me."

Day after day, God is persistently searching for us. Will you answer the call and give him your heart?

Prayer

God, thank you for loving me. I want to know you, because the more I know you the more I love you.

A Little Unhappy

For this world is not our permanent home; we are looking forward to a home yet to come.

(HEBREWS 13:14, NLT)

A fish would never be happy living on land, because it was made for water. An eagle could never feel satisfied if it wasn't allowed to fly. And we'll never be completely happy here on Earth because we're not supposed to be! Earth is not our final home; we were created for something much better.

In order to keep us from becoming too attached to Earth, God allows us to feel discontent and dissatisfaction in earthly life. Our deep longings will not be fulfilled until eternity. This explains why followers of Jesus experience hard times, sadness, and disappointment in this world. It also explains why some of God's promises seem unfulfilled, some prayers seem unanswered, and some things seem unfair. This is not the end of the story.

You will have happy moments here, but one day, if you accept Jesus' gift of salvation, you will know complete happiness and joy in Heaven with God.

Prayer

Life on Earth is full of sad and difficult times along with the happy moments, Lord. When it gets hard, remind me of your promise of the true joy to come.

In Deep Water

When the disciples saw him walking on the lake, they were terrified . . . Jesus immediately said to them: "Take courage! It is I. Don't be afraid." "Lord, if it's you," Peter replied, "tell me to come to you on the water."

(MATTHEW 14:26–28)

Unless you know how to swim, you don't head in to deep water. It's just not safe. But in your life, God wants to take you into the deep waters of faith.

Most people live in the shallow end. There's little depth to their lives or their relationship with God. Why? Because it feels safer in shallow water. They think, "If I get out into the deep water, there might be some waves. They might rock my boat, and it might overturn. So I'll just stay back here where it's safe and comfortable and fiddle around."

When God works in your life, it always means going deeper. Many Christians barely get their feet wet because they're afraid of getting in over their heads. They think, "What will my friends or family think? What if God asks me to do something bold for him?" So they miss out on a lot.

God's plan for your life is a good plan—the best. You can trust him. He will not let you drown. He will make your faith deeper and stronger in him.

Prayer

It's scary sometimes, Lord, to trust in your plans and get out of my comfort zone. Help me to be bold in my faith and trust in your good plan.

The Choice Is Yours

For we know that if the earthly tent we live in is destroyed, we have a building from God, an eternal house in heaven, not built by human hands.

(2 CORINTHIANS 5:1)

One day your heart will stop beating. That will be the end of your body and your time on Earth, but it will not be the end of you. Your earthly body is just a temporary home for your spirit. The Bible calls your earthly body a "tent" but refers to your future body as a "house." The Bible says, "When this tent we live in—our body here on earth—is torn down, God will have a house in heaven for us to live in, a home he himself has made, which will last forever" (2 Corinthians 5:1, TEV).

While life on Earth offers many choices, eternity offers only two: Heaven or Hell. God loves you so much, he wants you to meet him in Heaven. But it's your choice. Your relationship with God on Earth will determine your relationship to him forever. If you love and trust God's Son, Jesus, you will spend eternity with him. On the other hand, if you reject his love, forgiveness, and salvation, you will spend eternity apart from God forever.

What will you choose?

Prayer

I accept your gift of salvation, Jesus. Help me to choose to follow you every day.

The Final Word

You intended to harm me, but God intended it for good to accomplish what is now being done, the saving of many lives.

(GENESIS 50:20)

God is in control of the final outcome. He can take all our mistakes and all the sins that other people commit against us and turn them around. We may think everything is a mess, but God has the final say. He brings good out of bad.

Consider Joseph. He was nearly killed, sold into slavery, falsely accused, and put into prison. His life was heading downhill fast. But then God took those tragedies and brought good out of them. While Joseph was in prison, he made friends with the right-hand man of Pharaoh. A few years later, Pharaoh met Joseph and was so impressed with him that he made Joseph second in command over all of Egypt. In the end, Joseph saved Egypt plus several other nations from starvation.

God sees what is going on. And he will use bad choices and even bad situations to turn things around—Just hang on and watch what he does!

Prayer

Lord, help me to hang on even when I do not understand your plans. I trust that you know what is best for me.

Faith and Friendship with God

Perfect Every Time

He is the Rock, his works are perfect, and all his ways are just. A faithful God who does no wrong.

(DEUTERONOMY 32:4A)

Do you ever make mistakes? Of course! I make mistakes. You make mistakes. Everyone messes up. We are not perfect. But guess what—God never has to say, "Oops!" He never makes a mistake.

That means every single person is God's perfect creation. God has a plan for each one. He made you for a reason. He uses every situation in your life for his plan. He also uses every problem, even if you get yourself into trouble. And when something doesn't make sense to you, God uses that too.

He is in control of the universe, including the part of the universe you and I live in. You don't have to figure anything out by yourself. All God expects from you is that you turn to him and trust him. No one else could come up with a better plan than the one he has for your life. After all, he is perfect, and he does everything just right.

Prayer

God, you are in control of my life. Help me to turn to you in the happy times and in the tough times and trust in your plan for me.

Make It Your Own

Choose for yourselves this day whom you will serve, whether the gods your ancestors served beyond the Euphrates, or the gods of the Amorites, in whose land you are living. But as for me and my household, we will serve the LORD.

(JOSHUA 24:15B)

Joshua had seen a lot in his lifetime. First, he was born a slave in Egypt. Then he spent years learning valuable skills as Moses' sidekick. Joshua then inherited a homeless nation but saw God give victory after victory in a new land flowing with milk and honey (sounds sticky!). Maybe Joshua had a robe that said, "Been there, done that!"

When he was 110 years old, he gave one last speech of sorts. He challenged his countrymen to take a stand. Everyone listening to him had been raised to know about the one true God. But the Israelites still had a choice to make: They couldn't claim their parents' faith. They had to make faith personal.

How about you? Have you made the decision to build your life on God's ways? If your parents have, that's great. But your parents aren't you. Their faith is helpful and important. But it doesn't mean you automatically have a friendship with God because they do. At the same time, if your parents don't know God, you can choose to believe God for yourself. Be like Joshua. Make a choice, and boldly tell others about it.

Prayer

Today, God, I choose you. Faith in you and your love for me is my choice.

Mama Bird

He will cover you with his feathers, and under his wings you will find refuge; his faithfulness will be your shield and rampart.

(PSALM 91:4)

You've probably heard that you should never touch a nest, egg, or baby chick, since the mama will be able to smell your scent. Birds are super protective of their eggs and babies. Some go to crazy lengths to keep their chicks safe. The African palm-swift has amazing spit. The bird uses saliva to make a nest on the underside of a branch, creating a glue that holds the nest together and keeps the eggs in place. Another African bird, the hammerkopf, builds such a massive nest—six feet by six feet—that other smaller birds come over and use it for their eggs and babies too.

This little bit of bird trivia helps us understand why God compares his care for us to the way birds care for their young. He watches over his children with great care. He takes care of our needs. He builds protection for those in his family. Like the nest of a palm-swift or hammerkopf, God's family is a place safe from enemy attacks and a shelter from life's storms.

Prayer

Thank you, Lord, for protecting me and caring for me.

Grateful Heart

*Now this is what the L*ord* Almighty says: "Give careful thought to your ways. You have planted much, but harvested little. You eat, but never have enough. You drink, but never have your fill. You put on clothes, but are not warm. You earn wages, only to put them in a purse with holes in it."*

(HAGGAI 1:5–6)

In less than five minutes, you hear a friend say all these things: "I want another pair of shoes." "When are you gonna buy me a new bike?" "It's time for a new backpack; I don't like the one from last year." "I deserve more money in my allowance."

Selfish and ungrateful, don't you think? But would you still think the same of that kid if he only said one selfish thing a day? How about if he asked his parents for something new just once a month?

The timing doesn't matter. What matters is how content, or satisfied, you are with what you have. No matter if it's over an extra cookie or the latest and greatest bike, an ungrateful heart leads to waste. When you don't appreciate what you have, you don't enjoy or use it to its fullest.

The key to being content is thankfulness. Try this: Start each day this week naming five things you are thankful for. Each day, name a different set of five things. By the end of the week, you should notice less complaining and wanting. That will please God and your parents. Plus you will be happy with what you have.

Prayer

Thank you, Lord, for my home, my friends, my parents, my meals, and my clothes. Show me what else to be thankful for.

Word Power

*My soul is weary with sorrow; strengthen me
according to your word.*

(PSALM 119:28)

Animals have unique ways of showing agitation, fear, or sadness. Mad horses flatten their ears. Irritated iguanas whip their tales back and forth. And who can forget the freaked-out puffer fish? It blows up like a spiky balloon!

Unlike the puffer fish, humans don't worry about getting eaten by a sea snake. But we do get bummed out because of the messed-up world around us. To deal with those feelings, some people turn to sports or energy-burning physical activities. Others throw themselves into their hobby or look for (and usually find) trouble.

King David was no stranger to frustration, anger, or sadness. Yet his stress relief was a little unusual: he turned to the Word of God. The Bible isn't a few thousand pages of boring old history or rules. Those pages literally have the power to change lives. And as David showed, God's Word can give great strength to its readers.

It's awesome to kiss stress goodbye through sports, friends, or hobbies. But those things only give a temporary fix. For permanent peace, strength, and joy, crack open your Bible. Let the awe-inspiring words of God recharge your tired, scared, or confused soul.

It's a much better option than what the puffer fish has to do, don't you think?

Prayer

Lord, when I am angry or sad or frustrated, remind me to turn to you first. Help me to remember that you have my back. Your Word contains comfort and encouragement for every problem.

Happy to See You

*For the L*ORD *takes delight in his people; he crowns
the humble with victory. Let his faithful people rejoice
in this honor and sing for joy on their beds.*

(PSALM 149:4–5)

You start nodding off after a fun day at the beach with
your favorite friends. Then you jerk up your head, trying to stay
awake. Tomorrow you have to go back to school, and you don't
want the fun to end. So everyone keeps poking each other to try
to stay awake. Sometimes you just don't want a day to end.

God's people did the same thing because of God's blessings. When God gave the Israelites a victory, healed a dying
family member, or blessed them with good food and celebration—they laid on their beds singing to God because they just
didn't want a good day in God to end.

Once you are a follower of God, those days never end. Even
when you have a bad day at school or hear bad news at home,
God is still thrilled to have you in his family. He is right there to
remind you that he is large and in charge. So every night when
you go to bed, you don't have to worry that the goodness of
God will ever come to an end.

Prayer

I will sing praises to you, God, because you are good all the
time and I am one of your children. Thank you for loving me and
delighting in me.

Throw a Party

*The king contributed from his own possessions . . .
for the burnt offerings on the Sabbaths, at the New
Moons and at the appointed festivals as written in
the Law of the LORD . . . As soon as the order went
out, the Israelites generously gave the firstfruits of
their grain, new wine, olive oil and honey and all that
the fields produced.*

(2 CHRONICLES 31:3, 5)

State fairs, carnivals, festivals, parties, barbecues—if you think long enough, you can probably come up with a celebration for almost anything. If something notable happens in a town or country, the residents want to remember it—and it becomes an excuse to throw a party! "George grew the biggest pumpkin this year—so why not start an annual pumpkin contest, with a big fall festival?"

Do you know where the first celebration party was held? Long ago in Heaven, before Earth was ever created. The angels celebrated God and rejoiced over his goodness and love. God didn't want humans to miss out on the same joy. So God told his first followers to have fun: Celebrate your good farming seasons. Mark God's miracles on your calendar. Take a break from your toil for a big feast.

You might have thought that following God is anti-fun, but God himself is a partygoer. So the next time something good happens (good grades, winning a game, a new baby brother or sister), create your own festival or party. God would love to join you.

Prayer

Lord, how great that fun is part of your world and your command. Thank you for giving me joy and good things to celebrate.

DAY 70

An Awesome Friend

What, then, shall we say in response to these things? If God is for us, who can be against us? He who did not spare his own Son, but gave him up for us all— how will he not also, along with him, graciously give us all things?

(ROMANS 8:31–32)

How awesome would it be to have the cast from a Disney Channel show as your friends? Or the Olympic swimming team? Or Grammy-award-winning musicians? With friends like that, you wouldn't care if the rest of the world was full of enemies.

The right kinds of friends make you feel safe and secure. They watch your back. They help you worry less about what the bullies or popular kids say about you. You don't let a good friend go if you can help it. You know you have someone you can count on.

Don't you know that you've got the ultimate friend on your side? God is always for you. No one compares to him. He's more awesome than a lead singer. More powerful than swimmers. And cooler than Disney actors. He sent his Son, Jesus Christ, to Earth so you and he could be friends. One day, he even wants you to come live with him in Heaven. That's one awesome friendship. Don't let it go.

Prayer

Lord, thank you for your friendship and for being on my side. Remind me that I can always count on you to have my back.

Lots of Ways to Worship

Sing for joy to God our strength; shout aloud to the God of Jacob! Begin the music, strike the timbrel, play the melodious harp and lyre.

(PSALM 81:1–2)

We're not the only ones who enjoy a good concert. God loves when his people sing, cheer, and play instruments. He loves a good drum solo or a long series of runs on an electric guitar.

How do you worship God? Do you think it has to be one way? It doesn't. No one else sounds like you or worships like you. Maybe you like to drum everything in sight—pencils on the desk, fingers tapping your knees, head bouncing to the beat. God loves that. Maybe you can't carry a tune, but you and your buddies can rap. He'll be tapping his foot and bobbing his head with you. Maybe you play a mean trumpet—well, it brings a smile to God's face every time too.

God loves music made just for him. He loves to hear your praise. No matter what it sounds like, it brings a smile to his face.

Prayer

Lord, I love that you made me. You know my voice, and you love to hear it. I praise you today.

A Little Thanks, Please

*I will sacrifice a thank offering to you and call on the name of the L*ORD*. I will fulfill my vows to the L*ORD *in the presence of all his people.*

(PSALM 116:17–18)

Saying "thank you" isn't always easy. When a relative gets you a Rudolph sweater for Christmas or wraps up a big package of floral underwear for your birthday, it's tough to come up with nice words for that "thank you" card—or even when your mom puts a pile of veggies on your plate and is waiting for those magic words: "Thanks, Mom."

That's the way it works. When someone gives a gift, we say "thank you." We write the words. We put the smile on our face. We thank the person because we know that they love us. They are being kind and generous. Even when we don't really like the gift, we thank the giver.

God wants us to give thanks to him, even when we audition and don't get called back. Or when we try sewing a straight line and mess it up three times in a row. Or when we pray for sunshine and get rain. That's why it's called a "sacrifice of praise." We may not feel like it in the moment, but we know that God has good things for us, even if they're not what we want. We thank him anyway.

Prayer

Lord, thank you for today. Give me a thankful heart no matter what comes, because you are the giver, and you are good.

Full Expressions

Why, Lord, do you stand far off? Why do you hide yourself in times of trouble?

(PSALM 10:1)

The book of Psalms is a collection of worship songs or poetry to God. Sounds pretty tame. Certain chapters can definitely be calm and soothing, but there are just as many psalms that are angry, irritated, freaked out, or even a little whiny. "Wait!" you might think. "Aren't we only supposed to say nice things about God like 'Hallelujah' and 'Praise the Lord'?"

When David wrote Psalm 10, he was seriously miffed and not afraid to tell the Lord. He was sick of the neighborhood bully and angry with the local head honchos who lied and cheated their way to the top.

Sound familiar? Maybe you see the popular kid mocking the new girl at school, or you know a straight-A student who cheats on every history test and then brags about it. Your heart might wonder why God lets them get away with everything. But your head tells you to cork your complaints. After all, won't Jesus be mad if you vent about that soccer player who trash talks and plays dirty when the refs aren't looking? No way! Throughout the psalms, David questioned God, griped about the wicked, and told God he wanted him to do something about it. David used real language to tell the real God about real problems. It's okay to let God know how you really feel. Don't worry—your heavenly Father can handle it!

Prayer

Heavenly Dad, you like hearing about my day. Thanks for being a safe person I can tell anything to, even my anger or questions. I know you still love me anyway.

BFFs

The LORD confides in those who fear him; he makes his covenant known to them.

(PSALM 25:14)

Everyone wants a best friend—someone to talk to about who you like in class. Someone who promises to keep your secrets about what you want to be when you grow up. Someone who likes you because you are funny or quiet or cheerful. You may have a best friend or even a few. You'll find best friends from camp, swim lessons, your baseball team, art class, band practice, and more. When you move to a new town, a neighbor could become your new best friend.

Did you know there is a friend who can be a best friend for the rest of your life? God calls some people his friends. If you ask God to be in your life and you follow his ways, he will call you his friend too. And he will be the best friend you could have. He will never stop being your friend, even if you move to the other side of the country. He'll share his secrets with you. He'll tell you what he's doing in the world. Who knows—he may even ask you to help him! After all, that's what friends do for each other.

Prayer

Lord, I want to have you as my best friend. I don't quite understand how you can be when I can't see you, play with you, or spend the night at your house. But having you as my friend sounds like the best.

More Than a Song

God is spirit, and those who worship him must worship in spirit and truth.

(JOHN 4:24, NCV)

Did you know worship has nothing to do with the style or volume or speed of a song? God loves all kinds of music because he invented it all—fast and slow, loud and soft, old and new. You probably don't like it all, but God does! If it is offered to God, it is an act of worship.

Actually, worship was around before music. Adam worshiped in the Garden of Eden, but music isn't mentioned. If worship were just music, then all who are nonmusical could never worship. Worship is far more than music.

For many people, worship means music. They say, "At our church we have the worship first, and then the teaching." The truth is, every part of a church service is an act of worship: praying, Scripture reading, singing, confession, silence, being still, listening to a sermon, taking notes, giving an offering, baptism, communion, and greeting other people. Even outside of church, you can worship God in many ways. Where and how will you worship him next?

Prayer

I'm glad I can worship you, Lord, in so many creative ways and places! Thank you for the ability to praise you wherever I am.

Feel Good for God

For the LORD takes delight in his people.
(PSALM 149:4A)

God wired you with five senses, and he gave you feelings. Why? So you can experience pleasure. This is one of his greatest gifts. He wants you to enjoy what you see, hear, taste, smell, and touch. The reason you are able to feel happy, have fun, and laugh is that God made you in his image.

God has emotions too. He feels things very deeply. The Bible tells us that God feels compassion, pity, sadness, and sympathy as well as happiness, gladness, and satisfaction. God loves, delights, rejoices, enjoys, and even laughs!

When you enjoy life, you bring joy to God. You are a child of God, and you bring pleasure to God like nothing else he has ever created. The Bible says, "Because of his love, God had already decided to make us his own children through Jesus Christ. That was what he wanted and what pleased him" (Ephesians 1:5, NCV).

Prayer

God, thank you for the gift of emotions and for caring about your people so deeply. I want to bring joy to you and enjoy this life I have.

Crack Up

Sarah said, "God has brought me laughter, and everyone who hears about this will laugh with me."

(GENESIS 21:6)

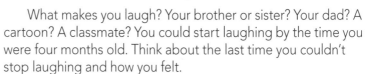

What makes you laugh? Your brother or sister? Your dad? A cartoon? A classmate? You could start laughing by the time you were four months old. Think about the last time you couldn't stop laughing and how you felt.

It may seem strange that the Bible includes many stories that tell us when people laughed. But God made laughter. He designed your brain to send signals to your mouth when something is funny, when you feel happy, or when you hear or see something that you enjoy. Laughing also happens when you are surprised. Sarah, Abraham's wife, laughed when God surprised her with a baby boy. She was happy.

How can you help your friends or family laugh? Bring some surprise and happiness to others. Laughter is like medicine; it makes you feel better. If you're feeling down, laughing can boost your mood. Even scientists say that if you laugh a lot, your health is better. God must have known that you would need a pick-me-up every so often.

Prayer

God, when my friends or family are sad or discouraged, I'd like to help them laugh. Will you give me ideas to bring happiness to others?

Party Crashers

Even though you bring me burnt offerings and grain offerings, I will not accept them. Though you bring choice fellowship offerings, I will have no regard for them.

(AMOS 5:22)

Your grandma is throwing you the coolest-ever birthday party. Guess how you get to celebrate? Helicopter rides! Awesome!

But when the big day comes, several not-so-nice classmates show up. Apparently, the bullies heard about the helicopters and sweet-talked your grandma into letting them come.

You're upset! You don't want people at your party who pretend to like you just so they can ride helicopters. You want real friends who actually care.

God is the same way. When people go to church, sing worship songs, give money, and donate time and talents to the community, he doesn't want it to be fake or for show. God wants us to be there because we love him.

The Israelites were sometimes guilty of being frauds. They went to church and sacrificed burnt offerings, but their hearts weren't sincere. And God wasn't buying it. "I hate, I despise your religious festivals" (Amos 5:21a).

It's great to give time, money, efforts, and talents to God. But if you're doing those things to get kudos from others, you've got it backward. God doesn't want you to crash the party—he wants your commitment and friendship.

Prayer

Lord, I don't want my "presents" to you to be fake. I want them to be from my heart. Will you help me as I learn to be real with you?

Misdirected

So all the people took off their earrings and brought them to Aaron. He took what they handed him and made it into an idol cast in the shape of a calf, fashioning it with a tool. Then they said, "These are your gods, Israel, who brought you up out of Egypt."

(EXODUS 32:3–4)

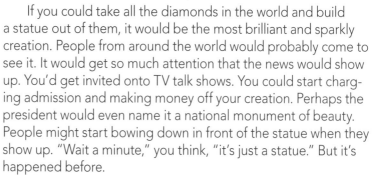

If you could take all the diamonds in the world and build a statue out of them, it would be the most brilliant and sparkly creation. People from around the world would probably come to see it. It would get so much attention that the news would show up. You'd get invited onto TV talk shows. You could start charging admission and making money off your creation. Perhaps the president would even name it a national monument of beauty. People might start bowing down in front of the statue when they show up. "Wait a minute," you think, "it's just a statue." But it's happened before.

The Israelites got really impatient with God. So they got creative. They collected all their gold. Then they made a beautiful sculpture out of it. It was so impressive that they got a little confused. They started thinking too much of their wonderful creation. Then they decided to eject God. Sounds crazy, doesn't it? But when people get too impressed with themselves or admire someone's work more than God, they get confused. They forget God and start treating something or someone like God. God is the Creator of everything beautiful. And he is always more impressive than anything any human could make.

Prayer

Lord, it seems crazy that people worshiped a statue. Please don't ever let me forget that you are the only God and the only one worthy of my praise.

Big Book of Reminders

A large crowd followed [Jesus], and he healed all who were ill. He warned them not to tell others about him. This was to fulfill what was spoken through the prophet Isaiah.

(MATTHEW 12:15B–17)

For thousands of years, God had been telling people in Israel about Jesus. God sent prophets, specially chosen men who got to talk directly with God. Prophets warned people about God's judgment and announced big news from God. But the Israelites didn't always pay attention. When they heard the news about a Savior (someone who would save their country), they listened. "When would he come?" they wondered. The clock kept ticking. Years went by. The people felt like God was taking a very long time to send a Savior. So when Jesus came to Earth, he had to remind them about what the prophets had said. "I'm the one the prophets told you about," Jesus told them.

God knows we forget important things. He also knows that we get impatient. But he reminds us about his promises. He tells us not to worry. If we forget something important about him, all we have to do is open that huge book he gave us. The better we know the Bible, the better we will know God.

Prayer

Lord, I don't know a lot about you yet, and I don't understand everything in the Bible. But I want to know you better and learn your ways.

They Did What?

About midnight Paul and Silas were praying and singing hymns to God, and the other prisoners were listening to them. Suddenly there was such a violent earthquake that the foundations of the prison were shaken. At once all the prison doors flew open, and everyone's chains came loose.

(ACTS 16:25–26)

When your parents ground you to your room, what's your reaction? Scream? Crank up the music to annoy your mom? Sing praise and thanks to God?

Wait! When we're in trouble, usually the last thing we want to do is praise God.

Paul and Silas chose praise when they found themselves in the hot seat. After Paul freed a demon-possessed slave girl, her owners were furious. She had no psychic powers left and wasn't earning money for her owners. So the local mob beat Paul and Silas and tossed them in prison.

These guys were probably cold, in pain, and tired. They could have thought, "Jesus, I've given up everything for you. And now you let me get kicked around. Thanks a lot!"

Instead, Paul and Silas prayed and worshipped. Then, an earthquake broke their chains and opened their cell doors! Not only were they freed, but several people also decided to follow Christ that night.

When we're going through rough times, it feels weird to tell Jesus how great he is. But that's exactly what we need to do.

Prayer

Jesus, you deserve my praise and love no matter what. I thank you for planning my "earthquake" even now!

Music to His Ears

Let the heavens rejoice, let the earth be glad; let the sea resound, and all that is in it. Let the fields be jubilant, and everything in them; let all the trees of the forest sing for joy.

(PSALM 96:11–12)

All of creation praises God. Like the best cartoon movies, where trees talk and dolphins sing, where crabs dance and bears wear tutus—all of creation was made to praise God. Okay, so maybe a dolphin won't actually sing *Amazing Grace*, but it can certainly leap high into the air. And a tree may not talk, but its bright, changing leaves chatter up a storm.

God made the animals, trees, the ocean, and everything in it. The colorful fish come straight from God's art box and are a living song of worship.

The next time something out in nature catches your eye, the next time a sunset or a puppy dog makes you happy, remember that it is a praise to God. The colors, the humor, the power, the beauty were all designed to make God and us smile.

You make God smile too. You are part of his song. Make today about praising him—with words, with song, with all that you are.

Prayer

I want to worship you today, God. I think you are wonderful! I praise you!

Props to the Name

You shall not misuse the name of the LORD your God, for the LORD will not hold anyone guiltless who misuses his name.

(DEUTERONOMY 5:11)

How many names do you have? Your first name. Your last name. Your mom's names for you: Sweetie, Honey. Your dad's names for you: Kiddo, Buddy, Whiz. When someone calls your name, you respond—unless maybe you know that you're getting in trouble for spilling orange juice on the carpet. When your mom or dad is upset with you, then hearing your name isn't as nice. "Jennifer Christine!" "Alex Custer!" You know what that means!

The way that someone says your name lets you know if they need you, like you, love you, or are about to come down on you.

If you sit down in a park or a shopping center and listen to the people walking by, you'll hear many people say God's name, but not in the I-love-God kind of way. People cry, "Oh my God!" "For the love of God!" and "Jesus Christ!" as exclamations of surprise or even in place of cuss words. That doesn't make God very happy. His name is the most powerful in the universe, and he only wants us to use it that way. So protect God's name. Use it only to tell him when you need him, that you love him, and that you want to know him.

Prayer

Lord, your name is so important. I want to protect your name. It is the name that gives love and forgiveness, not one that should be used casually. Help me to remember that.

Have You Noticed?

*Many, LORD my God, are the wonders you have done,
the things you planned for us. None can compare
with you; were I to speak and tell of your deeds, they
would be too many to declare.*

(PSALM 40:5)

You know that God does really big things, like parting the
Red Sea or raising Jesus from the dead. Did you know he also
cares about the little things? He'll do sweet things in the middle
of your day. He shines the sun on you when you're feeling down.
He sings a song to you through the radio or gives just the right
Bible verse when you're looking for answers.

The big things matter. But God also wants to be noticed and
remembered for the many little things he does to show us love
and care every day. Just like David, if you were to notice everything God does, you wouldn't be able to talk about it all. There'd
be too many moments to mention. God is working in your life, in
your friends, your family, and your church.

Do your best to notice him. When you see him in the details
of your day, tell others. Talk about the good that God has done
so others will learn to see him too.

Prayer

Lord, open my eyes to see your love today. Will you help me
recognize the little things you do to care for me? Thank you for
loving me in those ways.

Do the Happy Dance

Let them praise the name of the LORD, for his name alone is exalted; his splendor is above the earth and the heavens.

(PSALM 148:13)

Psalm 148 is just 14 verses, but it is a party of praise. If you read the whole chapter, count how many times it invites us to celebrate—more than the fingers on both your hands.

This celebration is worldwide. From the shining moon to the dark ocean deep, from the kings to the children, from planted trees to soaring birds, all are in a chorus of praise to God. And we can join in.

Why praise? Because when you get a glimpse of something awesome—God's goodness and love—it's natural to want to whoop it up. Plus, when you are in a party mood, nothing can get you down. There's no room for worry or fear. There's no room for sadness or jealousy. In the presence of a supernatural, almighty God, your heart is full of joy for the One who is worthy of praise.

The party has already started. Don't be shy. Join in!

Prayer

Lord God, you are worthy of praise, but I don't always act like it's time to party in celebration. I need to remember your goodness and love every day.

Full Up and Overflowing

"Blessed is the king who comes in the name of the Lord!" . . . Some of the Pharisees in the crowd said to Jesus, "Teacher, rebuke your disciples!" "I tell you," he replied, "if they keep quiet, the stones will cry out."

(LUKE 19:38–40)

Ever feel like you're about to burst with joy? Like in the middle of a worship song, while watching a spectacular sunset, or in the midst of roaring laughter with a best friend? That's the way it was when Jesus rode into Jerusalem. Those who knew him and loved him were absolutely bursting with joy. They couldn't contain themselves—they praised Jesus at the top of their lungs.

Nothing could take away the joy of the moment. Jesus even said the rocks would start singing if the people stopped.

Sometimes you might think of interaction with Jesus as subdued and quiet. And there are certainly moments that are quieter than others. But God wired you for exciting joy and loud praise. He created your happy laughter, gushy love, and squealing excitement. Does that surprise you? He loves our feelings and our interaction with him through worship.

Next time you feel praise bubbling up or joy that seems to broaden your smile and light up your eyes, let God know about it. Don't let the rocks steal the moment you could be sharing with God. Praise him from the bottom of your toes to the top of your lungs.

Prayer

Lord, I love that you are an expressive God. You gave us laughter and joy and happiness. I will sing your praises because I love you.

He Gets a Kick Out of You

The LORD directs the steps of the godly. He delights in every detail of their lives.

(PSALM 37:23, NLT)

God enjoys watching every detail of your life. He likes watching you study, read, and play. He smiles when he sees you jump, run, or spin. God even enjoys watching you eat and sleep. He doesn't miss a single move you make. That's how much he loves you.

God also likes to see you enjoy his creation. He gave you eyes to enjoy beauty, ears to enjoy sounds, your nose and taste buds to enjoy smells and tastes, and the nerves under your skin to enjoy touch. Every act of enjoyment becomes an act of worship when you thank God for it.

So you can do any human activity, except sin, to please God. Simply do it with a heart of praise. You can finish homework, build a fort, win (or lose) a game, finish chores, or help your parents make dinner for the glory of God.

Prayer

Lord, help me remember that everything I do can be an act of praise to you. Will you remind me to thank you more often for the little things in my life?

Never Overlooked

They came to Bethsaida, and some people brought a blind man and begged Jesus to touch him. He took the blind man by the hand and led him outside the village. When he had spit on the man's eyes and put his hands on him, Jesus asked, "Do you see anything?"

(MARK 8:22–23)

Sooo . . . Jesus spit on a guy's eyes? The whole idea of God coming to Earth was to experience what it feels like to be one of us. To taste, touch, see, smell, and hear our world.

But before you get too carried away with the fact that Jesus spit, look closer to see why Jesus did what he did. Jesus had a reputation for healing people, so friends brought a man who couldn't see to meet Jesus. Leaving the crowd behind, Jesus gave his personal attention to the man—just the two of them. Then Jesus reached out and touched him with his hands.

Jesus didn't have to touch the man. He could have just said, "Be healed!" But Jesus wanted to show this man with special needs that he was special to Jesus. That's what touch does. It communicates that someone matters. Jesus touched this man in the places that had caused him the most pain all his life.

Jesus wants to be personal with you too. Going to church is important. Listening to family devotions is good. But what Jesus wants most of all is to spend time with you one-on-one. Talk to him often. Tell him what's on your mind. Read his Word. Listen to what he says! Then you'll feel his touch.

Prayer

Lord, it's easy to feel overlooked in a group. There are times I feel like no one cares. But I know you care. Help me to remember you are my very best friend.

Smiling from Heaven

*But Noah pleased the L*ORD *. . . he walked with God . . . Noah did everything that God commanded him.*

(GENESIS 6:8, 9B, 22, NCV)

Noah loved God more than anything else in the world, even when no one else did! Actually, nobody outside of Noah's family loved God. They were outnumbered. Yet Noah trusted God, even when it didn't make sense to anyone else. Saving his family and the animal population from a worldwide flood required great attention and obedience. Everything had to be done just as God told him. Noah obeyed completely (in the way and time God wanted it done). That is called wholeheartedness. No wonder God smiled on Noah. Because Noah made God happy, you and I are alive today.

Do you want to make God happy? Then follow Noah's example. God smiles when you love him supremely. God smiles when you trust him completely. God smiles when you follow him with your whole heart. God smiles when you praise and thank him. And God smiles when you use your abilities to obey him.

Prayer

I want to make you happy, Lord, just as you were happy with Noah. I know you can help me love, trust, and obey you more. I want to make you smile and be proud of me.

Get Real

How long, Lord, will you look on? Rescue me from their ravages, my precious life from these lions.

(PSALM 35:17)

David was a man after God's own heart (read Acts 13:22). You would think a statement like that would refer to a guy who loved God all the time, always did the right thing, and never raised his voice. He definitely wouldn't be a guy who whines—would he?

But David had his moments. When he was in a bad mood or when he had a rough day, he was dramatic. He whined. He always told God what he was feeling. He was totally honest when he felt abandoned, scared, or angry. David was real with God. But David also knew that God would change his heart from the inside out. Psalm 35:18 proves the point: "I will give you thanks in the great assembly; among the throngs I will praise you."

You can be real with God too. When you tell him how you're feeling (which he already knows anyway!), he loves it. He loves time with you. He loves when you trust him enough to expose the negative emotions. And when you do trust him with those things, he is able to change your sorrow and anger into praise and joy. That's the nature of God. So don't be afraid to let it all out.

Prayer

God, I know that sometimes I have a bad attitude. Instead of spreading that attitude to other people, help me to bring it to you—to be real and honest with you so that you can change me from the inside out.

What Can You Give?

Tell the Israelites to bring me an offering. You are to receive the offering for me from everyone whose heart prompts them to give.

(EXODUS 25:2)

Think about the nicest gift you've ever received. It made you feel special. Now think about the best gift you've given to your mom, dad, or best friend. They probably smiled big when they opened it and gave you a hug. Gifts from the heart mean a lot. Heart gifts show how much you really care.

The Israelites brought gifts to God. Often they would make something for him, such as a fine piece of clothing or the best crops from their gardens. The strange thing is that some Israelites brought gifts to God that they didn't care about. They didn't think much about God to consider what he would really like.

The most important people get your best gifts. God asks to be one of the most important people in your life. So he wants gifts from your heart. You might write him poems, sing songs, make tasty cookies for a church potluck, or memorize Bible verses. When you do these kinds of things with your whole heart, you give a beautiful gift to God.

Prayer

Lord, I want to give beautiful gifts to you. What would you like from me?

The Real Deal

Hezekiah turned his face to the wall and prayed to the LORD, "Remember, LORD, how I have walked before you faithfully and with wholehearted devotion and have done what is good in your eyes." And Hezekiah wept bitterly.

(ISAIAH 38:2–3)

Step on a crack; break your mother's back. Swallow gum, and it stays in your stomach for seven years.

What do these statements have in common? They're old wives' tales, or superstitious sayings passed down through the generations. In fact, these old wives' tales are not true.

King Hezekiah probably heard his share of old wives' tales when he became deathly ill. A godly king, Hezekiah turned to the Lord instead of superstition and begged him to extend his life. And God granted his request! Hezekiah would not only live fifteen more years but also stay safe from the perpetually warring Assyrians (Isaiah 38:5–6).

To people who don't know God, prayer seems ridiculous, like an old wives' tale. "Wait," they might say. "You believe some invisible dude hears what you say in your mind or out loud, then answers you?" It sounds pretty weird, right?

Prayer is not a magical hotline, but it is a supernatural communication with a living, breathing heavenly Father who answers prayers. Prayer is real, and it works.

Prayer

God, it blows my mind to think you're hearing me, even right now. Thank you for listening to my prayers. Give me a chance to show your awesomeness to my friends.

Be You

How terrible it will be for those who argue with the God who made them . . . The clay does not ask the potter, "What are you doing?"

(ISAIAH 45:9A, NCV)

Do you ever wish you could be like someone else? Maybe another kid seems smarter or stronger or funnier. Or maybe you want to be older, faster, or better looking. Guess what! You only make God happy by being you. You don't bring glory to God by hiding your abilities or by trying to be someone else. Any time you dislike any part of yourself, you are rejecting God's wisdom and purpose in creating you.

Like a proud parent, God enjoys watching you use the talents and abilities he has given you. God gave each person different gifts for his enjoyment. He has made some to be athletic and some to be scientific. He has made some to be quiet and others to be loud. You may be gifted at art or math or listening or one of a thousand other skills. All your abilities can bring a smile to God's face. So be *you.*

Prayer

Lord, I can forget why I am special and wish I were someone else. But in those times, can you remind me that you love me just as I am?

Music Makers

Clap your hands, all you nations; shout to God with cries of joy. Sing praises to God, sing praises; sing praises to our King, sing praises.

(PSALM 47:1, 6)

The oldest instrument in the world is a flute made out of bone. Thousands of years old, the bone flute shows just how long music, rhythm, and dance have been around. In fact, your favorite band probably plays instruments that originated from simpler instruments used during Bible times, such as the lyre and flute. The people who lived during the Old Testament loved music. Some of their instruments are still played today: flutes, harps, cymbals, trumpets, and dulcimers. They made up songs on the spot when something marvelous happened or sang sadly when someone died. The kings and queens had singers and musicians who played in the royal court. The psalms were often songs, and King David composed many of them.

Music is a wonderful gift. Church services always include singing. Even the angels in Heaven create music for God. So if you love music or love playing a certain instrument, keep it up. Singing brings joy to others and to God. It can even improve your mood (David played music for King Saul to calm Saul down) and help you learn. So keep the tunes in your life.

Prayer

Lord, I see that music is important to you. I want all my singing and music to glorify you and bring joy.

Everywhere

Where can I go from your Spirit? Where can I flee from your presence? If I go up to the heavens, you are there; if I make my bed in the depths, you are there.

(PSALM 139:7–8)

This world is a gigantic place. If you started at the equator, your poor feet would walk (and swim!) nearly twenty-five thousand miles to get back to where you began in the United States. In fact, Earth is big enough to hold more than ninety-five billion football fields (that's a lot of foam fingers!).

You could spend your entire life traveling and still not see every country, mountain, desert, city, or forest. Yet no matter how huge this world is, it's still not enough to keep you from God's presence.

King David's mind wandered this direction while shepherding or chilling on his palace rooftop. He may have thought, "If I feel God's presence out here, is there any place I can go where he's not? Could someone ever run away from the Lord?" NO!

Some people think God's presence is only at church, so they try to outrun him. They bury themselves in work, school, or hobbies. But like David pointed out, that tactic won't work.

You could be an astronaut rocketing to the moon or a submariner exploring the ocean. Either way, God is there.

So explore the world and even the galaxy. Because no matter where you go, God will be with you.

Prayer

God, I love to dream about the places I'll go someday. This world is crazy-awesome! But it's so comforting to know you're with me all the time. Thank you for watching over and guiding me.

Never-Ending Friend

I speak to you as my friends, and I have told you everything that my Father has told me.

(JOHN 15:15B, CEV)

In Genesis, Adam and Eve had a good friendship with God. They didn't have a temple or church to go to. They just spent time with him every day. Adam and Eve delighted in God, and he delighted in them. That's the kind of friendship God wants with you.

But after the Fall (Genesis 3), Adam and Eve lost that relationship with their Father. Only a few people in Old Testament times had the privilege of friendship with God. Moses and Abraham were called friends of God. David was called a man after God's own heart. And Job, Enoch, and Noah had close relationships with God.

When Jesus came to Earth, he changed the situation. He paid for our sins on the cross and made it possible for anyone to have direct access to God again. So you can have a friendship with God just like Adam and Eve did before the Fall. It will be the best one you will ever have.

Prayer

God, thank you for being my friend. Teach me to be as good a friend to others as you are to me.

God's Love

Dear friends, since God so loved us, we also ought to love one another.

(1 JOHN 4:11)

In some ways, loving God is the easiest thing in the world. He's perfectly trustworthy, takes care of us, wants the best for us, and loves us completely. Before we even asked, he sacrificed his beloved Son to rescue us.

Loving other imperfect people is the tough part. Unlike God, they can be flaky, mean, hurtful, arrogant, and way more selfish than sacrificial.

Think of the cross that Jesus died on. It has the vertical piece and the horizontal crossbeam. God wants us to love him (the vertical expression) *and* love others (the horizontal expression).

It seems impossible to do until you look at the example of Jesus when he walked the earth. He showed us how it could be done and what it looks like to "know and rely on the love God has for us" (1 John 4:16). And he offers the Holy Spirit to help us do it. In relationship with him, we can do it.

Prayer

Lord, help me love like Jesus loves. Thank you for the Spirit who can help me do it.

Do I Know You?

Meanwhile, Simon Peter was still standing there warming himself. So they asked him, "You aren't one of his disciples too, are you?" He denied it, saying, "I am not." One of the high priest's servants, a relative of the man whose ear Peter had cut off, challenged him, "Didn't I see you with him in the garden?" Again Peter denied it, and at that moment a rooster began to crow.

(JOHN 18:25–27)

Have you ever slowly slinked away from a friend when he gets in trouble or makes too much noise or says something stupid in a crowd?

Peter, one of Jesus' best friends, did that. But instead of slinking away, Peter denied he even knew Jesus. Talk about a scaredy-cat!

Now imagine how it would feel if your best friend ditched you like that. Ouch! That would hurt. Peter knew Jesus was the mighty Son of God but was afraid to admit it. As painful as it was for Jesus to hear that Peter denied him, Jesus forgave Peter. They stayed friends. Later on, Peter got over his fears and talked boldly about Jesus Christ.

It's normal to feel scared. Don't be surprised if you are scared to acknowledge a certain friend or ashamed that you go to church. Here's the truth that will chase fear right out of you: Nothing is greater than God. Fear comes from thinking something else or someone else is greater than God. God is always greater.

Prayer

Jesus, I have been embarrassed to be associated with you. I don't know why I am afraid of others' opinions of you. You are greater than anyone or anything. Help me to remember that.

All the Time

*Praise God in the great congregation; praise the L*ORD *in the assembly of Israel.*

(PSALM 68:26)

Make a list of what comes to mind when you think of praising God. Jot down what that means to you. Maybe it's standing and singing in a church service or reading Psalms out loud. Sometimes "praise" seems like a churchy word that doesn't fit into our Monday to Saturday world. Could you praise in the middle of geography class? Praise during breakfast? What would that look like?

Praise is something we can do anytime, anywhere. It doesn't mean we have to stand up and start belting out a hymn on the school bus. Praise can be as simple as thanking God in our thoughts: "Thanks, God, for the eggs this morning." Praise also thinks about the goodness of God: "You are awesome, God. I love the way you made those mountains!"

Praise is something we can all do, every day, all the time. We just have to think about what we love about God and then tell him—in our thoughts, out loud, or even on paper. We were made to praise him, and it's a lot easier than we think.

Prayer

Lord, help me to remember to praise you today. Show me all the wonderful things about you so I can say them in my thoughts and in my words.

Need a Boost?

For physical training is of some value, but godliness has value for all things, holding promise for both the present life and the life to come.

(1 TIMOTHY 4:8)

"Eat your vegetables!" How many times have you heard that? Why do your parents or babysitters tell you that? Because vegetables are like power packs for your body. When you eat veggies, they fuel you with vitamins and nutrients. Your body works better when it gets all that good stuff. Being active is the same way; it trains your muscles, organs, and brain to grow and get stronger.

For an even bigger power boost, Paul told Timothy to go for godliness. Knowing God helps your life now and your life after Earth. You know how when you spend a lot of time with a friend, you start to have similarities? Training in godliness is like getting closer to a friend. The more time together, the more you laugh at the same things, know when the other is sad or happy, and communicate without words. Godliness builds in you as you become more like God. And it affects your mind and heart in powerful ways.

But don't give up your vegetables just yet. Your body still needs those.

Prayer

Lord, godliness sounds like a big task. But like eating healthy and being active, I understand how it is good for me. Will you train me in your ways so I grow in godliness?

Conversation Partner

For in him we live and move and are!
(ACTS 17:28A, TLB)

Wouldn't it be strange to have a silent friend? It wouldn't be much of a friendship if you never heard a peep out of that friend!

Being friends with God means he wants a talking relationship with you. He wants more than an appointment in your schedule. A common misconception is that spending time with God means being alone with him or going to church. Of course, you need both of those, but that is only a small part of your waking hours.

God wants to be included in every activity, every conversation, every problem, and even every thought. So share all your life experiences with him—just like you would with your mom or dad or best friend. You can carry on a continuous, open-ended conversation with him throughout your day, talking with him about whatever you are doing or thinking any time. Invite him to be a part of everything you do. You'll start to notice his presence more and become true friends.

Prayer

God, I'm sorry for the times I forget to talk to you. Help me talk to you more often and include you in every thought. I want to be better friends with you.

A Friend Full of Mercy

Now Peter was sitting out in the courtyard, and a servant girl came to him. "You also were with Jesus of Galilee," she said. But he denied it before them all . . . Then Peter remembered the word Jesus had spoken: "Before the rooster crows, you will disown me three times." And he went outside and wept bitterly.

(MATTHEW 26:69–70, 75)

Peter was one of Jesus' closest friends on Earth. Peter was ranked as the first disciple and often spoke for the rest of the followers of Jesus. So Peter was top dog among the guys and gals who hung out with Jesus. But Peter also made some big mistakes. In public. In front of Jesus. In embarrassing ways. During Jesus' hardest time, Peter even denied that he knew Jesus. What a letdown.

But you know what? Jesus always welcomed Peter with open arms. Peter was quick to recognize his mistakes and confess them. Jesus knew Peter wasn't perfect and didn't expect him to be. He knew he would never find perfect disciples; he wouldn't have wanted them anyway. He wanted regular guys and gals who make mistakes. Those who stick their foot in their mouth. Those who get impatient. Those who say the wrong things. Imperfect followers give Jesus the chance to show his love and grace. He gives both to everyone. And for those who confess their wrongs and want to do right, Jesus calls those people his friends. Are you one of those people?

Prayer

Jesus, thank you for asking me to be one of your followers. I want to be one of your friends. Help me see my wrongs and want to do what's right.

Chew on This

The LORD revealed Himself to Samuel at Shiloh by the word of the LORD.

(1 SAMUEL 3:21B, NASB)

To be God's friend, you have to know what he says. You can't love God unless you know him. You can't know him without knowing his Word. The Bible says God revealed himself to Samuel through his word. God still uses that method today.

While you cannot spend all day studying the Bible, you can think about it throughout the day. Remember verses you have read and chew them over in your mind. This is called "meditation." Meditation is simply focused thinking or putting your attention on one thing. Anyone can learn and use this skill.

When you think about a problem over and over in your mind, that's called worry. When you think about God's Word over and over in your mind, that's meditation. You just need to switch your attention from your problems to Bible verses. The more you meditate on God's Word, the less you will have to worry about. And the better you will know God.

Prayer

I want to meditate on your word, God, rather than worry. As I read the Bible, help me to focus on those words so I can remember them when I start to worry.

Sleeping Like a Baby

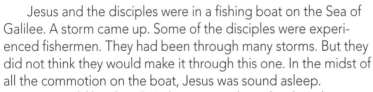

*He got up and rebuked the wind and the raging
waters; the storm subsided, and all was calm.*

(LUKE 8:24B)

Jesus and the disciples were in a fishing boat on the Sea of
Galilee. A storm came up. Some of the disciples were experienced fishermen. They had been through many storms. But they
did not think they would make it through this one. In the midst of
all the commotion on the boat, Jesus was sound asleep.

How could he sleep? He knew something the disciples
didn't know: God was in control. Then with one word from Jesus,
the storm stopped.

The disciple Peter learned something from that incident
about getting a good night's sleep. Some years later he was
arrested by King Herod and put in prison (Acts 12:1–19). God
sent an angel to rescue him. The angel had to strike Peter on
the side to wake him up because Peter was sleeping like a baby!
Why? Because he knew the Lord was in control. Peter was trusting God. That is real peace!

Prayer

Dear God, I want to have peace and security like Peter and
Jesus and know you are always with me. When I question if you
are there, remind me of your presence.

The Right Kind of Fear

The fear of the LORD is the beginning of knowledge,
but fools despise wisdom and instruction.

(PROVERBS 1:7)

Want to know how to be smarter—not just at school, but about everything? Then fear God.

Wait a minute! Does that mean you have to be afraid of God?

In the Bible, "fearing" someone didn't mean being afraid. The kind of fear that Solomon—the wisest man who ever lived—wrote about is different. Solomon learned that God was awesome and mighty. When he respected who God was, then he found out that God gave him the smarts to deal with disputes in his kingdom and hard decisions about running his country. Solomon also knew that if he disobeyed God's ways, the consequences could be severe.

When you are smart about obeying your parents, you are actually showing the kind of fear Solomon was talking about. Think about how when you obey and respect your parents, your life goes smoothly. But when you disobey them, there are naturally going to be consequences. When you respect God's words (the Bible) and follow his commands, you are fearing God. Choose to fear God, and you'll start to notice how much wiser you get about friends, school, and your parents. Because when you do things God's way, you're following the smartest path.

Prayer

God, I want to learn more about you so I can become wise. Teach me about who you are and how to live by your ways.

A Formula That Works

Is anyone among you in trouble? Let them pray. Is anyone happy? Let them sing songs of praise. Is anyone among you sick? Let them call the elders of the church to pray over them and anoint them with oil in the name of the Lord.

(JAMES 5:13–14)

At the beginning of the school year, you find out what subjects you will be learning. You're told what books to read, what math equations to memorize, and how many words to spell correctly. The formula is the same: study hard, memorize, pass.

A lot of things have proven formulas: Do this, and that will happen. Be nice to others, and then others will be nice to you. Obey your parents, and you'll avoid getting grounded. Mix sugar, flour, eggs, butter, and baking soda, and you'll have the base for cookies.

God offers "formulas" about prayer too. When certain situations occur, it's time to talk to God. In trouble? You bet that prayer is a good solution. Really happy? Don't keep it to yourself; praise God. Sick? Let the leaders at your church know to pray for you. God doesn't want to be left out of the important moments of your life. And prayer is the formula to keep him in the loop.

Prayer

Lord, thank you for clear direction on how and when to pray. I know I can talk to you any time.

Stronger Than Fear

Fear of man will prove to be a snare, but whoever trusts in the Lord is kept safe.

(PROVERBS 29:25)

Count how many things you are afraid of. It's normal to feel afraid of the dark, snakes, bugs, the woods, etc. The world has lots of scary things in it. And sin makes people do scary things. They make threats. They hurt others. They create monsters and horror movies.

But fear is not from God—ever! He actually wants to make you fearless. And you know what? He can.

We don't like to feel pain, so it's normal to fear things or people who can hurt us. This is where God steps in. He can make you stronger inside than any pain that you would feel outside of him. While he doesn't stop painful things from happening, he will change your heart and mind so that fear does not rule you. After all, the God of the universe is offering you strength and safety. Even the dark or creepy creatures don't scare our great big God.

Prayer

Lord, I am afraid of [fill in the blank]. But you aren't afraid of those things. Please fill me with your peace and make me fearless for you.

Turn on the Light

Your word is a lamp for my feet, a light on my path.
(PSALM 119:105)

At a sleepover, playing hide and seek in the dark or with flashlights can be fun. You pad yourself with pillows. You laugh and bump into each other. In the morning, though, someone suggests cooking breakfast in the dark. Huh? Without light, you could accidentally cook the yogurt and stir the eggs in with the fruit, not to mention the risk of burning down the house.

Yet stumbling through the dark is exactly what many people do—not in the kitchen, but in life. They may have heard about God and the Bible, but think they can manage their problems by themselves. They don't want the light of truth.

David knew that idea made as much sense as cooking in the dark. God's Word takes a murky situation and makes it clear. The Bible steers us around obstacles, protects us from enemy forces, and shows us our next move.

Will you study Bible verses like your life depends on it? Or will you leave the lights off and try to do it on your own?

Prayer

God, I want *your* words—not my friends' or the world's—to be my light. Thank you for providing the Bible to help me. When I'm in the dark, may my first thought be to reach for your Word.

Body Matters

Anyone with such a defiling disease must wear torn clothes, let their hair be unkempt, cover the lower part of their face and cry out, "Unclean! Unclean!"

(LEVITICUS 13:45)

Much of Leviticus reads like a medical book. Rashes. Skin sores. Bumps. What in the world was God doing with a book like that? Well, he knows everything about the human body. And he saw that the Israelites needed some medical help. They didn't have microscopes, shots, and hospitals like we do. If they weren't careful, one sick person could make the whole tribe sick. God was watching out for them.

God gave the Israelite leaders a book of guidance about health. They used it to examine illnesses, diseases, infestations, plagues, and other nasty matters. If someone was contagious, meaning they could infect others, the leaders or priests would send the sick person outside of the city until he got better. The priests weren't being mean. They were protecting everyone else.

That's how God looks after his people. He knows what they need and tells them what to do. If he hadn't done that with the Israelites, they may have never made it out of the wilderness and lived to tell about it.

Prayer

Wow, Lord! You know a lot, even about my body. Thank you for creating my body and all the amazing things it does. I know someone who is sick right now and needs your help. Please heal them.

Secret Keeper

I have hidden your word in my heart, that I might not sin against you.

(PSALM 119:11, NLT)

Think about your friends. Who is your best friend? What do you like about that person?

God considered Job and David his close friends. Know why? They prized his Word more than anything else. And they thought about it over and over. So they knew God really well. Job admitted, "I have treasured the words of his mouth more than my daily bread" (Job 23:12b). David said, "Oh, how I love your instructions! I think about them all day long" (Psalm 119:97, NLT).

Friends trust and care for each other. They also share secrets. It's true—God will share his secrets with you if you make a habit of thinking about his Word. God told Abraham his secrets, and he also told them to Daniel, Paul, the disciples, and other friends (Genesis 18:17, Daniel 2:19, 1 Corinthians 2:7–10). He wants to be that close to you too. Are you ready for a new best friend?

Prayer

God, it sounds really cool to be your best friend. As I read the Bible and talk to you, show me how to be better friends with you and learn more about you.

Chow Down

You, God, are my God, earnestly I seek you; I thirst
for you, my whole being longs for you, in a dry
and parched land where there is no water . . . I will
be fully satisfied as with the richest of foods; with
singing lips my mouth will praise you.

(PSALM 63:1, 5)

"I'm so hungry I could eat a cow!" Ever been that hungry? Or maybe you've even said, "I'm starving!" You're not really starving, but hunger pangs are yelling at you for something to eat. On a super-hot summer day, you feel the same way about water—so thirsty that you could drink a gallon in three gulps!

You don't drink or eat God. But did you know that your body and mind can get so used to spending time with God that you can get hunger pangs or feel "thirsty" if you miss him for a few days? Yep, just like your body tells you that it is past time to eat, your mind and heart will tell you when it's been too long since you talked to God or listened to his Word. You'll miss him. Seem strange? Hunger and thirst for God grow in you because your body begins to experience how good he is for you. You just can't live without him. So get your fill of God today.

Prayer

God, I am starting to understand what it means to feel hungry or thirsty for you. I want you to be as important as food and drink to me. Help me to grow in you and get used to having you in my life.

Wherever We Go, God Goes

God is our refuge and strength, an ever-present help in trouble. Therefore we will not fear, though the earth give way and the mountains fall into the heart of the sea.

(PSALM 46:1–2)

Have you ever felt an earthquake? Have you seen the destruction of a hurricane? It's powerful! Maybe you have had to run to a safe place when tornado sirens went off. Now that's scary. Natural disasters make us feel like fleas. We feel so helpless. There's nothing to do but wait it out.

No wonder we feel afraid. Everybody does. That's why Psalm 46 is worth reading again and again. It's a reminder that any time nature seems angry, our heavenly Father is in control. He is bigger than the biggest wildfires, blizzards, tsunamis, earthquakes, tornados, and hurricanes.

Sometimes the trouble we face comes as a personal "storm," like a bad injury or sickness or your parents losing their jobs. Those kinds of problems can rock our world too. When everything blows apart, we feel frightened and insecure.

But listen to this great news: God is always with us. Wherever we go, he goes. Wherever we are, he is. The Lord is strong enough to keep us safe. Write Psalm 46:1–2 on a piece of paper and hang it on your bedroom wall if you are facing a storm.

Prayer

Lord, it's easy to forget that you are right beside me when the wind blows and the sirens sound. Thank you that you keep me safe. Thank you that you are stronger and bigger than any trouble.

Huh?

My son, pay attention to what I say; turn your ear to my words. Do not let them out of your sight, keep them within your heart.

(PROVERBS 4:20–21)

"Pay attention" usually means you're in trouble or you got caught daydreaming. A friend could be telling you a long, boring story. You get distracted, and your friend notices. "Hey, I'm talking to you," your friend says. If your teacher sees you doodling instead of listening to a lesson, she might clear her throat and give you one of those looks—the kind that tells you that you'd better listen up.

When King Solomon wrote this Proverb , he was probably familiar with kids not paying attention all the time. And he wanted to make sure his son didn't miss something important— God's words and wisdom. Listen and watch those carefully. Everything you learn from God is so important that it needs to be hidden in the safest place you know—your heart. Know why? Because your heart is where everything you do and say comes from. If you keep God's words in your heart, you will live for him. It's just bound to happen. So pay attention—to people who teach God's Word, to your parents, to your teachers, and to godly friends. That way you won't miss anything important.

Prayer

Lord, it's not easy to pay attention all the time. Sometimes I don't even know why it matters if I listen in church or at school. Even my parents say things that I don't understand. Help me to pay attention to the important stuff.

Important Reminder

Make tassels on the corners of your garments, with a blue cord on each tassel. You will have these tassels to look at and so you will remember all the commands of the LORD.

(NUMBERS 15:38B–39)

Look at the refrigerator door. What's on it? A drawing you did last year? A list of chores for the week? A missionary card? Whatever is there is a reminder, like don't forget to do your chores. Appreciate your artistic skills. Pray for the family in Japan. Photos are similar. Your family probably has photos around the house of you biking with your dad or your last birthday party. The photos remind you of a good time you had together.

God likes us to remember important days and celebrations. Even more, he likes us to remember his Word, the Bible. The Bible is so big that you couldn't memorize the whole thing. But you could create reminders about reading it. The Israelites sewed tassels on their clothes to help them remember God. Tassels aren't really a stylish move these days, but perhaps you could put a cross in your room. Or wear a Christian T-shirt. If you are always on the computer, set up an alarm to read your Bible or pray. Each time you look at one of those reminders, spend a few minutes with God so you don't forget him.

Prayer

Lord, reminders help me do my homework and chores, but I need reminders for other important things, like you. What will help me remember to spend time with you? Will you show me?

Talk Freely

The Lord . . . is a friend to those who are honest.
(PROVERBS 3:32, NCV)

In the Bible, the friends of God were honest about their feelings. They often complained, second-guessed, accused, and argued with their Creator. God didn't seem to mind. In fact, he encouraged this kind of honesty.

God allowed Abraham to question and challenge him over the destruction of the city of Sodom. Abraham pestered God over what it would take to spare the city. God also listened patiently to David's many accusations of unfairness, betrayal, and abandonment. God did not shut out Jeremiah when he claimed that God had tricked him. Job vented how upset he was about losing his family and possessions.

Can God handle that kind of frank, intense honesty from you? Absolutely! Here's the thing: God is always honest back. He tells the absolute truth. Genuine friendship is built on openness. God listens to the passionate words of his friends. To be God's friend, you must be honest and share your true feelings.

Prayer

I want to be honest with you about my feelings, Lord. But it's hard to hear the honest truth back. Help me grow in openness and be able to hear the truth from you.

Happy to Obey

I have loved you even as the Father has loved me. Live within my love. When you obey me you are living in my love, just as I obey my Father and live in his love. I have told you this so that you will be filled with my joy. Yes, your cup of joy will overflow!

(JOHN 15:9–11, TLB)

Look at what Jesus said in John 15. He expects us to do only what he did with the Father. His relationship with his Father is the model for our friendship with him. Because Jesus loved God the Father, Jesus did whatever the Father asked him to do—no questions asked.

Love is the reason God created us. Love is the reason Jesus came to Earth. Love is the reason Jesus forgives our sins. It only makes sense that we obey him because he is so loving to us.

You may hear people say that Christians obey God out of duty or guilt or fear of punishment, but the opposite is true. God wants us to understand his love for us. Then we obey God because we love him and trust that he knows what is best for us. We follow Christ out of thankfulness. We have been forgiven and set free from sin. That is the reason for our joy!

Prayer

Jesus, I want to have a strong friendship with you. I am thankful that God loves me so much, and I want to follow where he leads me.

Always Available

Then the fire of the LORD fell and burned up the sacrifice, the wood, the stones and the soil, and also licked up the water in the trench. When all the people saw this, they fell prostrate and cried, "The LORD—he is God! The LORD—he is God!"

(1 KINGS 18:38–39)

God doesn't mess around. When his people call out to him, he's right there. Too bad the prophets of Baal didn't have God on their side. They kept trying to get their god to answer their prayers. They jumped. They danced. They sliced themselves with swords. "No one paid attention," verse 29 says.

Now that's a bad day.

Then Elijah called out to the Lord God, and God showed off big time. He burned up the soaking wet altar and sacrifice and everything around it—in front of all those other prophets.

The story is great, not just because it shows how awesome God is, but also because that's the same God who hears our prayers and answers us. So we can run to him with whatever is on our mind.

Is there something on your mind today? Let God know, and see how he will answer. He is always listening.

Prayer

Lord, thank you that I can come to you with anything that's on my mind. It's such a relief to know you hear my prayers and you care about me.

Special Privilege

My prayer is not for them alone. I pray also for those who will believe in me through their message, that all of them may be one, Father, just as you are in me and I am in you. May they also be in us so that the world may believe that you have sent me.

(JOHN 17:20–21)

Imagine the president is coming to town. He spends the day at your school. When he leaves, he gives you his phone number. "Call anytime," he says. "You can count on me for anything you need for the rest of your life." Seriously? The president just gave you his personal number? That would be awesome.

Jesus did something like that. He made a special visit to Earth. Right before he left to go back to Heaven, he prayed for his followers. He even prayed for you. He knew you were coming along one day. It's like he set up a special cell phone for anyone who believes in him. And when he got back to Heaven, he set up regular appointments with God to pray for your needs. With Jesus' private number—prayer—you have a line to the most important power in the universe. When are you going to call him? He's waiting to let God know your requests.

Prayer

Jesus, thank you for the awesome privilege of prayer. It's awesome to know that you will take care of me all of my life.

Jot It Down

My heart is stirred by a noble theme as I recite my verses for the king; my tongue is the pen of a skillful writer.

(PSALM 45:1)

King David wrote songs and poems—a lot of them—praising God and showing admiration. Writing was his way of putting his feelings before God. Miriam the prophet and Deborah the judge both wrote songs after big moments in their lives. Letting out their feelings, they created beautiful poetry for God. Using their pen was good for their soul and helped them remember all God had done.

Try writing for yourself. For the next two weeks, any time you feel sad or happy, grab a pen and a notebook or your tablet. Jot down your thoughts and feelings. Be completely honest. If you're fuming mad, write it. If you're glad God answered a prayer, create a thank-you note to him. Even if you feel like you hate someone, get it out on paper or your computer. After two weeks, go back and read what you wrote. Repeat it out loud to God if you're proud of it or need his help. If you notice that you need to address a problem or a sin, fess up. Then write a concluding prayer about all that you felt and thought about during those two weeks. Do this writing exercise any time you need to figure out your feelings or know that you need more time with God. It worked for King David. It will work for you.

Prayer

Lord, writing seems [hard or easy]. I don't know if it will help me, but if it worked for King David and many others in the Bible, it could work for me. Please show me how I can use writing to build my relationship with you.

Running Away

But Jonah ran away from the LORD and headed for Tarshish. He went down to Joppa, where he found a ship bound for that port. After paying the fare, he went aboard and sailed for Tarshish to flee from the LORD.

(JONAH 1:3)

———

You are sick and tired of your parents' rules. They just don't understand you. So you pack a bag and head for the door. How far would you go to run away?

Jonah wasn't running away from his parents, but he sure was mad. God wanted him to go tell the no-good, rotten scoundrels of Nineveh about God's love. No way! Jonah wouldn't do it. He'd run away before ever visiting Nineveh.

Can you understand how he felt? It just didn't seem fair to give the Ninevites a second chance to straighten up. They'd done too much wrong too many times.

God understood how Jonah felt, so God let Jonah run away. He let Jonah go far enough until Jonah started rethinking his choices. The smelly belly of a big fish was a lousy place to run away to!

When you don't understand something that God or your parents ask you to do, talk it over with God. Vent your frustration. Don't hold it in; otherwise you might run away and wind up in a stinking mess.

Prayer

God, why are there so many rules at home, at school, and at church? It seems like rules, rules, rules are everywhere. I know they are supposed to help and protect me, but I need faith to believe that's true.

You Better Believe It!

The centurion replied, "Lord, I do not deserve to have you come under my roof. But just say the word, and my servant will be healed . . . When Jesus heard this, he was amazed and said to those following him, "Truly I tell you, I have not found anyone in Israel with such great faith."

(MATTHEW 8:8, 10)

If your teacher told you that you'd get a pizza party when the whole class gets their vocabulary words right, would you believe him? Of course! Because you know your teacher. Now, what if you asked a man on the street if he'd give you a hundred dollars and he said "yes"? Would you believe him? No way! You don't know him.

With Jesus, when you ask him something, do you really believe he will answer you? That's a harder question.

The centurion answered "yes" in a second. He hadn't even met Jesus. But he'd already heard plenty about him. The centurion knew enough about Jesus' reputation as the Son of God who did miracles. So he just asked Jesus to heal his servant and believed that Jesus would do it. He didn't even need Jesus to come to his house or get doctors to prove that his servant was better.

You can trust Jesus, God's Son. When you talk to him or ask him for things, he will answer you through the Bible, people, or in your heart. You can count on him.

Prayer

Jesus, you ask me to trust you, but sometimes it's hard when I haven't met you face-to-face. Will you show me how to believe you and see your answers?

Pleased As Punch

It is better to obey than to sacrifice.
(1 SAMUEL 15:22B, NCV)

Jesus was unknown for most of his life. He wasn't out teaching truth and saving the world until he was thirty years old! Yet when John baptized Jesus, God spoke from Heaven: "This is my Son, whom I love, and I am very pleased with him" (Matthew 3:17b, NCV). What had Jesus been doing for thirty years that made God so happy? The Bible says only one phrase in Luke 2:51: "He went back to Nazareth with [his parents], and lived obediently with them" (MSG). Thirty years of pleasing God were summed up in two words: "lived obediently"!

Before Jesus was ever famous, he obeyed God in many small ways when no one but his family could see him. Big opportunities may come once in a lifetime, but small opportunities surround us every day. Even in simple acts like telling the truth, being kind, and obeying our parents, we bring a smile to God's face. God treasures simple acts of obedience. No one else may notice, but God does. He considers these acts of worship, and they bring you close to his heart.

Prayer

I want to follow Jesus' example of being obedient. God, help me in everyday moments, like when it is hard to obey or be nice to other people.

Constant Chatter

Pray all the time.
(1 THESSALONIANS 5:17, MSG)

How is it possible to pray all the time? Let me tell you how many Christians have done it for centuries: "breath prayers." You choose a brief sentence or a simple phrase to say to Jesus in one breath, like "You are with me." "I'm depending on you." "I want to know you." "I am your child, God." "Help me."

You can also use a short phrase of Scripture, like "God is my strength." "You will never leave me." Pray it as often as possible so it is rooted deep in your heart.

You can also create reminders that God is with you and wants to hear from you. You might post little notes that say, "God is with me right now!"

This practice will help you make prayer a habit. Just as musicians practice scales every day in order to play beautiful music, practice thinking about God at different times in your day. Before long, you'll be praying all the time.

Prayer

God, it seems hard to pray all the time. But I want to make prayer a constant habit so I can talk to you more and more.

Who Are You Trying to Please?

By myself I can do nothing; I judge only as I hear, and my judgment is just, for I seek not to please myself but him who sent me.

(JOHN 5:30)

You can't please everybody. By the time one friend is happy with you, another friend gets upset with you. Even God doesn't please everybody. So why would you to try to do something that even God doesn't do?

But God does want you to make him happy. Jesus knew this and lived out an example of pleasing God. He had no questions about it: "I'm going to please God the Father." And he did. In Matthew 3:17, God the Father said, "This is my Son, whom I love; with him I am well pleased."

If we focus on pleasing God, we will always do the right thing regardless of what anybody else thinks. So how do we make God happy? Turn to the Bible, and learn about God and his instructions for life. Follow them, and focus on him. Then one day, he will say, "I am pleased with you."

Prayer

God, I look forward to the day when you say you are pleased with me! Guide me in your ways, because I want to make you happy.

Follow the Leader

In all your ways submit to him, and he will make your paths straight.

(PROVERBS 3:6)

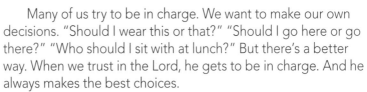

Many of us try to be in charge. We want to make our own decisions. "Should I wear this or that?" "Should I go here or go there?" "Who should I sit with at lunch?" But there's a better way. When we trust in the Lord, he gets to be in charge. And he always makes the best choices.

The apostle Paul was at peace because he knew God was directing his life. Even when he was locked in a Roman prison, he could write, "I have learned the secret of being content in any and every situation, whether well fed or hungry, whether living in plenty or in want" (Philippians 4:12b). What's the "secret" he learned? He depended on God's strength. That's called trust.

Paul had to learn to trust God. It didn't come naturally to him. Once he did, he was content and peaceful. You too can learn to trust the Lord and allow him to guide you. The safest place to be is following God wherever he wants to take you.

Prayer

Lord, I want the amazing peace Paul had. Even when it is not easy to trust and depend on you alone, I know you truly are in control and will take care of me.

The Only Judge

*I care very little if I am judged by you or by any
human court; indeed, I do not even judge myself.
My conscience is clear, but that does not make me
innocent. It is the Lord who judges me.*

(1 CORINTHIANS 4:3–4)

Have you ever watched a beauty pageant? Dozens of
attractive girls try to impress a panel of judges with their bodies,
smiles, and intelligence. Eventually those judges award a gigantic tiara and shiny sash to just one girl. What that bling says is,
"This girl is prettier, smarter, and better than all the other girls."
And the audience eats it up!

Of course, beauty pageants aren't new. Esther became
queen because she won a beauty pageant (read Esther 2).
People are still the same—they love to judge. "I don't want you
on my team; you're too fat." "You'll never win the science prize
because you're not smart enough." "I don't like your sister, so I
don't like you either." Judgmental words like that really sting!

Paul knew that being judged was no fun. So he talked about
whose words we should really pay attention to: God's, not
people's. So your teammate thinks your clothes and shoes aren't
cool? Your neighbor says you're weird for going to church? The
cool kids mock you for not watching the latest reality show? It
might hurt temporarily, but in the end it doesn't matter.

Don't try to impress people. Instead, focus on God, the ultimate judge who looks past your body, talents, background, and
flaws to the real you—and loves what he sees.

Prayer

People think they know me because they know things about me.
But Lord, that's not who I really am. When others judge me, help
me concentrate on pleasing you, not the crowd.

Lip Service

With all my heart I will praise you, O Lord my God.
(PSALM 86:12A, NLT)

You are made in God's image, so you are a spirit living in a body. And God designed your spirit to communicate with him. Worship is how your heart responds to God. One way you can worship is through praise.

Praise is not just a matter of saying or singing the right words; you must mean what you say. God looks past our words to see our attitude. God gave you emotions so you could praise him with deep feeling—but those emotions must be true.

Many forms of praise are mentioned in the Bible: confessing, singing, shouting, standing in honor, kneeling, dancing, making a joyful noise, testifying, playing musical instruments, and raising hands (Hebrews 13:15; Ezra 3:11; Psalm 149:3, 150:3; Nehemiah 8:6). The best style of praise is the one that best represents your love for God, based on the personality God gave you. How will you praise God today?

Prayer

I want to praise you, Lord! Thank you that you accept all kinds of praise, and everyone is uniquely created to praise you. Today, show me ways to honor you.

Where Is God?

"I came naked from my mother's womb," he said, "and I shall have nothing when I die. The Lord gave me everything I had, and they were his to take away. Blessed be the name of the Lord."

(JOB 1:21, TLB)

When God seems distant, you may feel that he is angry with you for some sin. In fact, sin does disconnect us from intimate fellowship with God. But often this feeling of being alone has nothing to do with sin. It is a test of faith, and everyone faces it. Will you continue to love, trust, obey, and worship God, even when you have no sense of his presence?

This happened to Job. On a single day he lost everything. Most discouraging—God said nothing for several days!

How do you praise God when you don't understand what's happening? How do you keep your eyes on Jesus when they're full of tears? Don't worry. God is there. So you do what Job did. Praise God for still being God—always the same even when life changes around you. The next time you are having a hard time, turn to praise. God will meet you and build your faith.

Prayer

I'm sorry, Lord, for the times I have sinned against you. I don't understand why some things happen in my life, but thank you for still being God who is in control.

Faith in Action

When Jesus saw him lying there and learned that he had been in this condition for a long time, he asked him, "Do you want to get well?" "Sir," the invalid replied, "I have no one to help me into the pool when the water is stirred. While I am trying to get in, someone else goes down ahead of me." Then Jesus said to him, "Get up! Pick up your mat and walk."

(JOHN 5:6–8)

"I have no one to help me," the handicapped man told Jesus.

And Jesus' response doesn't seem very nice: "Get up and walk." Jesus knew the man couldn't use his legs. But he wanted to see the man's faith and his willingness to take action if Jesus told him to do something.

God tells us to have faith. Faith is believing in God's power to do anything. Sometimes faith is being ready to take an action. For example, if you asked God to help your parents pay their bills, they might take action to cut expenses by walking more. But they believe God will take care of supplying enough money to pay the bills that they can't pay on their own.

When you need God's help, tell God the truth about what you need, but be ready to build your faith by taking action. When you pray for help on a test or improvement in a sport, God may very well want to answer "yes." But he may tell you to study hard or practice a lot. Like he told the man with a disability, it's time to get up and do something.

Prayer

Dear God, I don't know how much faith I really have. It is hard to take action when I don't know what you will do in response. Please increase my faith.

In the Dark

*Then they gathered around him and asked him,
"Lord, are you at this time going to restore the
kingdom to Israel?" He said to them: "It is not for
you to know the times or dates the Father has set by
his own authority."*

(ACTS 1:6–7)

How many times have you pestered a teacher or parent by asking "Why?" Or you read a book or article that goes over your head, so you want someone to explain it to you? Curiosity is natural. But we don't always get the answers that clue us in.

The disciples asked Jesus lots of questions. Often he sat them down and explained God's ways until they understood. And sometimes he had to remind them of what he had already explained. But this wasn't always the case. Before Jesus left Earth to go back to Heaven, the disciples wanted to know Jesus' full plan. "What's the scoop?" they basically asked. "Fill us in, please." The only answer Jesus gave was that they didn't need to know. Jesus told them they were going to do great things for him, but that was all.

Though we don't know why Jesus didn't answer their final questions, we do know that he knew they weren't ready for the answer. He may answer you the same way. If you ask him to explain why someone in your family got sick or why your family had to move, Jesus may not let you in on it because he knows it won't help you. That can make it tough to have faith. But Jesus will always give you what you need. Even if what you need is not what you want to know.

Prayer

Jesus, I want to understand your ways and know why bad things happen. It's hard to accept that you won't always explain everything to me. Still, give me faith to trust you when you don't fill me in.

Still Unsure?

They were startled and frightened, thinking they saw a ghost. He said to them, "Why are you troubled, and why do doubts rise in your minds? Look at my hands and my feet. It is I myself! Touch me and see; a ghost does not have flesh and bones, as you see I have."

(LUKE 24:37–39)

So let's think about this: If the disciples had a tough time believing Jesus was truly back among them, we will probably have our moments too—moments when we doubt if he is around and paying attention and helping us when we need him. Jesus isn't surprised when we have questions or doubts.

But Jesus didn't get mad at the disciples, and he doesn't get mad at us when we have doubts. He actually wants us to ask questions. He wants us to take a closer look. Asking questions doesn't mean we don't have faith. It just means we need to spend more time getting to know Jesus.

Prayer

Lord, you know my heart. You know my worries, fears, and doubts. Teach me to ask you questions, knowing you will hear and answer.

Tap into the Supernatural

Those who trust in the L<small>ORD</small> are like Mount Zion,
which cannot be shaken but endures forever.

(PSALM 125:1)

Ever tried to move a mountain? How about pushing a small hill? Sliding a large mound of dirt perhaps? You'd need a bulldozer for the mound, and an earthquake for the hill and mountain—unless you have supernatural powers.

Why not tap into God's supernatural power? It's free for those who trust in him, although he doesn't pass it out all willy-nilly so people can go around moving geological features.

The more you trust God and the less you trust yourself, God builds your inner strength. God's stability makes you solid and sure like a mountain. Bulldozers of life, problems that shake, and trials that quake will not move you. Sure, you will experience the emotions that come with life's troubles just like everyone else. And you won't be immune to sadness, fear, or nerves. But when you trust in God, those things are not as scary because you have the only superpower taking care of you.

Prayer

Lord, please build my trust in you. When trouble comes and scary things happen, I want to run to you and trust that you will take care of it.

What Are You Afraid Of?

Where God's love is, there is no fear, because God's perfect love drives out fear.

(1 JOHN 4:18A, NCV)

Do you ever feel afraid of the dark? Of being made fun of? Or failing a class? Or being hurt? There are hundreds of scary things that can drive your life.

Many kids—and adults—let fear be in charge of their lives. Fears can result from an accident or trauma, a failure, or even a genetic impulse. Some fear is natural protection, such as staying away from a rattlesnake or the edge of a cliff. But fear of trying something new, being bold for God, speaking truth, or taking a risk is like putting yourself in a prison. Fear can keep you captive. No matter the cause, fear-driven people often miss great opportunities because they're afraid to do anything. Instead they always play it safe.

Being afraid all the time will keep you from becoming what God wants you to be. Guess what fights fear? Faith and love. So leave fear behind by putting your faith in God and embracing his love.

Prayer

God, help me live boldly, knowing that you love and care for me. I want to be all you created me to be.

Hand Them Over

*This is what the L**ORD** says—your Redeemer, who formed you in the womb: I am the L**ORD**, the Maker of all things, who stretches out the heavens, who spreads out the earth by myself.*

(ISAIAH 44:24)

So many problems are very big. How can God help families who don't have enough to eat? Children all around the world who are dying from disease? People who have to flee their homes because of war? Such big problems seem impossible to fix. Can God *really* do anything about them?

God likes to remind us how big he is. He made each and every person. Before God ever placed you in your mother's womb, he designed your eyes, ears, fingers, and toes. He worked out every detail to make each person special—that's more than seven billion unique creations on Earth right now. If that doesn't seem like a big enough God, then look at the stars and the planets. Our galaxy, the Milky Way, has anywhere from 200 to 400 billion stars. Those numbers only account for two of God's creations.

Nothing is too big for our God to handle. We can tell him about everything that worries us. We can pray for our family, our friends, and all the bad news happening around the world. Our God is big and mighty, strong and able. If he can make the Big Dipper and something as small as a tooth, he can handle any problem we toss at him.

Prayer

Lord, help me to remember that there is nothing too big for you to handle. Thank you!

True Peace

Do not be anxious about anything, but in every situation . . . present your requests to God. And the peace of God . . . will guard your hearts and your minds in Christ Jesus.

(PHILIPPIANS 4:6–7)

What is peace? Peace is a feeling of calm and quiet in your heart. Worry is the opposite of peace. If you are worrying, you can't feel peaceful. If you are peaceful, you can't be worrying.

God is the only one who gives true peace. If we want God's peace, we need to ask for it. Notice the order in Philippians 4—first prayer and then peace. This is cause and effect. Prayer is the cause; peace is the effect. If you are not praying, you are likely worrying.

So whenever you start to worry, turn your cares into prayers. God will not be stressed out by what you tell him. He already knows it all and loves you very much.

When Jesus is in charge of your life, you will experience true peace. That doesn't mean you won't have any trouble, but it means God's presence will calm your heart in any situation.

Prayer

It is a comfort to know that if I ask you for help, you will take care of my worries. You promise me peace if I pray, and I thank you for that.

Call Him Up

I call out to the LORD, and he answers me from his holy mountain.

(PSALM 3:4)

God lives in Heaven. From there, he sees and hears everything. Even if a million people are praying all at the same time, he can hear each one. You could be praying about school at the same time a boy or girl halfway around the world in Thailand is praying for a peaceful night's sleep. God doesn't take prayers for just a few hours of the day. You can talk to him any time. He wants to hear from you. He wants to know what you are worried about, when you are happy, and about scary situations. Each time someone talks to God, he gets closer to that person. It's like he says, "I was just waiting to come over to see you. Thanks for calling." How do you know God is talking to you? His words are in the Bible. He also uses nature and other people to share what he wants to say. Sometimes he speaks right to your heart or through a situation the next day.

King David, one of the greatest kings of Israel, where much of the Bible was written, believed he could talk to God any time. Whatever God said, King David trusted him. You can talk to God any time too. Thank him for hearing your prayers, and ask him to help you accept his answers.

Prayer

Lord, thank you for hearing my prayer and the prayer of every person on Earth. I want to hear your answers.

Doubts

"Lord, if it's you," Peter replied, "tell me to come to you on the water." "Come," he said. Then Peter got down out of the boat, walked on the water and came toward Jesus.

(MATTHEW 14:28–29)

If only the story ended at verse 29. Peter steps out of the boat and walks toward Jesus. Wow! Can you picture the whole scene? Peter's walking on water! The wind is blowing, so maybe the water is lapping up over his shoes. Then maybe a wave or two splashes up his legs. He takes his eyes off Jesus and starts freaking out. How did his thoughts go south so fast? He probably started thinking, "This is so amazing! I'm walking on water! I'm really doing it!" And then . . ."I wonder how deep it is right here. Do fish like to eat fishermen? What if I sink? This could be bad. This could be really, really bad!"

Now we don't know if that's what Peter thought. But we do know that he went from trusting Jesus enough to walk on water to doubting Jesus and beginning to sink.

Does this happen to you? You believe Jesus will help you with something, but then you get freaked out by what's around you. Maybe God has called you to talk to a friend about Jesus, try out for a sport, or build a new friendship. Whatever it might be, don't take your eyes off Jesus. Don't get swayed by the doubts that might make you sink. Jesus has faith that you can do it, so keep your eyes on him.

Prayer

Lord, I want to walk on water! I want to faithfully do whatever you ask me to do and trust that you will give me everything I need.

Spill Your Guts

Those who hate me without reason outnumber the hairs of my head; many are my enemies without cause, those who seek to destroy me.

(PSALM 69:4A)

Ever felt like the whole world is picking on you? David did. As a famous, rich, and powerful king, he had plenty of enemies. He also had a quarreling, drama-filled family and an entire country to run. Phew!

To unwind and recharge, he wrote in his journal. Not knowing his words would one day be read by billions, he really let loose! He didn't sugarcoat anything; he told God how he felt. David often felt caught between a rock and a hard place.

Sound familiar? Perhaps you don't have soldiers or family members trying to mow you down with chariots, but you may have new stepsiblings to get along with or face bullying from the cool kid at school.

Life is hard, but you don't have to struggle through it alone. Just like David, we have a God who hears our questions, doubts, shouts, and groans. Whether it's in a journal, blog, or something else, the Lord loves it when we spill our guts to him.

So the next time you feel like pulling out your hair, try telling God about it instead. He'll welcome you with open arms.

Prayer

God, I don't always know exactly what I'm feeling, but I know I can tell you as much or as little as I want. Teach me to bring you my thoughts first and always. Help me make it a lifelong habit.

Welcome God Home

After David had constructed buildings for himself in the City of David, he prepared a place for the ark of God and pitched a tent for it.

(1 CHRONICLES 15:1)

Head to your bedroom with a notebook or tablet to take an inventory. Write down what takes up the most space in your room besides your bed (like clothes, hair accessories, or books). Next, write down what you like to do in your room (sleep, play games, read mysteries, etc.). Now walk around your house, and make notes about what your house says about your family—are you messy or clean? Do you like lots of color or plain rooms? Do you spend time together in the same rooms or prefer your private space?

When David finished building his house, he wanted to create a place for God. So he set up a special tent for a temple. That way David and all his people could visit with God close to their homes.

Now look in your room and around your house again. Is there a special place for God? If not, how can you make a spot that is just for reading Bible stories, writing prayers, or singing songs? If your parents believe in God too, ask them to work with you on creating a God space in the house.

Prayer

Lord, you are important enough to be in my room and my family's house. We need reminders of your greatness and that you are near to us always.

PURPOSE 3

Your Part in God's Family

Made for Family

*The Spirit we received does not make us slaves again
to fear; it makes us children of God. With that spirit
we cry out, "Father." And the spirit himself joins with
our spirits to say we are God's children.*

(ROMANS 8:15–16, NCV)

The entire Bible tells the story of God building a family. It's a family who will love him, honor him, and reign with him forever. Sounds like a good family to be part of!

God is love—that's why he treasures relationships. He even identifies himself in family terms: Father, Son, and Spirit. The Trinity is God's relationship to himself, and it's based on perfect love.

Since God has always existed in three persons, he has never been lonely. He didn't need a family. But he wanted one! So he created us, including you. You were formed for his family. He wanted you to be a part of it before you were even born. The choice is yours. If you say "yes," he will welcome you and share all he has. This would make God very happy.

Prayer

God, thank you for including me in your family! I am honored that you want each of us to be a part of your family, and we are all called children of God.

God's Kid

All honor to God, the God and Father of our Lord Jesus Christ; for it is his boundless mercy that has given us the privilege of being born again so that we are now members of God's own family.

(1 PETER 1:3A, TLB)

God created every human being, but not everyone is a "child of God." The only way to get into God's family is by being "born" into it. You became part of the human family by your first birth, but you become a member of God's family by a second birth.

When you place your faith in Christ, God becomes your Father. You become his child, and other believers become your brothers and sisters. The church even becomes your spiritual family, which includes all Christians in the past, the present, and the future.

Guess what—your spiritual family is even more important than your physical family, because it will last forever. Our families on Earth are wonderful gifts from God, but they are temporary and fragile. Your parents may be divorced. Your grandparents may not be alive. You may not even be close to your earthly family. Even if you are, eventually everyone grows old and dies. Yet your spiritual family will continue long after that. In Heaven we will enjoy God's family forever. That family will never break down or split up. God holds it together. It is a much stronger union and a more permanent bond than blood relationships.

Prayer

Jesus, you welcomed me into your family when I accepted you as my Savior. Thank you for my family here on Earth and for my family that lasts forever.

Love Everybody?

All the believers were one in heart and mind. No one claimed that any of their possessions was their own, but they shared everything they had . . . There were no needy persons among them.

(ACTS 4:32, 34A)

Count how many people you love. Two or three, five, ten? Perhaps you have a big family and lots of good friends and could say that you love (or at least like!) twenty people. Now, count how many of those people you would share anything you own with. Did the number just drop?

Just after Jesus left Earth, his followers were so full of love that they all loved each other—literally. They made sure everyone had enough to eat and a place to sleep. They brought their possessions together and gave them away. It was like the first band of Robin Hood and his merry men.

These days, it's hard to love others in quite the same way. Or we only love a few people enough to help them any time they need it. But the cool thing is that God gives his love to us so we can pass it on to others. And when we really love others, it's not hard to share or help them out. True love will just flow out of us. So why not ask God to expand your circle of love? It could grow to more than twenty someday.

Prayer

Lord, will you fill my heart with love for those around me and even for people I don't want to love? Your true love is amazing.

You're Invited

Then he said to his servants, "The wedding banquet is ready, but those I invited did not deserve to come. So go to the street corners and invite to the banquet anyone you find."

(MATTHEW 22:8–9)

Jesus liked to tell stories called parables. Each parable had a lesson. Often the people listening didn't understand what Jesus was teaching. With the story of the wedding dinner, Jesus wanted the people to know some important things about God. One lesson is that God's gifts are for anyone. Some Jews thought that the Messiah or Savior was going to be just for them. They wanted special privileges and thought they were better than others. No one else was special enough for God's gift of Jesus.

But God's gifts—love and salvation and Heaven—are for anyone who believes in him and asks for him to be in their life. It doesn't matter who you are, what you look like, how much money your family has, what your name is, or where you live. Isn't that great? Doesn't it seem like everyone would want gifts from God? Sadly, many people will reject these wonderful gifts because they don't understand they are free or that everyone is equal in God's eyes. Spread the word that God's table is open to everyone. No special qualifications—just accept his invitation to be part of his family.

Prayer

God, I want to be part of your family. I believe your gifts are for me. Please take charge of my life and allow me to show others your wonderful gifts.

All the Parts

If the whole body were an eye, where would the sense of hearing be? If the whole body were an ear, where would the sense of smell be? But in fact God has placed the parts in the body, every one of them, just as he wanted them to be.

(1 CORINTHIANS 12:17–18)

Wouldn't it be nuts if your nose decided to speak up and tell your mouth to take a hike? "You're doing a lousy job," your nose says to your mouth. "This body would be better off without you!" First, you'd think you must have been dreaming, because you've never heard your nose talk (that's the mouth's job!). Second, you'd say, "Hold on! How will I eat or drink without a mouth? You can't tell my mouth to get lost."

Christians are like one big body working for God. And even though you might get annoyed with other people who follow God, everyone has a place in the Body of Christ. Unity with all Christians is how people who don't know God can see the love of God. But unity is hard. You'll hear Christians complain about other Christians and churches that split up because of disagreements. Unity is possible only if everyone is connected to the same heart—the heart of God. That way his love is flowing through everyone's veins. Sure, the hands might not want to spend a lot of time with the ears, but they can work together to spread God's Good News to the world.

Prayer

God, thank you for creating a place for every one of your children to serve you and others. Please show me what my role is in the Body of Christ.

Family Act

Therefore, go and make disciples of all the nations, baptizing them in the name of the Father and the Son and the Holy Spirit.

(MATTHEW 28:19, NLT)

Have you been baptized? Jesus says this beautiful act is important for everyone in his family. Why is baptism so important? It publicly announces to the world, "I am not ashamed to be a part of God's family." And, it symbolizes one of God's purposes for your life: participating in his eternal family.

Your baptism says:

"I have faith in God."
"Jesus died and rose again for me."
"Jesus gives me new life."
"I'm so happy to be part of God's family."

In the New Testament, people were baptized as soon as they believed. At Pentecost, 3,000 were baptized the same day they accepted Christ. An Ethiopian leader was baptized on the spot after learning about Jesus from Philip, a disciple. Paul and Silas baptized a Philippian jailer and his family at midnight.

Your baptism is a physical picture of a spiritual truth. It doesn't make you a member of God's family; only faith in Christ does that. But baptism shows you are part of God's family.

Prayer

God, sometimes it can be scary to publicly announce that I'm a follower of Jesus. It's easier to just keep it to myself. Help me be bold and share my faith with others through baptism.

Shut Your Mouth

Gossips can't keep secrets, so never confide in blabbermouths.

(PROVERBS 20:19, MSG)

Nobody likes a gossip. But everyone has done it. We hear a story and can't believe it's true. So we tell the juicy news, rather than considering the person we're talking about. Gossip, or talking about others behind their backs, is never kind.

Spreading gossip is also always wrong. God even says gossipers are troublemakers. And you shouldn't listen to gossip either. People who gossip *to* you will also gossip *about* you. You can't trust them. If you listen to gossip, God takes it seriously. It's like accepting stolen property—it makes you just as guilty of the crime.

When someone begins to gossip to you, have the courage to say, "Please stop. I don't need to know this." Or "Have you talked directly to that person?" Then bust away from that troublemaker.

Prayer

It's easy to get sucked in to gossip, Lord. Next time I gossip, help me remember to say encouraging and uplifting things rather than unkind words. When others gossip, please help me to nicely remind them to say encouraging things too.

Big Bro

A crowd was sitting around [Jesus], and they told him, "Your mother and brothers are outside looking for you." "Who are my mother and my brothers?" he asked. Then he looked at those seated in a circle around him and said, "Here are my mother and my brothers! Whoever does God's will is my brother and sister and mother."

(MARK 3:324–35)

———— ❧ ————

Jesus is your big brother. You are his sister or his brother.

In this scene from Mark 3, you might be concerned about Jesus' family if they overheard him saying, "Who are my mother and my brothers?" They might have thought, "Seriously! What are we? Chopped liver?"

But there's something important to know about Jesus that makes this family scene understandable. He is love. His family knew that he loved them. He'd grown up with them. Their relationships were solid. Jesus wasn't offending his family, and they knew it. He was building up the people sitting in his presence. He was letting them know that by choosing him, doing his will, and calling themselves followers of Christ, they weren't just part of a congregation. They weren't in a cool fan club. They were truly part of his family.

And so are we. We are family with the Savior of the world. He is our big brother with all the best big brother traits: strong, protective, loving, playful, kind, and good.

That's your Jesus.

Prayer

Jesus, what an amazing thought! You truly are my family. My brother. When things get tough, remind me that I'm your sister/brother, that you love me, and that you will protect me. Thank you.

Church Workers

For Ezra had devoted himself to the study and observance of the Law of the LORD, and to teaching its decrees and laws in Israel.

(EZRA 7:10)

What do you hope to become one day? A racecar driver? A teacher? A vet? No matter what you do when you grow up, you'll spend years picking up the skills for it. You'll study. You'll practice. You'll watch. You'll learn.

Ezra spent his time learning to be a priest, which is like a pastor or minister today. Can you imagine spending hours and days and weeks studying the Bible? It's a tough but important job. Pastors and church leaders study the Bible's history, its meaning, and how to lead people. Then they have to preach, teach, counsel, visit, pray for, and listen to people day after day, year after year. Would you want to do all of that for a group of demanding churchgoers? Leading a church and teaching God's Word are big responsibilities. But like any calling, God puts a heart's desire inside those he calls to minister. He'll put a desire in you, too; you may already know what it is.

While you may not get the call to become a church leader, say thanks to your pastor for all he does to serve God and God's people.

Prayer

Lord, working in a church must be hard. Please bless the leaders in my church for their hard work and dedication.

Love – Sacrifice

This is how we know what love is: Jesus Christ laid down his life for us. And we ought to lay down our lives for our brothers and sisters . . . Dear children, let us not love with words or speech but with actions and in truth.

(1 JOHN 3:16, 18)

"I love you!" is probably not something you say a lot. Your parents may say it when they leave for work or drop you off at school. You may hear girls say it all the time to their best friends. It's even thrown around on TV, such as when singing contestants say it to their fans, or vice versa. You probably say it when someone does something nice. "Hey, my mom packed an extra snack for you today," a friend says. "I love her!" you might respond.

But love isn't that simple, so being slow to use the word is definitely okay.

Jesus Christ set the standard for love—he died for our sins out of love. Your parents might be willing to die for you. But no one else in his right mind would die for a singer, band, or school friend—and definitely not for a favorite snack.

Love is actually a kind of sacrifice. If we really love someone, we would give up something big for that person. Most of the time when people say they "love" someone or something, it really means, "I like you," "I think you're awesome," or "Thanks so much."

A real "I love you" comes from a deeper place. So is there anyone you really love?

Prayer

Lord, I don't know that I'm ready to really love anyone. But you love me and call me to love others. Show me how to find that deep place that your love comes from.

Share a Little or a Lot

*All these people gave their gifts out of their wealth;
but she out of her poverty put in all she had to live on.*
(LUKE 21:4)

Which would be harder: sharing one cookie if you only had two or sharing three cookies if you only had six? Unless you don't like cookies, it'd be harder to give up one cookie if it left you with only one. Now, think about the person you love the most in the whole world. If you had to share with your favorite person, would you feel better giving up the one cookie?

How much you love someone makes it harder or easier to share. So does how much you have. Jesus pointed out a poor woman who had almost nothing. In fact, when she gave money to God at the temple, she gave away the last of her cash! But she loved God so much that she didn't mind sacrificing her last coins to him. Giving or sharing when you only have a little bit is called sacrifice. God loves sacrifice. He may ask for a sacrifice from you many times in your life. You won't always want to give away what you own. Sacrifice is often hard to do. When love fills your heart, though, you'll be happy to share with others.

Prayer

God, sacrifice doesn't sound so bad if I get to choose whom I share it with. But it would be hard to give up something I really like or to share with someone I don't like. Fill my heart with love for you and for others so that I will gladly give when you ask me to.

Seriously Tough Love

As he approached Jerusalem and saw the city, he wept over it.

(LUKE 19:41)

"Hey," you say to the biggest, meanest kid in your class. "Do you need some help with your math homework? I know this cool fraction trick."

It took guts to talk to that kid. Apparently, he didn't appreciate that fact, because now you hear he's looking for you, and not to say thanks. Gulp! Why would he want to hurt you? You were only trying to help! This nasty kid definitely doesn't give you fuzzy feelings of love and concern. That would make no sense.

So what was up with Jesus in Luke 19? He knew that the hateful crowds would soon cheer for his death. Yet the Bible says Jesus cried over the lost people in Jerusalem, the ones who wanted to kill him. Why?

The same reason he was willing to die for us: his big love. He had been trying to help those people, even though they mocked him and spit on him. Still, Jesus pretty much said, "If I don't die, then everyone will spend an eternity away from my Father." That thought was a million times worse than the mind-blowing pain and humiliation he would face. He wasn't upset about how people were treating him. He was upset that they were missing out on God's love.

He wants you to know that love too. When you know it and believe it, you too will want others to find God's love—no matter how they treat you.

Prayer

Jesus, it's hard to understand your deep love for me. It's crazy! Thank you for providing life when everyone's sin, even mine, caused your death. I accept that gift of salvation from you.

Show Me!

I call on you, my God, for you will answer me; turn your ear to me and hear my prayer. Show me the wonders of your great love, you who save by your right hand those who take refuge in you from their foes.

(PSALM 17:6–7)

David knew he could count on God. He knew God would hear his voice—not only that, David knew that God would answer. David didn't shy away from asking God for his love. "Show me the wonders of your great love," he said. Most kids don't think to be that bold with God. Some of you even wonder if God loves you at all. But not David. Even though he made some pretty big mistakes, he was confident that God was crazy about him.

God isn't stingy with his love. He loves you, and he will show that in a million different ways. He shows it through incredible sunsets, majestic mountains, and the roaring oceans. You can feel it in the warmth of the sun and the cool breeze—as you run, ride a bike, or race across a field. God's love also comes through the loyalty of a friend, the smile of a stranger, and laughter with people you love.

Ask God for eyes to see his love for you. Look for it. Then respond. Tell him, "I love you too." And watch how your relationship grows.

Prayer

God, thank you for loving me. Thank you for pouring out your love in so many different ways. Give me eyes to see your love and a heart to respond.

Where Is the Love?

If I have the gift of prophecy and can fathom all mysteries and all knowledge, and if I have a faith that can move mountains, but do not have love, I am nothing.

(1 CORINTHIANS 13:2)

Think of the biggest mountain around your home. If there aren't any mountains, think of the biggest hill. Imagine walking outside one day and seeing that mountain is gone. Someone moved it from one side of town to the other. Wow! Now imagine it was a friend of yours that prayed a prayer, and—*poof!*—that's how the mountain moved.

You would think your friend is super close to God, that there is sure some incredible faith there! God teaches that a person can do really amazing things through faith in him, including miracles that knock your socks off—but if that person doesn't have love, it doesn't mean a thing.

Love matters to God. It matters more than miracles, moving mountains, or doing everything right. He wants us to love him. He wants us to love each other. So when you look at your day today, think about how you can love God and love others. It will make his day—and yours!

Prayer

God, I'd love to do the big miracles, but the best thing I can do is to love you and other people. Fill me up with love today.

Dealing with Meanies

If your enemy is hungry, give him food to eat; if he is thirsty, give him water to drink. In doing this, you will heap burning coals on his head, and the LORD will reward you.

(PROVERBS 25:21–22)

If you won a free pizza party for ten, you would invite your best buds, of course. How about adding a spot for the guy who always snickers at your clothes? No way. He'll just ruin the party. Plus, he probably wouldn't come.

An interesting thing happens when you are nice to someone who does not deserve it. It catches him off guard. Why would someone he's mistreated be nice to him? It plays with his head, because it doesn't make sense. In the end, extending kindness to an enemy will pierce his heart.

It's no big deal to treat your friends well, but it's hard to be nice to mean people. It takes God-size kindness to treat an enemy like a friend. God will bless you for it. And don't be surprised if the mean guy makes a change for the better.

Prayer

Lord, this is tough instruction to follow. Mean people don't deserve to be treated nicely. But if it is the better way to go, then I need your help to do it.

The King's Fabulous Fam

*But you are a chosen people, a royal priesthood, a
holy nation, God's special possession, that you may
declare the praises of him who called you out of
darkness into his wonderful light.*

(1 PETER 2:9)

Better than any club. More worthy than being popular. More important than any team—we are royalty! When we join God's family, we become princes and princesses. God is our King, and we are his sons and daughters.

It sounds wonderful, but living it out can be hard. It's not like you can show up to school wearing a crown and carrying a scepter. (Well, you could, but you might get made fun of!) You don't live in a castle or get to ride in a chariot to church. But someone very important calls you into his own family, and one day he will share his riches with you.

Does knowing that make you stand taller? Smile bigger? Be thankful? If an earthly king adopted you, you sure would.

Thank God for including you in his family. Then tell him how wonderful he is, and tell others too. Let your royalty shine by following his laws and caring for his subjects.

Prayer

God, I don't know any royalty, but I've read enough stories to know it would be awesome to be a prince or princess. Thank you for inviting me to your royal family. I want to serve you well and show your Kingdom to others.

Show It Off

Let love and faithfulness never leave you; bind them around your neck, write them on the tablet of your heart.

(PROVERBS 3:3)

How in the world are you supposed to tie love and faithfulness around your neck or write them on your heart? There's no way to get a pen to your heart. Plus, no one could see it even if you could. You could walk around with a big silver heart necklace, or hang a sign around your neck that reads "Love and Faithfulness Here." But God had something else in mind.

God wasn't exactly saying to hang a sign or literally write something on your heart (which is impossible anyway!). Certain ideas from God are so important that he uses a word picture to make his point. He was saying that love and faithfulness (being loyal to his ways) need to be part of who you are. Then others will see them. When you love God and your family—when you are faithful—it's like wearing a glittering sign with golden letters. Others will notice how you act. If your heart is in tune with God's ways, then your outside shows it. Sure, you could show it off with bling, but it's even better if your actions naturally show what God has put inside you.

Prayer

Lord, show me how to become more loving and faithful so others see it and ask about you.

Peace Out

Blessed are the peacemakers, for they will be called children of God.

(MATTHEW 5:9)

Jesus didn't say, "Blessed are the peace lovers," because almost everyone loves peace. Neither did he say, "Blessed are the peaceable," who are never disturbed by anything. He said those who work for peace are blessed.

Peacemakers are rare because peacemaking is hard work. It doesn't mean avoiding problems. Pretending conflict doesn't exist or being afraid to talk about it is actually cowardly. Peacemaking is working to get along with others, caring for them, and ending fighting or disagreements. Jesus is the Prince of Peace because he restores us to a peaceful relationship with God, despite our sin.

You can bring peace to any problem you have with someone else. Here's how: pray for the Holy Spirit's continual guidance. Discuss the problem with God. All your relationships would go smoother if you would just pray more about them.

Emphasize peace and a good relationship with someone else, rather than on solving a problem. When we focus on reconciliation (making the relationship right), the problem becomes less important.

Then use your ears more than your mouth. Listen to people's feelings. Admit your own mistakes or sin. Jesus said that's the way to see things more clearly (Matthew 7:5).

Prayer

Although it's overwhelming to think of creating world peace, help me focus on making peace with someone right around me. Lord, show me someone in my life you want me to reconcile with.

Frenemies

If you love those who love you, what credit is that to you? Even sinners love those who love them. And if you do good to those who are good to you, what credit is that to you? Even sinners do that.

(LUKE 6:32–33)

Dealing with friends and enemies would be a lot easier if Jesus didn't say this kind of thing. After all, don't you love the warm fuzzies that come from good friends? But when someone hurts your feelings, stabs you in the back, or totally blows you off, it's tough not to withdraw, pout, or badmouth that person—"What a lousy, no good, rotten . . ."

But to love that person who's mean? *How are we supposed to do that, God?*

Then God reminds us that love like that is exactly what God gives (Luke 6:35). When you didn't know God, when you make bad choices, when you are mean to others or blow them off—God loves you even then.

God asks you to love others like that. But the only way to do it is when you believe God loves you, even when you're not very nice. When you remember that God loves you when you are messy, it makes it easier to love others when they are messy too.

Prayer

Lord, it's not easy to love people who make me angry. Will you help me? Will you give me your love for them? I want to love people the way you love me.

Helping Hand

It is better not to eat meat or drink wine or to do anything else that will cause your brother or sister to fall.

(ROMANS 14:21)

So what was a newly saved Christian Jew to do when eating with a Christian Gentile buddy? Gentiles could eat anything, but Jews weren't allowed to eat pork. Should the Jew offend the host by not eating? Or should he chow down the pig and live with the guilt?

Paul had the answer. He told Christ followers that there was no need to stick to a legalistic rule just to brag that they had. He also said not to rub your freedom to do something in your friends' faces. Instead, consider their feelings and how your actions will affect their walk with God.

So if your parents allow you to watch a movie with a certain rating, but your friend's parents don't, consider how you might feel in that person's place. You wouldn't want others to make fun of you or pressure you into disobeying your parents. You'd rather hear them say, "That's okay. Let's play a board game instead."

We're all different. Some of us may be new Christians while others were practically born in a church pew. But everyone is called to love and encourage each other as Jesus does us. Don't cause your brother or sister to fall but give a helping hand.

Prayer

Help me to see how my friends are feeling, God. I don't want to be a stumbling block. I want to be a starting block for my friends' faith, encouraging them to work on building a closer relationship with you.

Join the Club

When you believed, you were marked in him with
a seal, the promised Holy Spirit, who is a deposit
guaranteeing our inheritance until the redemption of
those who are God's possession—to the praise of his
glory.

(EPHESIANS 1:13–14)

Without asking, you can usually size up other kids and figure out where they fits in. Their accessories (or lack of them), backpack, and kind of clothes clue you in to their preferences.

It's nice to be associated with a group of friends whom you really like and have things in common with. How about a club that you could always be a part of? When you believe in God and ask Jesus Christ to forgive your sins, you receive a special mark. It's the Holy Spirit. He is with you forever and identifies you as one of God's forever children. Everyone in this club will receive a great inheritance from God—the gift of Heaven. Now, that's a group worth being associated with.

Prayer

Thank you, Lord, for the opportunity to join your heavenly club. Please forgive me of my sins and send the gift of your Holy Spirit to seal me as yours forever.

Life of Love

*By this everyone will know that you are my disciples,
if you love one another.*

(JOHN 13:35)

One of the best things in the world is feeling loved. Think about who loves you: your mom or dad, a grandparent, a best friend. How do you show them love?

God is all about love. In fact, he created it. And it's the most important action he wants you to learn. When you love others, you act most like him.

Learning to love unselfishly is not easy though. Why? Because we are often selfish. While your relationship to Christ is personal, God never intends it to be private. Love cannot be learned if you are always by yourself. So God tells us to be close with his followers, and he gives us a lifetime to learn to love.

Of course, God wants us to love everyone, but particularly others in his family. The reason: God wants his family to be known for its love. Jesus said our love for each other—more than anything else—is our greatest witness to the world.

Are you ready to start loving others? The more you practice it, the more God will fill your heart with love.

Prayer

God, don't let me keep my faith to myself. Help me love others unselfishly and be a great witness to those around me.

The Big House

*But I, by your great love, can come into your house;
in reverence I bow down toward your holy temple.*

(PSALM 5:7)

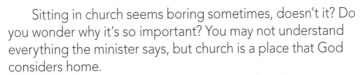

Sitting in church seems boring sometimes, doesn't it? Do you wonder why it's so important? You may not understand everything the minister says, but church is a place that God considers home.

Think about church like going to visit a friend. You go to hang out with that friend and play. You might eat a snack together, listen to music, or watch a movie. Going to church is like going to God's home for a visit. In God's house, though, he wants people to come to worship him. Worship means recognizing how wonderful God is and telling him. Worship often includes singing songs to him, praying to him, and enjoying the other people who are there with you. God's house is also a place to learn. The sermon is a lesson that teaches about God. And Sunday school or youth group is where boys and girls can learn too. He even wants people to take care of each other when they come to his house. If a family needs money or clothes or people are sick, God wants the people in his house to help them.

The next time you go to church, think about it as God's house.

Prayer

Lord, thanks for inviting me to your house. I want to enjoy my visits and learn more about you when I'm there.

Deep and Wide

The LORD is compassionate and gracious, slow to anger, abounding in love . . . For as high as the heavens are above the earth, so great is his love for those who fear him.

(PSALM 103:8, 11)

The next time you are at the top of a tall building or flying in an airplane, look down to see if you can see anything on the ground. Everything below is so far away. If you were to hike a mountain that put you into the clouds, the clouds wouldn't even be halfway to the heavens. That's a long way! The edge of space is fifty to seventy miles from Earth (scientists are trying to figure out exactly where the atmosphere ends and space begins).

God's love is that big—actually, it's bigger. Think about the most patient, loving person you know. Now imagine if that person were ten times more loving and patient. God's love is even greater than that. He waits and he waits. He forgives and he forgives. He loves and he loves and he loves. The next time you look up to the sky or down from a plane, thank God for his great big love.

Prayer

God, thank you for your amazing, massive love for me and for everyone in the world. I don't completely understand it, but I want to experience it and show it to others.

Glad Giving

All the officials and all the people brought their contributions gladly, dropping them into the chest until it was full. . . . The king and Jehoiada gave it to those who carried out the work required for the temple of the LORD. They hired masons and carpenters to restore the LORD's temple, and also workers in iron and bronze to repair the temple.

(2 CHRONICLES 24:10, 12)

You've saved your allowance for months to buy that awesome new tablet. But when Sunday rolls around, so does that offering plate. Your mom gives you a gentle nudge. Do you really have to hand over your money?

Churches need money because just like at home, things break and wear out. People who work at the church, like the pastors and janitors, need to eat. All those things cost money!

God's temple in the Bible was no different. In fact, when Joash was king, the temple was totally trashed. So Joash, along with Jehoida the priest, placed a money chest in front of the temple gates. Then people brought contributions gladly until they had enough to repair and restore the temple.

Did you catch that? The men and women gave gladly! They knew that they could never give so much to God that they wound up strapped. He would always take care of them and bless their offerings.

Hopefully, your church's pillars aren't crumbling like the temple's. Yet the Lord still calls us to give like the Israelites. Will you give reluctantly or gladly?

Prayer

Jesus, everything I own belongs to you, including my piggy bank. Will you change my heart from holding on tightly to gladly giving when you ask me to?

Who's in Charge?

*Now the family heads of the Levites approached
Eleazar the priest, Joshua son of Nun, and the
heads of the other tribal families of Israel at Shiloh
in Canaan and said to them, "The Lord commanded
through Moses that you give us towns to live in, with
pasturelands for our livestock."*

JOSHUA 21:1–2)

Think of someone you admire. You might look up to a
teacher, a team captain, a pastor, or the president. Leaders
teach, give advice, solve problems, and use wisdom to make
decisions. They help others. They always think about others.

God calls some people to be leaders in the church, such as
pastors, elders, or teachers. When God asks people to dedicate
their lives to working in a church or special ministry, God asks
other Christians to take care of those leaders. This idea started
many years ago in Israel. God called the tribe of Levites to be
the priests, which was like being a pastor. They took care of the
tabernacle, taught others, and conducted the sacrifices. Being a
priest required a lot of time. They didn't have time to grow crops
or earn a living outside of the church. So God told the other
tribes to share their land and food with the Levites.

Not every leader today is a volunteer who doesn't get paid.
Like your schoolteachers, coaches, and the president, most
pastors and church leaders get paid to do their jobs. But God
still wants you to show love and support to the leaders in your
church. Ask you mom or dad how your family can do that.

Prayer

Lord, my pastor and small group teachers are leaders, but I
don't think about how I can support them. As a kid, what can I
do to care for my leaders?

Crazy Love

*While Jesus was in Bethany in the home of Simon
the Leper, a woman came to him with an alabaster
jar of very expensive perfume, which she poured on
his head as he was reclining at the table. When the
disciples saw this, they were indignant. "Why this
waste?" they asked.*

(MATTHEW 26:6–8)

What's the most valuable thing you own? An autograph from
a sports star? A rare coin? Your iPhone? Maybe it's that old stuffed
animal you've had since you were a toddler. Would you ever
think of giving that away? Probably only to someone very special.
Surrendering something that means so much would be hard to do.

Just a few days before Jesus died on the cross for our sins,
he had dinner with some close friends. A woman interrupted the
meal and started pouring a bottle of very expensive perfume
on Jesus' head. Jesus' friends were shocked. They thought the
woman was being wasteful. She could have sold it for lots of
money and given it to the poor or used it for ministry. But Jesus
wasn't bothered by it at all. He knew the woman was showing
her love for him by giving her best gift.

Saying you love someone is easy. Showing your love can be
more difficult. One way to show the Lord how much you love
him is by giving something to someone in need. Do you know
anyone in the hospital or home sick in bed? How about a friend
who is sad? Give away your best gifts. It may seem crazy, but
God's love is crazy like that.

Prayer

Lord, I want to be willing to give something I value to a friend
who is going through a hard time. My friends might not understand, but I know it will make you happy and show love.

Missionary Calling

*By the power of signs and wonders, through the
power of the Spirit of God. So from Jerusalem all the
way around to Illyricum, I have fully proclaimed the
gospel of Christ. It has always been my ambition to
preach the gospel where Christ was not known.*

(ROMANS 15:19–20A)

Amy Carmichael and Bertha Smith were two brave women
who traveled to faraway places to help the poor and needy. Both
women spent many years telling people about God's love. In their
day and age, women traveling alone—much less as missionaries—
wasn't common.

A missionary calling, like the one Paul received from
God, comes with a passion to share God's message of salva-
tion with others around the world. Paul traveled all over the
Mediterranean and the Middle East. Amy Carmichael worked in
India. Bertha Smith worked in China. God gave them confidence
and excitement to leave home and live with very little.

God still calls missionaries. He asks many people to spend
their lives traveling near and far to tell his message. One day, he
may call you or someone you know to missionary service. Whether
or not you go yourself, you can be part of missions by praying for
missionaries, writing letters, and sending gifts. They need encouragement from friends and family, just like you do at home.

Prayer

Being a missionary seems like a special calling, God. If that will
be part of my life, please start preparing me. If not, show me
ways that I can support those who go into missions.

Bustin' Pots for God

This is what the Lord says: "Go and buy a clay jar from a potter. Take along some of the elders of the people and of the priests and go out to the Valley of Ben Hinnom, near the entrance of the Potsherd Gate. There proclaim the words I tell you . . . Then break the jar while those who go with you are watching."

(JEREMIAH 19:1–2, 10)

Jeremiah was unusual. He had the tough job of being a prophet when his country was acting up in a very bad way. So he was creative in getting their attention and making God's point.

Long before teachers at church used movie clips or crafts or games to illustrate God's ways, Jeremiah was cutting edge. Instead of just telling people what God was going to do with them, Jeremiah would say, "I have something to show you." He'd grab a clay pot and then smash it on the ground. "Now that I have your attention, ladies and gentlemen . . ." Even when he was put into the wooden stocks, Jeremiah turned it into a teachable moment.

God speaks in a variety of ways—through prophets, grand displays of power, quiet whispers, nomads, simpletons. He may send a message through someone you dislike or your neighbor's pets. He knows how to get our attention, and he is creative. What is he trying to teach you? Are you listening?

Prayer

Lord, please speak to me through specific people and things. I need to learn how to be open to your word, however it comes to me.

Game Time

Let's see how inventive we can be in encouraging love and helping out, not avoiding worshiping together as some do but spurring each other on, especially as we see the big Day approaching.

(HEBREWS 10:24–25 MSG)

Soccer players don't go out on their own to face an opposing team. They go with their team. They know they need each other. Christians need each other too. We are on God's side, but there are opposing spiritual forces of evil out there (Ephesians 6:11–18). But Christians who know the score realize they need each other. They see church as a place where they can get filled up and tuned up and prepared to go back on the field.

One strong team of Christians for God was the Roman Christians. Their secret was they were good together (Romans 15:14–15). They met together regularly. They challenged and encouraged and supported one another in their faith.

Our closeness with other believers is designed to encourage us to live good lives in an evil world. God is the one who gives us strength and protects us from evil, but one of the most powerful ways he does that is through a team of his children working together.

Prayer

God, I'm glad I don't have to live out my faith alone. I'm glad you are by my side.

God's House

Better is one day in your courts than a thousand elsewhere; I would rather be a doorkeeper in the house of my God than dwell in the tents of the wicked.

(PSALM 84:10)

Think about your favorite place to be or a place that you really, really want to visit. Would you love to live at Disney World year-round and go to the park every day for free? Totally! Maybe you want to live in Hawaii and swim and surf every day.

King David had a favorite place, but it wasn't what you would expect from a king. He absolutely loved God's house. David loved to worship and talk with God. When he was there, he couldn't imagine any other place he would rather be.

That might sound crazy, because church may not seem like the best place on Earth to you. It's even normal if you dread going sometimes. Next time, though, ask God to help you be aware of his presence when you are there. Once you understand what he wants you to experience in his house, Disney World won't even compare.

That's what David would tell you. If he could have, he would have spent every day in God's house. Will it ever be on the top of your list?

Prayer

God, I want to experience being in your presence, either at church or when I'm at home talking to you. I'd like to know the same wonder and awe that David felt when he spent time with you.

Better Together

The human body has many parts, but the many parts make up one whole body. So it is with the body of Christ.

(1 CORINTHIANS 12:12, NLT)

For the organs of your body to work right, they must be connected to your body. You can't leave your brain or stomach at home all day. If an organ is somehow severed from its body, it will shrivel and die. It cannot exist on its own, and neither can you as a part of the Body of Christ.

You were created for a specific role in life. You discover what that is through your relationships with others. If you are disconnected and cut off from other Christians, your faith will wither away.

The Bible says a Christian without a church (a group of believers) is like an organ without a body, a sheep without a flock, or a child without a family. It is unnatural. When we come together in love as a church family from different backgrounds, races, and social status, we act as Christ's Body and bring his message of grace and love to the world.

Prayer

God, I know I am created for a special role in your community of believers. Thank you for such a diverse church family in which I can worship and serve you. Help me stay connected to others and you.

If You Can't Say Something Nice . . .

*I said, "I will watch my ways and keep my tongue
from sin; I will put a muzzle on my mouth while in the
presence of the wicked." So I remained utterly silent,
not even saying anything good.*

(PSALM 39:1–2A)

If your dad said, "Put a muzzle on it," you'd close your
mouth immediately because your dad probably means business.
Can you imagine how quiet you'd be if you actually put a muzzle
on? You could hum or make noises, but you wouldn't get a word
out.

King David held his tongue when he was around evil people.
But if he was the king, why would he be worried about what he
said around others? Because he didn't want to be sucked into
bad conversation.

When you're around kids who are mean, stuck up, or bullies,
you can get sucked into insulting or badmouthing others or
laughing at dirty jokes that you'd never say at home. The pressure to go along with other kids can sneak up on you. Before you
know it, you cuss, insult a friend, or snicker behind someone's
back—and those are regrettable words. You never know when
a conversation can go bad, so practice muzzling your mouth.
Count to ten before you agree, disagree, or say something
mean. The longer you keep your lips tightly closed, the less likely
it is that wrong words will come out of your mouth.

After all, if you don't have something nice to say, pull out a
muzzle.

Prayer

Lord, it's not easy to keep my mouth shut when other kids are
saying mean things. Please remind me to hold my tongue or to
say only good things when those around me are mouthing off.

Group Training

And let us consider how we may spur one another on toward love and good deeds, not giving up meeting together, as some are in the habit of doing, but encouraging one another—and all the more as you see the Day approaching.

(HEBREWS 10:24–25)

Serious swimmers, soccer players, weight-lifters, and sprinters may spend up to twenty hours a week building strength and endurance for many years. You wouldn't walk over to a world-champion Olympic weight-lifter and say, "Go ahead and give me that two-hundred-pound barbell. I can lift it." That is, unless you are in the mood to crush your ribs.

You could stand there in the gym wearing a muscle tank top. You could put on a back brace. You could slick down your arms with oil. But you're still no weight-lifter!

Christians sometimes try similar spiritual shortcuts. We sleep in on Sundays, thinking we can catch church next week. Or you decide it's not a big deal to skip youth group since your favorite leader moved away months ago.

Just like weight-lifters may practice with a team and a coach, Christians need others to help them with their training. God made us to need others. Worshiping, reading the Bible, and learning about him with other God-followers is like long hours at the gym. These activities grow and stretch us into mature believers. So don't give up practicing with your crew (the church) or listening to your trainer (God).

Prayer

I don't always feel like going to church, God, and reading my Bible is hard. But I know these things will build my spiritual strength. Will you give me a fresh love for my church so I can share its blessings with family and friends?

More Fun with Others

Two are better than one, because they have a good return for their labor: If either of them falls down, one can help the other up. But pity anyone who falls and has no one to help them up.

(ECCLESIASTES 4:9–10)

Having a friend, sibling, or relative to play with, talk to, and share with (maybe not dessert!) makes life more fun. God enjoys the company of his Son Jesus and the Holy Spirit, and he likes having a relationship with you. He wanted you to experience the same pleasure.

While there's a place and time to be quiet and alone, God designed us for community, a group of people that cares for each other. As you grow up, your community will change from the schoolyard to the neighborhood to the workplace and possibly to around the world.

God never intends for us to be alone. He is always with you too. If you are feeling alone, ask him to bring friends and family to you. And when you have the chance to include people who are lonely, invite them into your community. Life is more fun when you share with others.

Prayer

Lord, sometimes I just don't care to be around people, but you've said they are important. Please show me how valuable others are to my life and how I can be a friend.

Be a Titus

But God, who comforts the downcast, comforted us by the coming of Titus, and not only by his coming but also by the comfort you had given him. He told us about your longing for me, your deep sorrow, your ardent concern for me, so that my joy was greater than ever.

(2 CORINTHIANS 7:6–7)

If you like airplane rides, here's a record to beat: the world's most-traveled man has flown over fifteen million miles. That's like rocketing to the moon and back thirty one times!

The apostle Paul's methods of transportation didn't include airplanes, but he certainly covered the ancient map while teaching about Jesus. Can you imagine how many "frequent camel miles" he must have racked up?

Going someplace new is exciting. But long hours on the road can also be boring, tiring, and even lonely. And though Paul had a strong relationship with God, he still needed friends, just like we do. That's why Paul was so thrilled when his good friend Titus joined him and Timothy in Macedonia.

God knows we need people who understand us and have fun with us. Sometimes, just seeing a friend's happy face is enough to change a bad day into a good one. So the Lord comforts us by sending friends.

Do you know a Paul—someone who may be lonely? Be a Titus, offer a smile, and invite that person over for some fun. You just might be God's comfort to someone who really needs it.

Prayer

Lord, my friends are important to me. They definitely cheer me up when I'm feeling down. Is there a guy or girl around me who needs a friend like that today?

It Takes Guts

*If we are thrown into the blazing furnace, the God we
serve is able to deliver us from it, and he will deliver
us from Your Majesty's hand. But even if he does not,
we want you to know, Your Majesty, that we will not
serve your gods or worship the image of gold you
have set up.*

(DANIEL 3:17–18)

Talk about gutsy guys! Shadrach, Meshach, and Abednego
would not budge. They had already been taken captive. They'd
already lost their families and their homes. As far as we know,
they only had each other—and God—to count on. But that was
plenty for them. Good friends and a good God were the last
things standing in their lives.

King Nebuchadnezzar was in charge, and he expected
everyone to obey everything he said! But these three friends
were not going to betray their faith, their God, or their country.
They had nothing left to lose, so they certainly weren't going to
sacrifice their faith.

How gutsy are you? Would you stand up to a harsh teacher
or a tough friend? That doesn't sound easy. It's no fun to risk
others not liking you or being shunned or hurt. These three
friends from Daniel's day are a great example of how awesome
God is. He wants to show you what an amazing God he is, so
that if you ever face something like Shadrach, Meshach, and
Abednego did, you'll have no doubt what your answer will be.
Your guts will tell you!

Prayer

Wow, God, I don't know if I have the guts to risk standing up
for you in the face of such threats. Teach me more about your
awesomeness, and provide me with good friends so that I never
doubt you are better than any earthly risk.

Stand Up!

When Reuben heard this, he tried to rescue him from their hands. "Let's not take his life," he said. "Don't shed any blood. Throw him into this cistern here in the wilderness, but don't lay a hand on him." Reuben said this to rescue him from them and take him back to his father.

(GENESIS 37:21–22)

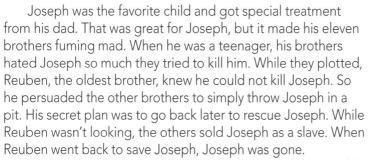

Joseph was the favorite child and got special treatment from his dad. That was great for Joseph, but it made his eleven brothers fuming mad. When he was a teenager, his brothers hated Joseph so much they tried to kill him. While they plotted, Reuben, the oldest brother, knew he could not kill Joseph. So he persuaded the other brothers to simply throw Joseph in a pit. His secret plan was to go back later to rescue Joseph. While Reuben wasn't looking, the others sold Joseph as a slave. When Reuben went back to save Joseph, Joseph was gone.

Reuben didn't stand up for what was right when he should have. He tried to do it sneakily. If he had protected Joseph from the very beginning, he would have saved Joseph and stopped his other brothers from such a terrible choice.

It can be tough to stand up for what's right—especially when other people want to do what's wrong. But God wants his children to do the right thing, even if it makes others mad and even if it's unpopular. Stand up for right, and you may help prevent someone from making a big mistake. Even if people don't listen, God will reward you for obeying him.

Prayer

Lord, please give me the courage to always stand up for what's right. I don't want to regret not helping protect someone from being hurt by others.

Tough Job

This is what each of you keeps saying to your friends and other Israelites: "What is the LORD's answer?" or "What has the LORD spoken?" But you must not mention "a message from the LORD" again, because each one's word becomes their own message. So you distort the words of the living God, the LORD Almighty, our God.

(JEREMIAH 23:35–36)

The misbehaving Israelites hated the prophets God sent. They didn't spare Jeremiah. They got so sick of hearing his prophecies that they started mocking him. The King James Version of the Scripture says Jeremiah used to say, "The burden of Jehovah . . ." then go on to preach to the people. So the people turned it around on him: "You old burden of Jehovah!" they called him. Then they would taunt him by sarcastically asking, "What's God's burden for us today?" What a tough crowd!

Jeremiah was cast out, shunned, and hated. Yet he was living for and serving God. How did Jeremiah keep going? God was more important than what anyone else could say or do to him. And God gave him strength to continue his tough job.

Pastors and church leaders have a tough job too. Not everyone likes what they have to say, and they work hard day and night. Even if you don't agree with or like a certain pastors or ministers, they are serving and living for God. Listen. Consider their words. Thank them for their service. God will bless you for recognizing the challenging job they have to do.

Prayer

God, please bless the pastor and leaders at my church. They have a hard job and need your strength to do it well, especially when people are tough on them.

Don't Put Down—Pull Up!

What right do you have to criticize someone else's servants? Only their Lord can decide if they are doing right, and the Lord will make sure that they do right.

(ROMANS 14:4, CEV)

Is it easier to encourage or criticize?

The Bible calls Satan "the accuser of our brothers and sisters" (Revelation 12:10). It's the Devil's job to blame, complain, and criticize members of God's family. Any time we do the same, we're being duped into doing Satan's work for him. No matter how much you disagree with another Christian, that person is not your enemy.

God warns over and over not to criticize, compare, or judge each other. Whenever I judge another believer, four things instantly happen:

I lose closeness with God.
I expose my own pride.
I set myself up to be judged by God.
I harm the closeness of God's family.

When you criticize another believer, you are interfering with God's business. It's best to let God be the judge. He's the only one who knows a person's heart and who sees everything. Instead, spend time building unity with encouraging words rather than pointing out someone's faults.

Prayer

God, you tell me not to judge others but instead to encourage them. When I start to criticize or judge another believer, can you remind me to say something encouraging instead?

Kind Words

Anxiety weighs down the heart, but a kind word cheers it up.

(PROVERBS 12:25)

Worry comes in all shapes and sizes. Since we live in a messy world, it's easy to worry about all kinds of things: friends, school, money, parents, brothers, and sisters—the list goes on and on. And we each have our own set of problems. You might worry about your dad while your best friend thinks a lot about math class and how much he doesn't like it.

So how can we help each other out? Sometimes we just need to pay attention, notice what might be bothering our friends, and then, like it says in Proverbs, say something nice: "I know that was a hard test in math, but don't worry, you'll do great next time. Maybe I can help you study."

When we say something kind, it helps a worried heart. And it not only helps our friends, it usually helps us to stop thinking about the things that drive us crazy too.

Prayer

Lord, help me to pay attention to my friends today. I want to be a good friend. Help me to say the right thing when they need it.

Today's Levites

[The Levites] will eat the grain offerings, the sin offerings and the guilt offerings; and everything in Israel devoted to the LORD will belong to them.

(EZEKIEL 44:29)

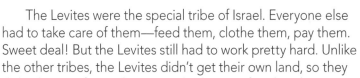

The Levites were the special tribe of Israel. Everyone else had to take care of them—feed them, clothe them, pay them. Sweet deal! But the Levites still had to work pretty hard. Unlike the other tribes, the Levites didn't get their own land, so they didn't have to farm. The Levites had a specific job—they were the priests for the whole country. Like church pastors and ministers today, the priests cared for the spiritual needs of others.

Priestly duties included running feasts and celebrations, cooking sacrifices, cleaning the altars and temple (like a church), praying for sinners, teaching God's laws, and more. They didn't have time to do anything else, much less take care of their own land or find a way to support themselves. So the people took care of the Levites.

The day-to-day duties of pastors today are different from Levitical priests. But they are still committed to serving and caring, and also equipping us to serve and care for others. They still count on us, the Body of Christ, to encourage and support them so they can provide spiritual leadership.

How does your family support your minister or pastor?

Prayer

God, thank you for the pastor at my church. Please bless our church leaders and their families and show me ways I can help support them.

Up-Lifters

Then Job replied: "I have heard many things like these; you are miserable comforters, all of you! Will your long-winded speeches never end? What ails you that you keep on arguing?"

(JOB 16:1–3)

Sometimes friends fall off the friend wagon. When you have a bad day, instead of standing up for you, they say the wrong thing. That's what happened to Job. Instead of looking out for Job and being good buds, his friends tell him his misery is his own fault! Who needs friends like that?

Take Job's story to heart, and be a friend who chooses your words carefully. If a friend is having a bad day, stand by her, no matter what happens. If her team lost, her parents yelled at her, or a mean girl pushed her around, hang out with her and let her know she has a friend in you.

It's easier to think of ways to criticize than encourage. There's a time to correct and be accountable to each other, but pray a lot before you offer any constructive criticism. Even if a bad day is your friend's fault, stick by her. Pointing out her faults right at that moment won't help a thing. Be a friend, an up-lifter and steady companion.

Prayer

Lord, it's easy to see an answer to friends' problems, but that may not be helpful. Will you give me wisdom to know what to say to a friend who is down?

PURPOSE 4

Becoming Like Christ

The Bigger Picture

God assured us, "I'll never let you down, never walk off and leave you," we can boldly quote, God is there, ready to help; I'm fearless no matter what. Who or what can get to me?

(HEBREWS 13:5–6, MSG)

You have a destiny. God's purpose is greater than any situation you will ever experience. God even has a plan beyond any of your problems. Because of this, it is dangerous to focus on your problems more than your purpose. You will start despairing if you keep your eyes on the problem rather than on God's love and plans.

You are not here on Earth just to take up space. No person is born by accident. God has a specific plan for your life. Storms are simply temporary setbacks toward fulfilling that purpose.

Absolutely nothing can change God's ultimate purpose for you unless you choose to disobey him. If you choose to reject his plan, he will allow you to do that, but no one else can change God's plan for you. You can either accept it or you can reject it. It's up to you.

Prayer

God, I know you have a plan for me, but sometimes I get caught up in my problems and forget. Guide me so that I can live out my true purpose and be obedient to you.

Awesomely Ordinary

When they saw the courage of Peter and John and realized that they were unschooled, ordinary men, they were astonished and they took note that these men had been with Jesus.

(ACTS 4:13)

Hanging out with Jesus makes us more than who we are without him. It's enough to make you smile: Peter and John weren't just unschooled, but they were ordinary too.

That means there's a whole lot of hope for the rest of us. Who hasn't felt stupid on occasion? Who doesn't feel ordinary or plain other times? God tells us this story to let us know: it doesn't matter. Jesus is the one who makes us special. He is the one who makes us extraordinary. He is the one who makes us smarter than we actually are. What a good God!

So on those days when you might be feeling ordinary, remember that you are in good company. Peter and John were two of the treasured disciples who made an amazing difference for good. If Jesus could work with them, he can definitely work with you.

Prayer

Lord, thank you that I don't have to be a scholar to be used by you. I'm special simply because you made me, and I am so grateful.

Ancient Celebrity

So Abram went, as the Lord had told him; and Lot went with him. Abram was seventy-five years old when he set out from Harran.

(GENESIS 12:4)

Abram was called the father of Israel. Abram's kids started a new country, and it was all because Abram loved and obeyed God. He had faith that became legendary.

Can you name someone who had long-lasting fame? You might know about Gabrielle Douglas or Michael Phelps, top athletes in Olympic history. Maybe you'd recognize the name of a writer of a classic book, such as Jane Austen who wrote *Pride and Prejudice* or C.S. Lewis who wrote *The Chronicles of Narnia*. Or you might know about Pocahontas, the Native American who helped English settlers that came to America. She's been widely known for more than five hundred years.

Abram (whose name was later changed to Abraham) is more famous than any of those people. Millions of people have known about Abram for thousands of years. People still talk about Abram today. He is known as one of the godliest people who ever lived. He moved when God said move. He prayed when he needed help. He trusted God even when he was old. God blessed Abram because of his faith. Following God's ways is the type of fame that will never fade.

Prayer

Lord, I don't want to get caught up pursuing fame or attention for the wrong reasons. I want my life to matter because I lived for you. Help me be an example like Abram.

Family Resemblance

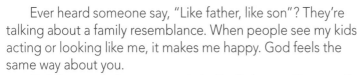

For God knew his people in advance, and he chose them to become like his Son, so that his Son would be the firstborn among many brothers and sisters.

(ROMANS 8:29, NLT)

Ever heard someone say, "Like father, like son"? They're talking about a family resemblance. When people see my kids acting or looking like me, it makes me happy. God feels the same way about you.

Only human beings are made in God's image. How cool! Here are a few ways we are like God:

1. Our spirits will outlast our earthly bodies.
2. We can think, reason, and solve problems.
3. We can give and receive real love.
4. We can figure out right from wrong.

Every single person possesses part of the image of God. But his image has been damaged by sin. So God sent Jesus on a mission to restore the full image that we have lost.

What does the full image of God look like? It looks like Jesus Christ! The Bible says Jesus is "the exact likeness of God," "the visible image of the invisible God," and "the exact representation of his being" (2 Corinthians 4:4; Colossians 1:15; Hebrews 1:3).

God wants his children to bear his image and likeness too. He wants you to grow up spiritually and become like Christ.

Prayer

God, I didn't get what it meant to be made in your image, but it's actually pretty cool! Thank you for making me. Help me grow to become more like you.

Mimic Me

Jesus gave them this answer: "Very truly I tell you, the Son can do nothing by himself; he can do only what he sees his Father doing, because whatever the Father does the Son also does.

(JOHN 5:19)

Growing up, most children watch their parents, grandparents, daycare providers, foster parents, and teachers, and they follow and take cues from the adult examples that are strongest around them.

Jesus did the same thing. He was quick to point out to the crowds that he was only doing what his heavenly Father did. What Jesus was teaching was the very thing he learned from God. So when Jesus healed someone who was suffering, he was behaving like his Father.

But unlike children, Jesus and his Father are really the same. This was Jesus' way of saying that he is God, just in human form. When you were little and mimicked an adult, it was pretending. But Jesus isn't pretending to be God. He really is God. When you read the gospels and look at everything Jesus did, you are actually seeing into the heart of God, not just an imitation.

Prayer

Lord, I like the way you treated people and showed us God's ways. I want to imitate you in the things I do and say.

Test Me, Please

Test me, LORD, and try me, examine my heart and my mind.

(PSALM 26:2)

❦

King David asked God to test him. Who in their right mind asks for a test? Would you go to class and ask your teacher to give you a test to show how well you are learning math? Even adults don't ask their bosses to test them. You certainly wouldn't ask your mom or dad to test your cleaning abilities. (But you might ask them to check your homework before you turn it in for a grade.)

Well, David had been serving the Lord, but his life was getting pretty tough. So he asked God why life was so hard when he was faithfully serving God. David was confident in his relationship with the Lord. He knew God would be honest with him and that he honored people who followed his ways. He also knew he'd been living right and studying God's Word. So David said, "Check me out."

Every now and then, it's a good idea to ask for a test. That may sound crazy. But letting God test you—and being ready for his grade—will help you see if you are living by his ways. You might even ask your parents or a close friend for a mini test on how you're doing when life gets tough. They can help you learn how to deal with trouble and problems in a way that is smart and makes the grade.

Prayer

God, I'm not sure if I'm ready for you to test me, but I want to learn more about you and your Word so when life is hard, I will turn to you and continue to follow your ways.

Words to Live By

But He answered and said, "It is written, 'Man shall not live on bread alone, but on every word that proceeds out of the mouth of God.'"

(MATTHEW 4:4, NASB)

God's Word is unlike any other word. It is alive. When God speaks, things change. Everything around you—all of creation—exists because God said it. He spoke it all into existence. God even spoke you into your mother's womb!

God's Word is the spiritual nutrition you must have to fulfill your purpose. The Bible is called our milk, bread, solid food, and sweeter than honey (1 Peter 2:2; Matthew 4:4; 1 Corinthians 3:2; Psalm 119:103). This four-course meal is the Spirit's menu for spiritual strength and growth.

Millions of believers are "starving to death" from spiritual malnutrition. Don't be one of them. To be a healthy disciple of Jesus, feeding on God's Word must be your first priority. It's the only way to grow strong faith for life.

Prayer

God, the Bible can be confusing to me. Will you please give me an appetite for reading it and help me when I'm lost? I want your words to be my ultimate source of fuel.

Not Cool

My son, if sinful men entice you, do not give in to them.

(PROVERBS 1:10)

T-E-M-P-T-A-T-I-O-N. A big word for a big problem. Temptation is when something that is wrong or hurtful seems appealing or fun *before you do it*. Have you ever thrown rocks at a window because a friend egged you on? Have you ever told your teacher you did your homework when you actually forgot? Those probably don't seem too bad. You'd have fun throwing rocks. And if your teacher never finds out about the homework, you might be home free.

Throughout your life, other people will tempt you to join them. Maybe they'll ask you to smoke or do drugs. Maybe someone will tell you to lie to your boss for him. Maybe you'll go along and insult someone who is weak and lonely.

The tricky part is that giving in to T-E-M-P-T-A-T-I-O-N may make you feel good for a short while. But it always involves lying, cheating, stealing, hurting, or hiding the truth. If you feel torn inside, that's a clue that you're facing temptation. Consider whether the kids asking you to join them are looking to do good or to get into mischief. Giving in to the big T word will always hurt someone else, God, or you in the end.

Prayer

God, help me to see temptation for what it really is. When others try to get me to do something wrong, I want to know what the right thing to do is.

Did You Hear That?

The disciples left, went into the city and found things just as Jesus had told them. So they prepared the Passover.

(MARK 14:16)

Do you wonder if the disciples ever got used to Jesus? In this particular scene, he tells them to go into town where they'll meet up with a man who has a large upstairs room. Jesus tells them exactly what to say and do when they get there. He even tells them exactly how it will play out.

The disciples did as they were told. Perhaps they talked about it on the way. Maybe they questioned how Jesus knew about the man with the upper room. Did they wonder or worry at all? By this time, they may have just accepted that when it came to Jesus, anything could happen.

The awesomeness of Jesus is that he never changes. Just like he told the disciples what to do and what to expect, he can tell *us* things as well. He knows what's coming and where we're headed. Our job is to learn how to hear his voice and then obey when he speaks—which will be through his Word, trusted adults, lessons at school and church, friends and leaders, and prayer. We may not always get it right, but as we grow up with God, we'll get better at hearing his voice and following his direction.

Prayer

Jesus, I want to hear your voice. Like the disciples, I want to have confidence to act on what you tell me and to trust that you have a plan.

Memory Check

Let the teaching of Christ live in you richly.
(COLOSSIANS 3:16A, NCV)

How good is your memory? Your memory is like a muscle. The more you use it, the stronger it will become. Your capacity to remember is a God-given gift. The truth is, you have thousands of ideas, truths, facts, and figures memorized. You remember what is important to you. If God's Word is important, you will take the time to remember it. There are enormous benefits to memorizing Bible verses. It will help you resist temptation, make wise decisions, reduce stress, build confidence, offer good advice, and share your faith with others (Psalm 119:11, 49–50, 105; Jeremiah 15:16; Proverbs 22:18; 1 Peter 3:15).

Begin by selecting a few Bible verses that you like and understand. Write or type them on something you can carry with you (notebook, tablet, phone). Then review them aloud throughout your day. You can memorize Scripture anywhere: while playing or eating or at bedtime. The three keys to memorizing Scripture are review, review, and review. Your memory will get stronger each time.

Prayer

Lord, I want to know your Word better and be able to have those words on my mind every day. Keep your Word close to my heart and mind.

How Do You Spend Your Time?

Jesus said to the people who believed in him, "You are truly my disciples if you remain faithful to my teachings."

(JOHN 8:31, NLT)

What do you spend more time doing? Playing games, reading books, reading the Bible, or watching TV?

We can't watch television for three hours, then read the Bible for three minutes and expect to grow. There are more Bibles in print today than ever before, but a Bible on the shelf is worthless.

Though there is a lot in the Bible that may be hard to understand, it's the most powerful book you will ever read. The Bible is much more than a guidebook. God's Word:

- Leads to life
- Forms our faith
- Changes us
- Heals hurts
- Builds character
- Spreads joy
- Defeats temptation
- Infuses hope
- Cleanses our minds
- Guarantees our future forever.

We cannot live without the Word of God! Never take it for granted.

Prayer

Lord, forgive me for those times I've taken your Word for granted. When I don't want to study or read the Bible, can you give me encouragement to pick it up? I want to know you better.

Pick a Side

Whoever is not with me is against me, and whoever does not gather with me scatters.

(MATTHEW 12:30)

Ever get in the middle of two friends who are fighting? It's not very fun. It seems easier to stay out of it—to avoid picking sides so that you don't make anyone mad. That's smart when it comes to friends. But it doesn't work as well when it comes to the fight between good and evil. In Matthew 12, Jesus had just finished arguing with the Pharisees about doing good things. The Pharisees were pointing fingers and saying that the only way Jesus could fight evil was if he was evil himself. Well, that is just silly. Evil doesn't beat up evil. Neither does good fight good. Jesus gets straight to the point and tells them so. Then he says that unless people take a stand for good, they are siding with evil.

There is no way to stay out of the fight when it comes to good versus evil. Either we love Jesus and take a stand for good, or we are working against him. There is no middle ground. We have to pick a side.

Prayer

Lord, help me to stand with you. I don't want to end up on the wrong side just because I'm afraid to get involved.

Bright Obedience

*The path of the righteous is like the morning sun,
shining ever brighter till the full light of day.*

(PROVERBS 4:18)

Getting up super early isn't fun. It's not even fun to get up at a normal time if you are tired. That's why more people watch sunsets than sunrises. Even fewer folks have watched what happens in the sky an hour or so before the sun actually comes up. On the horizon a glow of light appears that gradually gets brighter and brighter. The sun eventually rises, and the sky keeps getting lighter until it reaches its brightest at lunchtime.

The writer of Proverbs wants us to know something important about obeying God. Just like the sun making its way to the middle of the sky, obedience shines brightly. No one may notice at first when you do the right thing. But obeying God will shine on others. The more you do right, the more others will see God's light in you.

Some may think you're dumb for standing up for a kid at school. They may think you're ridiculous for refusing to cheat on a test (like they do). But the truth always comes to light. That's when you'll shine brightly.

Prayer

Lord, help me to shine for you, even when I don't see the value in obeying you. Remind me that it takes time for the truth to be revealed.

Champion for God

Let us run with perseverance the race marked out for us.

(HEBREWS 12:1B)

You want to become a chess champion. You read the rules, win one game, and then you never play again. But you claim you hold the title of chess champion extraordinaire. Um, that's not how it works.

Anything you want to do with your life that counts takes work and dedication. If you really want to be a chess champion, you are going to play over and over, learn strategy, and figure out how to read your opponents. To become a champion, you will play for years and keep practicing so you don't lose your title.

Giving your life to God is not a one-time deal either. You can confess your sin and ask Jesus Christ into your life, but that's not the end of the story. He wants to grow your faith and your friendship with him. That takes dedication. It takes practice. You can't skimp on the time. Are you ready to become a champion for God? He's waiting to teach you the rules and the strategy. Will you take the time?

Prayer

God, there are many things I want to do with my life. Serving you needs to be first, but I need the dedication to do it. Please show me how great a champion I can be for you if I put in the time.

Getting What We Ask For

*And the L*ORD *told him: "Listen to all that the people are saying to you; it is not you they have rejected, but they have rejected me as their king.*

(1 SAMUEL 8:7)

Israel was definitely different than other countries. None of their neighbors had special rules about what they could eat or wear or where they could live. On top of that, Israel had no king! Unlike other nations, Israel was guided by an invisible God, not by a man with a crown.

But Israel grew tired of being different from everybody else. They wanted a king with a palace, big muscles, and fast chariots. And they wanted him *now!* So God gave Israel a king—with a big warning. Sometimes, even when we ask for something that is bad for us, God allows us to have it because it will teach us that God's way is always best.

How about you? Like the Israelites, we sometimes ditch God to fit in. We let friends, favorite TV shows, and songs guide us instead of following God's advice in the Bible and through prayer.

It was a lesson Israel learned the hard way. Its long line of kings often led the nation into war, sin, death, and poverty. Wanting to have friends is good. But hiding our differences—like believing in God and who we are as Christians—just to be like everyone else is not.

Prayer

Lord, you made me to need friends. But sometimes I make them more important than you in my life. I'm sorry for rejecting you like that. Help me to always keep you as "king" over my life.

Are You a Baby?

When Jesus was leaving, he saw a man named Matthew sitting in the tax collector's booth. Jesus said to him, "Follow me," and he stood up and followed Jesus.

(MATTHEW 9:9, NCV)

God wants you to grow up.

Sadly, millions of Christians are stuck. It's like they are spiritual babies in diapers—and they don't want to grow. But who wants to be a baby forever?

Your heavenly Father's goal is for you to develop the characteristics of Jesus Christ. Discipleship—the process of becoming like Christ—always begins with a decision. You must want, decide, and make an effort to grow. When the first disciples chose to follow Jesus, they didn't understand all he would require. They simply responded to Jesus' invitation. That's all you need to get started too.

Once you decide to get serious about growing spiritually, start to act in new ways. Just like you started putting on your own clothes and feeding yourself a few years ago, you will need to let go of some old routines. Develop some new habits like reading the Bible on your own, asking your mom or dad or a teacher about God, and praying for your family. The Holy Spirit will help you with these changes. And soon you'll leave those baby ways behind.

Prayer

God, I want my faith to mature and grow. It doesn't sound easy, but would you please help me get into a routine to deepen my faith?

Thinking of Others

We should think of their good and try to help them by doing what pleases them. Even Christ did not try to please himself.

(ROMANS 15:2–3A, CEV)

Want to be more grown up? Start thinking like Jesus. He considered others, not just himself. Part of becoming more mature is knowing more of the Bible and what it means. But that's not the whole story. Maturity includes your behavior and character. Your beliefs must be backed up with Christ-like behavior.

Christianity is all about relationships—with God and others—and how you live. Thinking of others is the best proof of growth. How do you think of others? You consider how your words and actions will affect others. Will what you say show love or insult? Will what you do show that you care or that you are selfish? This kind of thinking is rare and difficult. Fortunately, we have help from the Holy Spirit and the example of Jesus. Ask the Holy Spirit to guide your thoughts, and read the gospels to see how Jesus treated others.

Prayer

Holy Spirit, guide me in my walk with Jesus. I want to mature and think and act Christ-like to those around me, but I need your direction.

Schooled

He replied, "Because you have so little faith. Truly I tell you, if you have faith as small as a mustard seed, you can say to this mountain, 'Move from here to there,' and it will move. Nothing will be impossible for you."

(MATTHEW 17:20)

Pop quiz: who's your favorite schoolteacher? Maybe it's a funny math instructor or that science teacher who lets you blow things up. No matter what, your favorite teachers are probably never boring.

Jesus' teaching methods were definitely not boring. Instead of using fancy words in a fancy sermon, like most religious teachers of the past preferred, Jesus taught people about God by using everyday language and everyday situations. At the time, his style was pretty radical.

Take the boy with the demon in Matthew 17. Jesus' disciples couldn't heal him, but Jesus could. His clueless disciples didn't get it—why couldn't they heal him? Instead of a yawn-worthy diagram or long lecture, Jesus answered with an object that everyone immediately recognized: a mustard seed. They knew right away what Jesus was talking about. They didn't have to work up a miracle. They just had to believe in Jesus' power.

If Jesus were here today, he might teach you about life using your drum set, chessboard, or cell phone. Jesus isn't a sleep-inducing lecturer; he's a genuine father who loves you and is interested in your everyday life. He'll use things you know well to teach you about himself.

Prayer

Jesus, thank you for being the ultimate teacher who cares about my life. Help me follow your example of being real with my friends, family, and teachers every day of the week.

Change the Channel

Turn my eyes from worthless things, and give me life through your word.

(PSALM 119:37, NLT)

Have you ever watched a food commercial and suddenly felt you were hungry? Have you ever heard someone cough and immediately felt the need to clear your throat? That is the power of suggestion. The more you think about something, the stronger it takes hold of you.

It's like a classmate who is about to read her book report out loud and keeps repeating to herself, "Don't be nervous . . ." Of course she's going to be nervous!

This is why the battle for sin is won or lost in your mind. Whatever gets your attention will get you. Every time you try to block a thought from your mind, you drive it deeper into your memory. You don't defeat temptation by fighting the feeling of it.

Since temptation always begins with a thought, the quickest way to neutralize it is to turn your attention to something else. For example, the classmate about to speak should focus on anything except her feelings. She could focus on God or her book. So when temptation comes your way, don't fight the thought. Just change the channel of your mind and get interested in another idea.

Prayer

God, when I have a tempting thought, help me to redirect that strong thought toward something else. You are the one who provides peaceful thoughts at the times I need them.

Kinda Confused?

Whoever finds their life will lose it, and whoever loses their life for my sake will find it.

(MATTHEW 10:39)

Jesus Christ, the Son of God, said a lot of things while he lived on Earth that didn't make sense when people first heard them. Lose your life to find it? Find it then you'll lose it? What was he talking about? Jesus spoke in ways that sounded like riddles. He wanted people to scratch their heads in curiosity. Plus, he was talking about God's ways, and the human mind doesn't always get God's ways.

Think about it like this: you are in elementary school or middle school, but you probably know someone who is in high school. You could easily talk to the high school student, and he would understand what you're talking about. But if the student started telling you about his calculus homework, you'd be lost. That doesn't mean the high school student doesn't know what he's talking about. He just knows more than you do.

Jesus knows way more than anyone. He's the ultimate know-it-all—but in a good way. So when you read or hear something from the Bible that doesn't make sense to you, ask Jesus to help you understand. If you still feel like you're in the dark, trust that he knows a lot more than you do.

Prayer

Jesus, there are many things I don't understand in the Bible or at church. But I want to believe your words whether I know what they mean right now or not.

Holy Spirit Help

*We . . . are being transformed into the same image
from one degree of glory to another. For this comes
from the Lord who is the Spirit.*

(2 CORINTHIANS 3:18, ESV)

The Bible compares spiritual growth to a seed, a building, and a child growing up. Seeds must be planted and watered, buildings must be constructed; they don't just appear. And children must eat and exercise to grow. But guess whose job it is to grow you? Not yours. It's the Holy Spirit's.

You cannot reproduce the character of Jesus on your own strength. Best intentions or wishing really, really hard are not enough. Only the Holy Spirit has the power to make the changes God wants. This is called "sanctification."

Most of the time the Holy Spirit's power comes into your life in quiet ways you aren't even aware of and can't feel. He often nudges with "a gentle whisper" (1 Kings 19:12). How does this happen in real life? Through the choices we make. We choose to do the right thing and then trust God's Spirit to give us his power, love, faith, and wisdom to do it. We choose to act differently and depend on his Spirit to help us actually do it. Before you know it, you're growing strong and sure.

Prayer

God, help me make choices that are pleasing to you. I know I can't do it by myself, but the Holy Spirit gives me the wisdom and strength to act differently. Thank you for the Holy Spirit working in my life.

No Compromise

To show partiality is not good—yet a person will do wrong for a piece of bread.

(PROVERBS 28:21)

A young man says he will never work for the evil queen. Then the evil queen offers the young man a magic potion that will solve any problem—but he has to do one small favor for the queen. The guy's family is so poor that he could really use some money to restart their lives and knows the potion will help him get it. So he agrees—just this once. The rest of the story? You know how it goes: He makes more compromises and gets in too deep with the queen's evil rule.

Though evil queens are for fairy tales, you could still face similar temptations. As you grow up, you will have friends, classmates, and maybe family members try to persuade you to set aside what's right and wrong. They will figure out what motivates you: money, power, popularity, opportunities, etc. Then they will use that to get you to compromise just once for something you really need or want.

Compromise is hard once, slightly challenging twice, not so bad the third time—after that, you won't even care. Make it clear that you follow God's standards, which are more valuable than anything someone else could offer you.

Prayer

Lord, I see how feeling desperate for something could make it easy to compromise. I need your wisdom to know my weaknesses and beware of others who will try to get me to turn from your ways.

Choked or Growing?

The seed that fell among thorns stands for those who hear, but as they go on their way they are choked by life's worries, riches and pleasures, and they do not mature.

(LUKE 8:14)

Aren't online games and apps fun? And the more you play, the better you get. Texting with your friends is pretty fun too. Technology has made life a whole lot easier and enjoyable. Just ask your parents.

Your parents could tell you how complicated life was before computers. But they could also tell you how much simpler the world seemed before they had so much stuff. Money allows you to buy cool games and devices. But the more you have, the more you have to worry about. And the more you have, the easier it is to forget God.

Although Jesus did not grow up in a wealthy family, he knew very rich people. He could see how money and stuff choke out what is most important. More than anything, Jesus wanted his disciples to mature in their faith. He wants the same for you.

So how do you keep growing spiritually? For one thing, make room for the Lord every day. Before you start texting away, tell the Lord what's on your mind. Tell him you're sorry for putting other things first. You can be sure he will forgive you!

Prayer

Lord, there are so many distractions to take my mind off you. It's hard to be focused when there's a new game to play or something else to watch on TV. Please help me today to put you first.

The Way

Jesus answered, "I am the way and the truth and the life. No one comes to the Father except through me."

(JOHN 14:6)

During Jesus' life, he showed people how to really love each other—even their enemies. He was peaceful, kind, selfless, and caring. But lots of famous men and women throughout history have been considered peaceful. So was Jesus any different than Buddha, Confucius, Gandhi, Muhammad, or other religious figures?

Many people say "no," that Jesus was just another good teacher. But read the verse above again about what Jesus had to say.

Did you catch that? Jesus didn't say, "There are lots of ways to the Father, as long as you're a good person." No—he said he was the only way and that no one could have eternal life without him!

In today's world, it's popular to treat faith like a restaurant buffet line. "Hmm, I like that part about Christianity, so I'll take that, but I don't like that other thing, so I'll replace it with a little bit of this religion instead." That line won't fly with Jesus.

As an all-or-nothing kind of God, he doesn't want half of your heart. He wants it all! People who say Jesus was a good teacher are right. So listen to what he says—find your way to God through him.

Prayer

Jesus, thank you for being the way and the truth and the life. You aren't afraid of my questions about you and the Bible, so I bring them to you now, knowing you are faithful to answer all of them.

Slowly, Slowly

This will continue until we all come to such unity in our faith and knowledge of God's Son that we will be mature in the Lord, measuring up to the full and complete standard of Christ.

(EPHESIANS 4:13, NLT)

You are a work in progress. It takes years to grow up. You'll get taller. You'll get stronger. You'll get smarter. Your voice and tastes will change. So don't worry about trying to grow up too fast. God designed you to grow slowly.

Becoming like Christ takes time too. It's a slow process of growth. Even when you're physically an adult one day, spiritual maturity will take the rest of your life. Sometimes it can feel like it's taking forever. And it will! Your growth won't be completed here on Earth. So relax! It will only be finished when you get to Heaven or when Jesus returns. Whatever work is left will be wrapped up then. The Bible says that when we are finally able to see Jesus perfectly, we will become perfectly like him (1 John 3:2).

Prayer

Jesus, I look forward to the day when I can see you perfectly. When I get discouraged about my spiritual growth, encourage me to keep pressing on toward perfection.

How Temptation Works

Temptation comes from our own desires, which entice us and drag us away. These desires give birth to sinful actions. And when sin is allowed to grow, it gives birth to death.

(JAMES 1:14–15, NLT)

We think temptation lies around us, but God says it begins within us. We want something, so a temptation attracts us because of the desire we already have. Temptation always starts in your mind, not in circumstances.

Temptation starts when Satan suggests (with a thought) that you give in to an evil desire, or that you fulfill a good desire in a wrong way or at the wrong time. It may be a sinful desire, like the desire to steal something or lie, or it may be a normal good desire, like the desire to be loved or to feel happy. Satan whispers, "You deserve it! You should have it now! It will be exciting . . . fun . . . or make you feel better."

When you finally act on a thought you have been toying with in your mind, you give in to temptation. What began as an idea is born as sinful behavior. You give in to whatever got your attention. You believe Satan's lies and fall into the trap that James warns about. If you are on your guard, you'll recognize temptation when it comes. And God will always be there to help you resist it.

Prayer

God, you know my heart and what I struggle with. Continue to show me the places where I'm tempted and help me resist those sinful desires.

Ripe Fruit

Walk in a manner worthy of the Lord, to please Him in all respects, bearing fruit in every good work and increasing in the knowledge of God.

(COLOSSIANS 1:10, NASB)

Have you ever eaten gassed tomatoes? That is what you purchase at the grocery store. If farmers picked ripe tomatoes and shipped them, they would get smashed on the way to market. So the farmers pick tomatoes green and spray carbon dioxide on them just before they go to market. That gas ripens green tomatoes into red very quickly. Now, there is nothing wrong with those tomatoes. But if you have ever eaten a tomato straight from a garden, there is no comparison. It takes time for fruit to ripen—on the vine or in your life.

God needs time to ripen the spiritual fruit in your life. Begin the process by telling God you want to be a productive, fruitful Christian. Commit yourself to reading, studying, and memorizing the Bible. Ask God to change the way you think. Pray and talk with him about everything. Ask him to help you respond to difficult people and unpleasant situations as Jesus would. God wants to produce the fruit of the Spirit in your life. Will you let it ripen?

Prayer

God, I want to be a stronger follower of Christ. Help me talk to you about everything happening in my life and grow. I want to be a fruitful follower.

Life Changer

He was accompanied by Nicodemus, the man who earlier had visited Jesus at night. Nicodemus brought a mixture of myrrh and aloes, about seventy-five pounds. Taking Jesus' body, the two of them wrapped it, with the spices, in strips of linen. This was in accordance with Jewish burial customs.

(JOHN 19:39–40)

Most of us know John 3:16: "For God so loved the world that he gave his one and only Son, that whoever believes in him shall not perish but have eternal life." But do you remember to whom Jesus was talking when he said that? It was Nicodemus, a Pharisee and Jewish ruling council member. Nicodemus risked his reputation by speaking to Jesus.

Apparently that conversation stuck, because when Jesus died, Nicodemus did something even riskier. He went with Joseph of Arimathea, another well-known, well-off guy, and asked Pilate for Jesus' body.

Nicodemus wrapped the body mummy-style with seventy-five pounds of spices and lotions—an expensive sign of love and respect. The men then laid Jesus in Joseph's family tomb. Criminals never received that sort of lavish burial!

Jesus made a difference in Nicodemus' life. Suddenly the Pharisee went from being a spiritual scaredy-cat to boldly asking a dangerous political leader if he could bend the rules to show his devotion to Christ. Has Jesus changed you like that?

Prayer

Jesus, sometimes I feel like the first Nicodemus. I'm scared to admit I talk to you or know you. Please change me from the inside out, giving me courage to live out my faith and belief in you.

The Right Choice

*Then Balak's anger burned against Balaam. He struck
his hands together and said to him, "I summoned
you to curse my enemies, but you have blessed them
these three times. Now leave at once and go home!
I said I would reward you handsomely, but the LORD
has kept you from being rewarded."*

(NUMBERS 24:10–11)

The country of Moab had a bad king, King Balak. King Balak
and the Moabites did not like God's people, the Israelites. The
Moabites were afraid the Israelites would muscle their way in
and take over their land. So King Balak hired the prophet Balaam
to help him.

The king offered to pay a lot of money if Balaam would
simply put a curse on God's people. But God wanted to bless
Israel, and Balaam knew it. He had a hard choice to make. Do
wrong and get rich, or do right and leave the results to God?
Fortunately, Balaam made the right decision even though the
king was angry. God was happy with Balaam.

How do you feel when kids at school or on your team ask
you to do wrong with them? It seems tempting. When you
choose to do the right thing, God sees. Even if others pull away
from you because you choose to do right, God will reward you in
ways that your friends cannot. Being a godly girl or boy can be
lonely and seem costly. But, in the end, God will bless you.

Prayer

Lord, help me to do the right thing even when it seems hard.
Help me to do the right thing because I know it will make you
happy.

Dreaming Big

Whatever you do in word or deed, do all in the name of the Lord Jesus, giving thanks through Him to God the Father.

(COLOSSIANS 3:17, NASB)

Have you started thinking about activities you want to do in high school? Or even what you want to be when you grow up? Maybe you really like astronomy and want to go to space camp one day. Maybe you enjoy helping out in the kitchen and think it'd be cool to become a chef. It's great to pray about dreams like that. God puts some dreams in your heart to lead you into his plans for you. But do you know what's even more important to God? Your character.

We worry when God seems silent on specific questions such as "What should I do over the summer?" or "What should I sign up for after school?" or "Which sport should I try out for?" The truth is, there are many activities that could be in God's will for your life. But he's far more interested in what you *are* than in what you *do*. We are human *beings*, not human *doings*. God is much more concerned about your character. Here's why: you only take your character into eternity; everything else stays behind.

Prayer

Thank you, God, for caring about the little details of my life. Although it's important to think about what I want to do and be, you also want me to be a person of character. Help me to be like Jesus.

School for the Wise

"I, wisdom, dwell together with prudence; I possess knowledge and discretion."

(PROVERBS 8:12)

Imagine your little sister is a classic know-it-all. She thinks she's always right and never wrong. One day she announces she doesn't need school anymore. Her reasoning? There's nothing else to learn—she already knows everything.

You would laugh. After all, if she quit now, she would never learn her multiplication tables, U.S. capitals, or how to write a story. Not only that, she would miss out on getting her driver's license or joining a cheerleading squad.

But guess what? We often pull the know-it-all act with God. We think that because we memorized the books of the Bible, we're pretty good Christians. Or because we're usually nice to others and obey our elders, there's nothing more for us to learn from Jesus. We count ourselves as pretty wise.

Wisdom isn't just about knowing facts; it's about knowing what to do with those facts, which is called discretion. Your sister might recognize numbers. But until she can learn to drive, a thirty-five-mile-an-hour speed limit sign probably means nothing to her.

So will you settle for only knowing *about* God? Instead, learn how to use that knowledge every day. As Proverbs 8:17 promises, you won't be disappointed: "Those who seek me find me."

Prayer

Lord, I know I can't become wise by myself. I need you for that. Help me correct my know-it-all attitude so I can find your wisdom.

Get Out of There!

Run from anything that gives you the evil thoughts that young men often have, but stay close to anything that makes you want to do right.

(2 TIMOTHY 2:22A, TLB)

Temptation begins by capturing your attention. What gets your attention arouses your emotions. Then your emotions activate your behavior. The more you focus on "I don't want to do this," the stronger it draws you into its web.

Ignoring a temptation is far more effective than fighting it. Once your mind is on something else, the temptation loses its power. So when temptation calls you on the phone, don't argue with it. Just hang up! Sometimes this means physically leaving a tempting situation.

It is okay to run away. Get up and turn off the TV. Walk away from friends who are gossiping. Leave. Go. Flee. Just like you would stay away from a beehive to avoid being stung by bees, do whatever you need to do to get away from temptation.

Prayer

Lord, give me the courage and strength to get away from temptations. It's easier to not do anything to fight it, so I need your help.

From an Acorn to an Oak

*I tell you the truth, a grain of wheat must fall to the
ground and die to make many seeds. But if it never
dies, it remains only a single seed.*

(JOHN 12:24, NCV)

God takes two days to make mushrooms, but he takes sixty
years to make an oak tree. Do you want to be a mushroom or an
oak tree? Growth takes time.

When you examine your growth, you may wonder, "Why is
it taking me so long?" Notice what Jesus said in John 12:24. He
was talking about his death, but it applies to us as well. When
Jesus says, "I tell you the truth," he means, "Now get this! Tune
in! This is really important."

The point Jesus was making is that death precedes life. Just
as a grain of wheat must die to produce fruit, so must we die to
our own selfishness to see growth. But we like to dig up the seed
every now and then and check on its progress instead of trusting
God to grow us. Christ will produce fruit in our lives if we remain
in him. Remaining in Christ means depending on him, living for
him, and trusting him.

God is pleased with you at every stage of your spiritual
growth. He is not waiting until you are perfect to begin loving
you. Remember that growth takes time.

Prayer

God, I get impatient about growing in Christ. I know that it takes
time. Help me to remain in you and trust that you're working in
my life.

Soil Prep

*But the fruit of the Spirit is love, joy, peace,
forbearance, kindness, goodness, faithfulness,
gentleness and self-control. Against such things
there is no law.*

(GALATIANS 5:22–23)

Every good farm has crops—corn, sunflowers, wheat, soybeans—and the crops depend on the climate and soil. But crops don't grow overnight. The farmer doesn't go out and plant the seed one day and then pick some fully ripe corn the next. It takes months for the corn to grow with the right amount of sunshine and water.

Just like crops, our character takes time to grow. It's easy to think that we should be kind, good, faithful, and gentle the minute we ask God to save us from sin and change our lives. "If I am a Christian," we think, "I should be perfectly good in every way."

But that's not how it works. Love, joy, peace, and kindness grow in us as we spend time with Jesus and read the Bible. Then the fruit of the Spirit will grow. It's our job to do our part but let God be the farmer that helps it to grow inside our hearts.

Prayer

Lord, help me to do my part—to spend time with you, talk to you, and read the Bible—so that your fruit will grow in my heart.

Who's Your Idol?

You shall not make for yourself an image in the form of anything in heaven above or on the earth beneath or in the waters below. You shall not bow down to them or worship them.

(EXODUS 20:4–5A)

Did you know the Ten Commandments are more than a bunch of rules? They are all about good relationships with God, parents, friends—and enemies. The second commandment doesn't quite seem to fit for today: building idols? Bowing down to statues? Do you know anyone who travels around looking for statues to sit down in front of and sing to? But the second commandment is still important.

You may not realize you have idols in your life. Maybe you think highly of a certain singer, actor, or athlete. The sure-fire way to know if someone or something is an idol? You think about that person or thing *all the time.* You may even think that your life will be better if you get to meet that celebrity or be like him or her. God knows there are things that can easily distract us. Are idols taking God's place in your life? He is the only one who deserves your full attention and one hundred percent admiration. And he is the only one who can change your life.

Prayer

God, it's easy to be distracted by celebrities and earthly things. I don't want to idolize anyone or anything but you. Please remind me to put you first in my life.

Be an Example

Jesus, knowing their thoughts, took a little child and had him stand beside him. Then he said to them, "Whoever welcomes this little child in my name welcomes me; and whoever welcomes me welcomes the one who sent me. For it is the one who is least among you all who is the greatest."

(LUKE 9:47–48)

Jesus used all kinds of lessons to teach his followers. He used fish. He used bread. He even used olives and figs. A few times Jesus used children to teach the adults. He said that everyone needed to be like a child to be part of God's way of life. Did that mean he didn't want people to grow up? Not at all. But children are important to God too. Girls and boys, no matter their age, can have a relationship with God.

At your age, you probably don't have to worry about work, making money, buying food, or caring for a family, because you trust the adults in your life to provide for you. Jesus didn't want the adults to forget what they had learned as children. He wanted them to remember to focus on God first. To keep life simple enough that they don't forget God's ways. To let God be in charge instead of worrying about how they would take care of life. So he says, "Hey, take a look at your children. They trust you. I want you to trust me like that."

Did you ever think you'd be an example for your parents or other adults? You might just help them remember to trust God.

Prayer

Lord, thank you for my parents or guardians who love me and provide for me. Please provide for them and show love to them Help us all to trust you no matter how grown up we get.

God's Team

*For our light and momentary troubles are achieving
for us an eternal glory that far outweighs them all.*
(2 CORINTHIANS 4:17)

Professional athletes work hard to get strong and win
games. They wake up early in the morning for practice. They
spend hours training. Their bodies get tired. They might pull a
muscle, get hit by a ball, or wear themselves out preparing for
games. But they do it because the hard work and pain can lead
to a top performance and winning team.

Life is similar to hard training. It throws challenges at us
like friends letting us down, parents getting sick, or bad things
happening. God wants us to look at those hardships as part of a
training program. He is the coach who will help us steer through
the obstacles. He will help us recover from pain. He is in charge,
and he won't let anything knock us down without being there
to pick us up. He's making us stronger. Building us up. Training
us. The big game—Heaven—is just around the corner, and for
those who have joined God's team, they are guaranteed to win.

Prayer

God, sometimes life is hard. Help me to trust you. Help me to
remember you are training me for something better.

He Gets It

Because he himself suffered when he was tempted,
he is able to help those who are being tempted.

(HEBREWS 2:18)

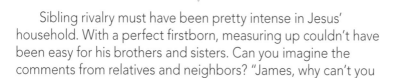

Sibling rivalry must have been pretty intense in Jesus' household. With a perfect firstborn, measuring up couldn't have been easy for his brothers and sisters. Can you imagine the comments from relatives and neighbors? "James, why can't you behave like Jesus?" or "Simon, will you ever get it together like your brother?" Jesus had to be a tough act to follow.

Jesus was sinless from birth, but that doesn't mean that he never wanted to sin. He may have thought about snapping at the annoying kid in Sabbath School. He was fully God, but also fully human, meaning he still knew the pull of temptation.

Jesus knows exactly how it feels to be tempted. He isn't some distant deity who doesn't get what we're going through. He understands when we really, really want to sin, because he faced similar situations.

So the next time you feel like going against God's guidelines, take a deep breath. Pause and pray. Remember, you have access to someone who's been there, done that. Ask for Jesus' help; he was your age once. He is more than willing to help you win the very fights he faced before.

As the perfect older brother, he won't even rub it in your face.

Prayer

Jesus, it's so good to know you understand me. Thank you for your strength when I want to stray and your grace when I blow it. I want your presence to be stronger than my next temptation.

Making the Grade

Whoever can be trusted with very little can also be trusted with much, and whoever is dishonest with very little will also be dishonest with much.

(LUKE 16:10)

———❧———

"I'll give you five dollars for your allowance each week this month," your mom says. "If you figure out how to use five dollars well, then next month, I'll bump up your allowance to ten." Sweet! You're excited about the possibility of more money in just a month. Hold on, though—your mom has a catch. She wants to know if you're going to blow the money as soon as you have it or if you will think through how to use it. She's testing you. You might think you're ready for ten dollars a week, but your mom isn't so sure.

You may think you're ready to get in the game rather than sitting on the bench at soccer practice. You may think you're ready to bake brownies by yourself rather than only mixing ingredients your mom gives you. If you are truly ready, you'll prove it. Not by whining about it. Not by demanding that your parents or coach trust what you say. You prove it with your actions. Be thoughtful with the few dollars you have. Follow your mom's instructions on mixing the brownies. Encourage your teammates even when you don't get to play. That's what Jesus meant when he said that if you can be trusted with very little, then you can be trusted with much. Think about it: if you gripe and complain to your coach or ignore your mom's advice to be careful with money, why would either of them let you have more?

Prayer

Jesus, I get impatient sitting on the sidelines. I feel like I'm ready for more responsibility, but I need to continue doing well with the small jobs I've been given first. Please help me be patient as I wait for more.

Pop Quiz

No test or temptation that comes your way is beyond the course of what others have had to face. All you need to remember is that God will never let you down; he'll never let you be pushed past your limit; he'll always be there to help you come through it.

(1 CORINTHIANS 10:13, MSG)

Did you know God gives tests? The good news is that God wants you to pass the tests of life. So he never allows the tests to be greater than the strength he gives you to handle them.

Words like trials, temptations, refining, and testing occur more than 200 times in the Bible. God continually tests people's character, faith, obedience, love, honesty, and loyalty.

God tested Abraham by asking him to offer his son Isaac. God tested Jacob when he had to work extra years to earn Rachel as his wife. The Bible gives many examples of people who passed a great test, such as Joseph, Ruth, Esther, and Daniel.

God constantly watches your response to people, problems, awards, sickness, and even the weather! Even when you open a door for others, pick up a piece of trash, or are polite, God pays attention.

Every time you pass a test, God notices and makes plans to reward you in eternity.

Prayer

God, you pay attention to everything I do. So when I'm tested, please be with me and help me through those hard times.

Time to Fly

God blesses those who patiently endure testing and temptation. Afterward they will receive the crown of life that God has promised to those who love him.

(JAMES 1:12, NLT)

A mother eagle will take the nest of her young and stir it up. She will make them uncomfortable and miserable, then kick them out and force them to learn to fly—for their own good. God does that in our lives: he makes us uncomfortable sometimes because he wants us to grow. He will allow a problem, irritation, or frustration to push us toward what is best for us.

When God wants to change us, he starts by getting our attention, such as putting us in a frustrating situation beyond our control. We cannot win, and we just keep getting more and more tired in the struggle. God uses these kinds of experiences.

If you are facing a problem right now, God may be getting ready to change you for the better. We usually don't change until we get fed up with our current situation and uncomfortable enough to turn to God. When we become motivated to let God do something in our lives, then he pushes us out of the nest so we can learn to fly.

Prayer

God, it's not fun feeling uncomfortable or dealing with problems. Even though change is hard, I know you do it for my good. Help me to trust that you will take care of me.

Stick with It

When the man saw that he did not prevail against Jacob, he touched his hip socket, and Jacob's hip was put out of joint as he wrestled with him. Then he said, "Let me go, for the day has broken." But Jacob said, "I will not let you go unless you bless me."

(GENESIS 32:25–26, ESV)

Jacob was committed. He was not going to give up easily—even though he was in a situation he didn't like. In fact, he was in pain. It was frustrating. He was getting tired. But he kept wrestling with God until he worked it out.

Here is the point: after God gets our attention with a problem, he does not solve it right away. He waits to see whether we really mean business. Most people cop out or get discouraged. Instead of hanging in there and saying, "God, I'm not going to let go of this until you bless me, until you turn it around," they give up and end up missing God's best.

This kind of commitment can be tough. We are so used to having instant everything—instant mac 'n cheese, instant online purchases, on-demand movies—so if we don't have an instant answer to one prayer, we could easily say, "Forget it, God."

Whatever you do, don't give up. You don't want to miss God's best because you give up too soon. There is hope. Hang in there. Keep asking God for an answer, no matter how long he takes.

Prayer

God, it's easy to give up on prayers if an answer doesn't come instantly. Prompt me to keep coming to you through prayer and not give up.

Tough Stuff

You are my portion, LORD; I have promised to obey your words.

(PSALM 119:57)

In every superhero movie, the good guy has a tough time. The bad guy is constantly bugging him. The good guy doesn't have as much money, as many cool toys, or as flashy a uniform as the villain. Only in the end does the superhero finally triumph. The beginning and middle often belong to the bad guy.

What's up with that? After all, our parents teach us that if we obey God's rules, then good things happen. On the other hand, we aren't immune from the consequences of other people's sin.

As we get older, we learn that our parents can't control the world. They're not there when we go to school, basketball practice, friends' houses, or even youth group. And suddenly, following all God's laws—being kind, respectful, honest—doesn't automatically mean our lives are problem-free.

In fact, sometimes hard things happen because we are listening to the Lord! Remember all the trouble King David faced? Just like David, keep obeying God. On Earth, no one gets a problem-free life, because sin is everywhere. But obeying God brings his goodness and friendship to your side. And even though the bad guys might be ahead for a little while, God always wins in the end.

Prayer

Getting bashed wears me out, Jesus. Sometimes I wonder if it would be easier to follow the crowd. Please give me strength to not give in and the courage to keep following you when it's hard.

One Problem after Another

*Friends, when life gets really difficult, don't jump
to the conclusion that God isn't on the job. Instead,
be glad that you are in the very thick of what Christ
experienced. This is a spiritual refining process, with
glory just around the corner.*

(1 PETER 4:12–13, MSG)

No one gets to skate through life problem-free. Like math class, every time you solve one problem, another is waiting. Not all of them are big, but all are significant in God's growth process for you.

God uses problems to draw you closer to him. Here are a few examples: God could have kept Joseph out of jail (Genesis 39:20–22), kept Daniel out of the lions' den (Daniel 6:16–23), kept Jeremiah from being tossed into a slimy pit (Jeremiah 38:6), kept Paul from being shipwrecked three times (2 Corinthians 11:25), and kept the three young Hebrew men from being thrown into the blazing furnace (Daniel 3:1–26)—but he didn't. He let those problems happen, and every one of those people got closer to God because of it.

Problems force us to look to God and depend on him instead of ourselves. You will never know God is all you need until God is all you've got. When you're in pain or facing a problem, stay focused on God's plan. That is how Jesus endured the pain of dying on the cross. We can follow his example.

Prayer

When I have little or big problems, Lord, I want to turn to you for help and guidance. I sometimes want to fix them myself, but I know you've got them handled. I trust you.

Dragging Your Feet

GOD said to Moses, "Go to Pharaoh and tell him,
'GOD's Message: Release my people so they can
worship me. If you refuse to release them, I'm
warning you, I'll hit the whole country with frogs.'
(EXODUS 8:1–2, MSG)

Sometimes it's hard to change your mind. You've believed something for so long it just feels right. And then you find out maybe what you believe isn't completely true or right.

Like the Pharaoh, who believed the Israelites were there to serve the Egyptians. He believed he had every right to have them as slaves for his people. But God, through Moses, tried to teach Pharaoh differently. And time and again, Pharaoh promised to let them go only to change his mind—even in the face of the suffering of his own people! You and I do this all the time. We put off changes that we know will be good for us or others around us. Why? Maybe we are too lazy or maybe we are afraid. Maybe we are too proud or stubborn. Whatever the reason, we procrastinate.

It is one thing for me to tell you that Jesus Christ can help you conquer the problems you are facing right now. But it is quite another matter for you to actually let him begin to do it now! Are you going to put it off until tomorrow?

Prayer

Jesus, I know you can help me with the problems I'm dealing with. Today, I ask that you meet me where I am, problems and all, and help me change what I need to change right now.

Real Joy

We can rejoice, too, when we run into problems and trials, for we know that they are good for us—they help us learn to be patient.

(ROMANS 5:3, TLB)

Ever wish you could get rid of a mean teacher or annoying kid? Then you'd be happy! But the truth is, even if you got rid of those problems, other ones will come up. Joy is enjoying life in spite of problems. Joy is not the absence of suffering but the presence of God. That is why Paul says we rejoice in suffering, because God is always with us.

Paul is not saying you should fake it. He is not talking about putting a plastic smile on your face, pretending everything is okay, and acting as if nothing is wrong. God does not want you to be fake. He is not saying we rejoice because of our suffering. He is not even saying we enjoy suffering. He is saying we rejoice in it because we know there's a purpose behind it. Christians can be positive even in a negative situation because we know God has a reason for allowing that problem.

Prayer

God, thank you that there's a purpose behind everything I go through, even if I don't understand or know it. Thank you that I can be real with you and show all my emotions. You love me, and I find joy in that!

More Than Meets the Eye

So then, it was not you who sent me here, but God.
He made me father to Pharaoh, lord of his entire
household and ruler of all Egypt . . . I will provide
for you there, because five years of famine are still
to come. Otherwise you and your household and all
who belong to you will become destitute.

(GENESIS 45:8, 11)

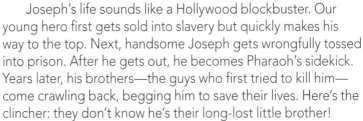

Joseph's life sounds like a Hollywood blockbuster. Our young hero first gets sold into slavery but quickly makes his way to the top. Next, handsome Joseph gets wrongfully tossed into prison. After he gets out, he becomes Pharaoh's sidekick. Years later, his brothers—the guys who first tried to kill him— come crawling back, begging him to save their lives. Here's the clincher: they don't know he's their long-lost little brother!

Now would be the scene where Joseph gleefully says, "I'm ba-aaack!" right before booting his brothers into a pit. Instead, an emotional Joseph reveals he's still alive—and he's not mad!

Joseph knew that sometimes God lets us experience rough stuff for a reason—in this case, to save an entire nation from starvation. He wasn't bitter. He saw the bigger picture: "It was not you who sent me here, but God," he told his family.

What has God allowed you to go through for a reason? Maybe you partner with the meanest kid in science class or warm the bench during basketball games. Though it probably isn't fun, these things teach patience, trust in God, kindness, and lots of other good qualities—if you let God show you.

Prayer

Lord, it's so hard to see past my problems, but I know you want to shape me through them. Give me eyes to see your hand in it all, and help me trust in your perfect timing.

Knocked Down

But he knows the way that I take; when he has tested me, I will come forth as gold.

(JOB 23:10)

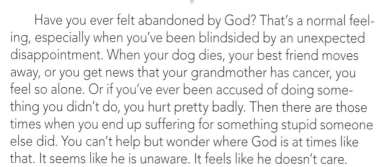

Have you ever felt abandoned by God? That's a normal feeling, especially when you've been blindsided by an unexpected disappointment. When your dog dies, your best friend moves away, or you get news that your grandmother has cancer, you feel so alone. Or if you've ever been accused of doing something you didn't do, you hurt pretty badly. Then there are those times when you end up suffering for something stupid someone else did. You can't help but wonder where God is at times like that. It seems like he is unaware. It feels like he doesn't care.

That was Job's experience. He was a good guy who loved God. He had an enviable life. But then out of the blue came darkness. Yet Job didn't turn into a bitter man. The fiery trials that he faced revealed a precious faith that shimmered like gold. Job was convinced that God knew exactly what was playing out in his life. Job was able to believe that God had a plan and that all things would work out in the end. He trusted God to use the bad stuff for a bigger plan that would glorify God.

Prayer

Lord, I want to have faith like Job. Forgive me when I doubt your goodness in bad times.

Anchor Yourself

I belong to God, and I worship him. Last night he sent an angel to tell me, "Paul, don't be afraid! You will stand trial before the emperor. And because of you, God will save the lives of everyone on the ship."

(ACTS 27:23–24, CEV)

Storms can never hide us from God. We may not see him, but he sees us. We may think God is a million miles away, but he is with us and is watching us. In Acts 27, God sent a personal representative, an angel, to remind Paul he wasn't alone.

Just like with Paul's shipwreck, God's plan was at work in the storm. God was part of it all. Over and over the Bible says that wherever we are, God is right there with us. We never go through anything by ourselves. No matter what situation you are going through, God is with you. Even if your life seems like Paul's ship, tossed around on rough seas, you are going to make it. You may lose the cargo. You may lose the ship. You may even get wet. But you are going to make it because of the promise of God. He is the anchor you can trust.

Prayer

God, thank you for being with me through everything. You are my rock and my anchor.

Bullied

Rescue me, Lord, from evildoers; protect me from the violent, who devise evil plans in their hearts and stir up war every day.

(PSALM 140:1–2)

Bullies are everywhere—in the neighborhood, at school, and even at church. Some kids try to prove their toughness by picking on kids who are shorter, less athletic, or less intelligent. Battles on the ball field are a familiar scene during recess or after school. It isn't the kind of war reported on the nightly news, but these frontline skirmishes are just as real.

The psalmist had his own battles with bullies. Being a good and godly guy didn't exempt him from problem people. He knew that living in a broken world includes living with broken people who make life miserable for others. But he also knew where to turn when verbal grenades and flying fists found him. He turned to the Lord. He called on his heavenly Father to protect him.

God cares when you're blindsided by bullies. Because you belong to him, he has a personal interest in protecting you. He will give you the courage to stand when you feel like running away. You can count on that. All you have to do is call out to him.

Prayer

Lord, I'm encouraged by the words of the psalmist. He was totally honest with you when he was being attacked. He didn't pretend everything was okay. Neither will I.

1–800-HELP!

Call upon Me in the day of trouble; I shall rescue you, and you will honor Me.

(PSALM 50:15, NASB)

Heaven has a twenty-four-hour emergency hotline. God wants you to ask him to help you overcome temptation. When temptation strikes, you don't have time for a long conversation with God; you simply cry out. David, Daniel, Peter, Paul, and millions of others have prayed this kind of instant prayer for help in trouble. This is called a "microwave" prayer because it is quick and to the point: Help! SOS! Mayday!

The Bible guarantees that our cry for help will be heard, because Jesus understands our struggles. He faced the same temptations we do, "yet he did not sin" (Hebrews 4:15, NLT). God's love is everlasting, and his patience endures forever. If you have to cry out for God's help two hundred times a day to defeat a particular temptation, he will still be eager to give mercy and grace, so come boldly. God never gets irritated, bored, or impatient when we keep coming back to him. Ask him for the power to do the right thing, and then expect him to provide it.

Prayer

Jesus, you understand temptation, and you welcome my cries for help. You don't get sick of me. I need your help, love, and kindness every day.

Peace in Tough Times

*Three times I was beaten with rods, once I was
pelted with stones, three times I was shipwrecked, I
spent a night and a day in the open sea, I have been
constantly on the move.*

(2 CORINTHIANS 11:25–6A)

People get sick. People die. People are born with handicaps
or wind up wheelchair-bound after an accident. Some people
live with hungry stomachs. Some live with broken hearts and
broken families. Suffering is a consequence of the sin in the
world. But God is still with us in pain and heartache.

The apostle Paul faced plenty of suffering. Among other
things, he was stoned and left for dead. Three times he survived
shipwrecks. The poor guy didn't have the security of living in
one place. He was always on the move and often running for
his life. Paul's detailed description of the suffering in his life is
gut-wrenching. But Paul's love for his Lord did not grow cold.
His faith remained strong in spite of being extremely weak. How
does that make sense?

Paul understood that following Jesus comes with peace and
love that makes this sinful world bearable. While having Jesus in
your life is not a guarantee against trouble, he is a rock to support
you so that hardship will not wreck you. Stand firm on him.
Let him take the pain and suffering and comfort you. Without
him, you're on your own in a tough, rough world.

Prayer

Lord, it's good to know that my problems aren't a surprise to
you. Remind me to lean on you for strength when tough stuff
comes my way.

Lifeguard on Duty

When you pass through the waters, I will be with you; and when you pass through the rivers, they will not sweep over you.

(ISAIAH 43:2)

Not knowing how to swim can be scary. As long as you can touch the bottom of the pool with both feet, it's okay. You can play in the shallow end for hours and not think a thing of it. But once you dive into the deep end of the pool, well, that's another story. And you never do that in a pool without a lifeguard or adult who's ready to help you if you start to sink. It all changes when you learn how to doggie paddle your way to the edge of the pool.

The Lord knows that the swimming pool isn't the only time we feel "in over our heads." Many things in life scare us, like getting lost in a crowd, losing something valuable, and trying to prove ourselves on a team made up of kids who are better than we are. God is like a lifeguard watching over our lives. Instead of worrying about the things that frighten us, we should remember that he is in control and always with us. We are never out of his sight or beyond his reach. When we are in trouble or feel insecure, we can call on him. He will jump into the situation to save us.

Prayer

Lord, it helps to know that you are keeping an eye on me everywhere I go. I'm grateful I don't have to be afraid.

Comfort for a Hurting Heart

The Spirit of the Sovereign LORD is on me, because the LORD has anointed me to proclaim good news to the poor. He has sent me to bind up the brokenhearted, to proclaim freedom for the captives and release from darkness for the prisoners.

(ISAIAH 61:1)

Have you ever been so sad that your insides felt achy? Or so upset that your stomach turned in knots? Your body shows the effects of what you are feeling, even when you're not physically sick. Heartache, sadness, and depression can make your body and mind feel awful.

Who do you turn to for comfort? The person who makes you feel better when you are sad or hugs you until you cheer up. It could be your mom or dad, a grandparent, or a good friend.

Did you know that one of Jesus' biggest reasons for coming to Earth was to comfort you while you're in pain? He read this prophecy from Isaiah and announced that he would fulfill it. He wanted to comfort hurting hearts, set people free, and bring good news that would heal bad feelings inside and out. Next time you are down and out, turn to Jesus. Ask him to be your comforter and healer. He'll touch your heart.

Prayer

Jesus, when I feel sad or upset, I don't always think to turn to you. But you can do more for me than anyone on Earth. Please touch my heart when I need it most.

The Best Hiding Spot

You are my hiding place; you will protect me from trouble and surround me with songs of deliverance.

(PSALM 32:7)

Where is your favorite hiding place? Under your bed? In your closet? In the backyard? Under an oak tree in the neighborhood park? When you're afraid or tired of being with people, where do you run?

Seems like everyone has a secret place where they go when they want to be alone. Even the president of the United States probably has a place he likes to use as a getaway. We all want a place to hide and be safe.

King David called God his hiding place. When the king was in trouble or afraid, he "ran to God" and told God what was going on. Since God is everywhere, David could stay right where he was. All he needed to do was start talking to God. As he talked about what was bothering him, he could feel God's protection. The king felt like angels were hovering around him, singing. Pretty neat.

Here's an idea: go ahead and go to your hiding place every day. But instead of just reading or playing, why not pray too? Thank the Lord that he is bigger than the things that make you afraid. Thank the Lord that he is a safe place.

Prayer

Lord, when I feel like hiding, please take care of me. You know the things that make me scared. When I run to my hiding place, will you also be my safe place?

Ow! That Hurts!

A woman giving birth to a child has pain because her time has come; but when her baby is born she forgets the anguish because of her joy that a child is born into the world.

(JOHN 16:21)

Has anybody told you that you were a real pain? Well, you were. Just ask your mother. On the day you were born, you caused her quite a lot of pain. Giving birth to you wasn't a vacation. It was hard work. Maybe that's why they call it labor. But in the end, all that pain was worth it. You appeared!

Jesus referred to the "labor pains" almost every mother has experienced to teach a lesson about hard times. He wants us to know that we will have tough days. Being a Christian doesn't mean problems bounce off us. Sometimes they knock us off balance. We stumble. We fall. We get hurt. We cry.

But here's the deal: suffering is part of life. Yet it doesn't last forever. The "ouches" will turn into "yippees" if we are patient. And when we tough it out with the troubles that tackle us, we discover something else: our faith muscles get stronger. They develop, helping us deal with difficulties without being defeated.

Prayer

Lord, I know my faith muscles aren't as strong as you'd like them to be. If that's why you are giving me some heavy burdens, give me the strength of a weightlifter.

Forget about It

Brothers and sisters, I do not consider myself yet to have taken hold of it. But one thing I do: Forgetting what is behind and straining toward what is ahead, I press on toward the goal to win the prize for which God has called me heavenward in Christ Jesus.

(PHILIPPIANS 3:13–14)

Remember when you took your first steps? Probably not. But your mom remembers. Remember when you started school? Yes, but that was several years ago. Remember when you had your last birthday party? Or have you already forgotten? Remembering is an important part of learning, but sometimes it's best to forget.

Wait. What?

Paul said he practiced forgetting. He didn't want to get so stuck on the good times or the bad times that he missed what was happening in the moment. He didn't want the past to keep him from moving forward toward his goal of serving Jesus Christ every day.

Yes, it's good to remember the past for memories and lessons, but don't let the past rule what you do today. If you're stuck on how awesome your birthday was last year, you may not enjoy a quieter celebration this year. If you feel so bad about failing a grade, you may not appreciate having a second chance. Ultimately, we want to look toward Jesus and his plan for our lives so that nothing can hold us back—especially the past.

Prayer

Lord, it's hard to forget the past, whether it's good or bad. But today is a gift from you that I want to enjoy and make the most of. Will you keep me in the present?

Top of the Class

The king talked with them, and he found none equal to Daniel, Hananiah, Mishael and Azariah; so they entered the king's service.

(DANIEL 1:19)

Daniel, Hananiah, Mishael, and Azariah were four friends from Jerusalem. Like any teenage boys at that time, they probably led ordinary lives: hanging out after school, racing their donkeys, and staging slingshot contests. But when Babylon invaded Jerusalem, that all changed.

Nebuchadnezzar, the Babylonian king, wanted the best young men from Israeli royalty or nobility as his servants. Daniel, Hananiah, Mishael, and Azariah fit that description. So they entered a three-year "Serve the King" program, learning a new language and culture and even getting renamed. Their world was turned upside down. When three years had passed, Daniel and Company still came out on top.

Your chances of getting kidnapped, renamed, and forced to serve a foreign king are pretty slim. But what would happen if you met your mayor, governor, or even the president? Would he or she be impressed with your intelligence, ideas, physical fitness, and passion?

Remember, the friends didn't become class presidents and team captains overnight; it took steady time in training to pro-duce those qualities. Copy their playbook—make the Lord your top priority, and work hard at whatever comes your way. Even your enemies will be impressed.

Prayer

God, you say to ask for wisdom if I want it. So here goes: please make me like Daniel and his friends, rising to the top with my understanding, wisdom, insight, and people skills so that I can help others find you.

No One Will Notice, Right?

Whoever conceals their sins does not prosper, but the one who confesses and renounces them finds mercy.

(PROVERBS 28:13)

Fact #1: You detest Brussels sprouts.
Fact #2: For some unknown reason, your mother loves them. Therefore, those slimy, green globs show up on the dinner table way too often.
Fact #3: Luckily, your golden retriever feels the same as your mom. Problem solved.

At first glance, it looks like a win-win-win situation. But let's take a closer look.

First, your mom told you to eat your dinner. Disobedience—sin #1. Second, you deceived her with the dog trick. Double whammy—sin #2.

"Wait," you think. "Doesn't hiding my mistakes keep me from landing in hot water? If there's a way out, why not take it?"

Here's why: that way out is actually a way down and into more trouble. Covering your tracks doesn't work in the long run, but coming clean does. Maybe you won't get caught right away. But carrying around a secret sin seriously holds us back. Confessing, on the other hand, sets us free.

You don't have to love (or even like!) Brussels sprouts. But if you want to prosper, try dealing with your sins the right way. That's guaranteed to have a better ending than a dog full of veggies.

Prayer

Confessing what I did wrong *feels* hard, Lord. But this thing is tearing me up inside, and I want to let it out. Because of your mercy, I'm getting this sin off my chest and out of my life for good.

Still God

For what you have done I will always praise you in the presence of your faithful people. And I will hope in your name, for your name is good.

(PSALM 52:9)

Saul, the current king, was constantly trying to kill David, the future king. Others, like Ahimelech the priest, were often drawn into this game of cat-and-mouse—with killer results.

Ahimelech fed and armed David and his band of merry men (1 Samuel 21). Ahimelech didn't know he was helping a wanted fugitive. But Saul executed the innocent man anyway—and eighty-five other priests.

David felt responsible for all those deaths. So he threw his anger toward Saul (and Saul's shepherd, the tattle-tale who ratted Ahimelech out) into Psalm 52.

It's normal to question God or his love when we see death and mayhem. We know people who are being torn apart by divorce, illness, drugs, alcohol, or other pain, even in our own families.

So how do we react? By saying, "God, if you're real, you really screwed things up, and I don't want any part of you"? No! Follow David's example. In the middle of his sadness, he believed God was still God. David praised God's goodness and remembered that God gives hope. Bad things will happen in this world because of sin. But God is still good and still worthy of our praise.

Prayer

God, I see bad stuff happening everywhere, and it scares me. But I want to be safe and secure in you, like David wrote. Please make my faith strong.

Wise Guys

So give your servant a discerning heart to govern your people and to distinguish between right and wrong. For who is able to govern this great people of yours?

(1 KINGS 3:9)

These days, people say that it's okay to do whatever seems right to you. They say there isn't the same right and wrong for everybody. Sure, most people agree that murder is wrong. But they may say lying is okay to protect yourself. Or that stealing is okay if you take something to help out someone who needs what you stole. You can easily start to get confused about whether there is such a thing as right and wrong.

King Solomon faced this dilemma. He knew that certain people were clever—smart enough to make bad things sound like they were good and sly enough to get away with murder and make it seem right. But Solomon knew there is right and wrong, and it's based on God's words and ways. Anything that doesn't line up with God's ways falls into the "wrong" category.

Follow Solomon's lead. Ask God for wisdom to know right from wrong and to see past the tricks that others may try to sneak by you. It worked for Solomon. He wound up being the wisest man in the world. People still read his wisdom today.

Prayer

God, I want to be wise like Solomon and be able to discern your ways from the ways of sin. Open my eyes and heart to understand situations when it counts most.

Help, Please!

He turned the sea into dry land, they passed through the waters on foot—come, let us rejoice in him.

(PSALM 66:6)

Remember the first time you went camping with your scout troop or church camp? When you jumped into water that was more than a few feet deep, it's likely that you dog-paddled as fast as you could to the edge. If you were afraid you might drown, you wouldn't admit it to the other kids.

Back when the Israelites fled from Pharaoh, they faced really deep water. The Egyptian army was chasing them from behind, and the Red Sea was in front of them. It wasn't a swimming pool or a pond. It was like an ocean. They were trapped and didn't know what to do. But God divided the sea and gave the Israelites a dry path to get across. Boy, were they relieved. They were grateful too.

It's possible you are facing a problem that seems impossibly huge. It might have to do with friends or schoolwork or something you can't stop thinking about. It bugs you big time, and you don't know who to talk to about it. Like the Red Sea, it's way too big to cross by yourself.

The good news is that you don't have to handle this problem alone. Ask the Lord to "part the waters." Be honest with him about what's going on. That's the cool thing about prayer. You can tell God anything. He has a solution. You'll see!

Prayer

Lord, I'm so glad you are listening when I pray. Give me the faith to trust you for my sea-size problems.

Down and Out

Why, my soul, are you downcast? Why so disturbed within me? Put your hope in God, for I will yet praise him, my Savior and my God.

(PSALM 42:11)

Friends hurt you. Adults let you down. Your heart can go through a beating. Sometimes you can't even pinpoint which situation is making you sad. You're just done. Tired of it. Ready to give up.

David went through those moments a lot. It seemed like a lot of his life went wrong. Friends tried to kick him out. Wars broke out all around him. In Psalm 42, he wasn't sure what was going on inside his heart. But he knew he was sad and needed help.

When you're going through those rough times, be like David. Even when you don't know exactly what's got you down, go to God. Talk to him, and let it all out. David reminds himself, "Put your hope in God, for I will yet praise him." Sometimes we need to do that too. Tell God that you don't have a clue what's going on inside of you, but you choose to trust him. "I trust you, God, even though my heart hurts."

When you choose to trust even when you're hurting inside, God gives you strength to make it through.

Prayer

God, when I'm sad or upset, I don't usually think of telling you. Sometimes I don't even know why I feel that way. Remind me that I can talk to you and trust you no matter what comes.

Stay Away from the Peanuts

I saw among the simple, I noticed among the young men, a youth who had no sense. He was going down the street near her corner, walking along in the direction of her house.

(PROVERBS 7:7–8)

If you have a peanut allergy, a peanut factory is the last place you want to hang out. It doesn't matter how delicious peanut butter cookies taste. Breaking out in hives and struggling to breathe is not worth a peanut butter cookie!

So what would you do if you saw a friend with a peanut allergy who was dashing straight through a peanut factory's doors? You would grab his arm and scream, "What are you doing?"

Though peanut butter wasn't invented in King Solomon's lifetime, he saw a young man running right into a death trap, giving in to the pull of sin. The king knew that sin would destroy the young man's life both spiritually and physically.

See if you can spot the key to avoiding such a scary fate: "He was going down the street *near her corner*, walking along *in the direction of her house*." In this case, "her corner" and "her house" represent evil. Just as you would avoid a peanut factory if you knew it would kill you, so you want to avoid places that can "kill" you spiritually—meaning they lead you away from God. And if you see a friend heading that direction, do what you can to stop him.

Prayer

Lord, certain sins look and seem so cool at first. Remind me that's not true. Please give me eyes to see temptations and the courage to stay away.

Refuge

*The L*ORD *is a refuge for the oppressed, a stronghold in times of trouble.*

(PSALM 9:9)

A wildlife refuge is a place specially reserved for animals. They are safe from hunters there. People can't build homes or stores in a refuge. The land is a safe place for animals to live.

God is a refuge for people who believe in him. He takes care of his people. You can turn to him. He protects his people when trouble comes. For instance, if kids get rough at school, you can turn and talk to God. If you are worried about someone in your family who is very sick, you can go to God about it. God doesn't take the troubles away, but he provides a place for you to be safe.

Think about how you can go to your teacher for help if you are being teased at school. The teacher tells the teasers to stop. God stands up for you just like this. Running to him during trouble is like running into a castle and locking the door behind you. No one can get in to get you, and you are safe within its walls. The trouble is still out there. But in God's refuge, he will show you ways to handle the trouble when it's time to go back out and face it.

Prayer

God, when trouble comes my way, will you remind me that I can run to you for safety? Please protect me and show me what to do.

Always Good

And we know that for those who love God all things work together for good, for those who are called according to his purpose.

(ROMANS 8:28, ESV)

This verse does not say that everything is good. There is a lot of evil in this world, and God's will is not always done. But if you follow and believe in God, God makes all things—even the bad things—work out for good.

God is greater than any problem you will ever face, and he has your best interests at heart. He will even take a terrible problem and use it for good somehow. He will bring out greater glory in the long run. Of course, it is difficult to see how God is working in a bad situation while you are in it. But later, you may be able to see what God was doing. Many examples in the Bible show this: Joseph was sold into slavery but later became a leader who saved many people from famine. Daniel was thrown into a lions' den but he survived, astonishing the king who then worshipped God. Esther's people were doomed to die, but God used her to save them and rat out the schemer.

No matter what happens in your life, the final outcome is in God's hands. And that is always good.

Prayer

God, you don't promise that everything will be easy or problem-free. But you do promise to be there with me. You are in control. Help me to trust in you even when it's hard to.

Ruler of Everything

*In order to fulfill the word of the LORD spoken by
Jeremiah, the LORD moved the heart of Cyrus king of
Persia to make a proclamation . . . "Any of his people
among you may go up to Jerusalem in Judah and
build the temple of the LORD."*

(EZRA 1:1B, 3A)

Sweet and sour. Old and new. Black and white. Opposites—
they possess what the other does not have. Opposites
sometimes complement each other, or combine to create
something new, like the color gray coming from a mix of black
and white.

Some opposites, though, don't go together. Like oil and
water or an atheist and a Christian school. But that's not a
problem for God. God uses whatever he wants and whomever
he wants.

The Israelites were in captivity under King Cyrus. They didn't
expect him to be the one to let them go home and rebuild a
temple to God. He was the least likely choice. In God's world—
and it is all God's world—he chooses who, what, when, where,
why, and how.

We could easily think that because someone isn't godly,
God can't use that person in our lives. Or we may think that a
tragedy or crisis isn't part of God's will. That's not the case at all.
God is the ultimate ruler. Everything, all the opposites, are under
his control.

Prayer

I cannot understand, Lord, how you can turn evil into good or
use something hard for good. But I believe it is your world, and I
know your rules are in charge of everything. So I will trust you to
use whatever you want to use in my life.

A Good Mystery

No, we declare God's wisdom, a mystery that has been hidden and that God destined for our glory before time began.

(1 CORINTHIANS 2:7)

We all like a good mystery. We like shows where the adventurous kids discover a map, figure out the clues, and find the buried treasure. We like when a cereal box has a secret code on the back—a code we can crack while we munch our sugary flakes in the morning.

God says that he has mysteries for us too—things we find out once we know him. The Bible says that the Spirit of God searches out the deep things of God—mysteries, treasures, all from God's heart.

The wonderful thing is that the Spirit of God lives inside us when we give our lives to God. That means the more we get to know God by reading the Bible and spending time with him, the more we'll know about his mysteries, such as what is true wisdom and how he works in miraculous ways. Though we can never understand everything about God, God will open our minds to amazing things that are way better than the secret message on the cereal box or buried treasure in the woods.

Prayer

God, I want to know your mysteries! Help me to trust in your mysterious ways even when you don't reveal their secrets to me.

Sleuth for Truth

The devil led [Jesus] to Jerusalem and had him stand on the highest point of the temple. "If you are the Son of God," [Satan] said, "throw yourself down from here. For it is written: 'He will command his angels concerning you to guard you carefully.'"

(LUKE 4:9–10)

A friend asks you to "partner" with him on a test. He says you'll be sharing with each other and will both do better in class. But the teacher said this was a solo exam—no sharing, no cheating. Then your friend says, "Remember how the teacher told us that she wants us to help each other?" He's right. Your teacher did say that. That's what is so sneaky about temptation. The devil is sly. As a fallen angel, he knows God's truth, and he uses little bits of truth to lure people into temptation. He even tried that trick on Jesus.

You see, if the Devil used full lies, people would catch on. "Hey, that's a lie! We're not falling for that trap," they'd say. But if a temptation includes just a little truth, then it's easier to go along with it. For instance, your friend reminded you what the teacher said about helping each other, but he left out the part about not cheating. It can be confusing. But real truth is complete. It is true one hundred percent of the time, not sometimes or only when it's convenient. That's why knowing God's Word is important for spotting temptation. "Aha!" you'll be able to say. "That is a temptation that will lead me to sin. I won't be taken in."

Prayer

Lord, temptation seems scary. Please help me not to be afraid but to trust you to lead me in truth and recognize lies that will lead me to sin and away from you.

Beware of the Liar

Not only is [the Devil] a liar himself, but he is also the father of all lies.

(JOHN 8:44, CEV)

Satan cannot tell the truth. He is called "the father of all lies." Anything he tells you will be untrue or just half-true. Satan offers his lie to replace what God has already said in his Word. Satan says things like, "You'll be wiser like God. You can get away with it. No one will ever know. It will solve your problem. Besides, everyone else is doing it. It is only a little sin." But a little sin is still a sin that separates you from God.

It helps to know that Satan is entirely predictable. He has used the same strategy and old tricks since Creation. All temptations follow the same pattern, which Satan used on Adam and Eve and also on Jesus. Satan tries to get you to doubt what God has said about the sin: "Is it really wrong? Did God really say not to do it? Didn't God mean this rule for someone else or some other time? Doesn't God want me to be happy?" Watch out! Don't let doubts make you turn away from the living God. Keep your eyes and mind on God. His truth will help you spot Satan's lies every time.

Prayer

God, Satan's lies steer me away from you so easily. I want to listen to your voice and hear your truth. When I doubt, turn me toward your Word.

Check Your Reflection

As water reflects the face, so one's life reflects the heart.

(PROVERBS 27:19)

At a lake or pond, lean over the edge to see how clearly the water reflects your face. (Live far from water? Fill a bucket to try the same thing.) On a calm, sunny day, you should be able to make out everything from your hair down to your nostrils and eyelashes. If the water is rough, you'll still see the outline of your head and swirly reflections of your features.

The way you act is like water. It reflects what is in your heart. Think about new neighbors you've met. Based on how they dress, talk, and treat each other, you might be able to guess what they do for work or what is important to them.

The same can be told about you. Your reflection reveals whether you give in to temptation and never repent; you won't be able to hide it. It'll show up in how you treat your siblings and friends and whether you obey your parents. Your face and actions reveal what's inside you.

Check your reflection. Is it showing godliness?

Prayer

Jesus, what does my behavior reflect these days? I would like it to reflect a good image that pleases you, but I need your help.

What Did You Do?

In all that has happened to us, you have remained righteous; you have acted faithfully, while we acted wickedly.

(NEHEMIAH 9:33)

Why is it so hard to admit when we're wrong? The Israelites were the same way. They were great about letting God know when life wasn't going their way and they wanted him to do something about it. But they weren't very honest when they messed up. The Israelites knew they'd made a lot of bad decisions in their past. They could see where they lied or worshipped other gods. When they took a really close look, they could see that they had done a lot of things wrong, while God had done a lot of things right.

Instead of always looking or thinking about things we want God to do, it helps to take a good look at our own lives and be honest with him.

I lied to my parents.

I didn't study for that test.

I wasn't very nice to my brother.

As we are honest, we can also be thankful that God isn't like us—he never lies. He has done good things, even while we've messed up. A little honesty from us will go a long way in improving our relationship with him and with others.

Prayer

Lord, forgive me for what I've done wrong, and help me to value honesty. Please remind me of all that you've done right.

S-O-S!

He reached down from on high and took hold of me; he drew me out of deep waters. He rescued me from my powerful enemy, from my foes, who were too strong for me.

(PSALM 18:16–17)

In Psalm 18, David was in "deep water." He was so overwhelmed by his enemy, a gang of guys who were out to get him, that he felt like he would drown. "Deep water" was the way he described being in over his head or up to his neck in trouble. These guys were stronger than he was. But God came through and pulled him out just in time. David knew it and gave the Lord credit for saving his life.

Do you remember a time you felt like you were being taken down? You may have faced a gang of mean kids on the playground or bullies at the swimming pool. In those kinds of situations, call out to God for help. You don't even need to actually speak out loud. God can hear what you say inside your heart. Then when God rescues you from frightening episodes, do what David did: give God credit for saving you.

Prayer

Lord, I don't think I thanked you for helping me out the last time I was being bullied. As hard as it was, you got me through it, and I'm really grateful.

No Biggie

The only temptation that has come to you is that which everyone has. But you can trust God, who will not permit you to be tempted more than you can stand. But when you are tempted, he will also give you a way to escape so that you will be able to stand it.

(1 CORINTHIANS 10:13, NCV)

Satan does not have to tempt those who are already doing his evil will; they are already his. Temptation is a sign that Satan hates you. It is not a sign of weakness or worldliness. It's a compliment! It is also a normal part of being human and living in a fallen world. Don't be surprised or discouraged by temptation. You will never be able to avoid it completely.

It is not a sin to be tempted. Jesus was tempted, yet he never sinned. Temptation only becomes a sin when you give in to it. A priest named Martin Luther said, "You cannot keep birds from flying over your head but you can keep them from building a nest in your hair." You can't keep the Devil from suggesting thoughts, but you can choose not to dwell or act on them.

Sometimes while you are praying, Satan will suggest a bizarre or evil thought just to distract you and shame you. Don't be alarmed or ashamed by this. Satan fears your prayers and will try anything to stop them. Treat it as a distraction from Satan and immediately refocus on God.

Prayer

God, when Satan tries to tempt me, help me to not give in. Give me thoughts on pure and admirable things instead.

Sin Leads to Stupid

*This day I call the heavens and the earth as witnesses
against you that I have set before you life and death,
blessings and curses. Now choose life, so that you
and your children may live and that you may love the
LORD your God, listen to his voice, and hold fast to
him.*

(DEUTERONOMY 30:19–20A)

Chocolate cake guaranteed to make you throw up or chicken soup that will cure your cold in five minutes. Working with a tutor for an A+ on a test or a blind exam without any studying? Which would you choose? The answers seem obvious! Wouldn't it be stupid to choose the one that would make you sick or get a failing grade? Of course.

Well, sometimes the mind doesn't cooperate with the truth or what makes sense. If you could go back in time and ask any Israelite, they would agree. God delivered the Israelites from Egypt. Then he gave them clear instructions: follow me and be safe. Turn away and others will destroy you. But every so often, the Israelites lost their minds. They turned away from God. Then they suffered the consequences like losing their homes, facing famine, and being kidnapped back into slavery. Seems stupid, doesn't it? That's what happens with sin. Stepping into sin and staying there makes you stupid.

God always gives a clear choice from the beginning. Don't let stupid get the best of you and make you turn away. Choose the option that puts you on God's side and in safety.

Prayer

Lord, serving anything but you doesn't make sense. But people do it all the time. I don't want sin to make me stupid. Show me the clear way of following you so that my life is always in your hands.

Crowd Control

But with loud shouts they insistently demanded that he be crucified, and their shouts prevailed. So Pilate decided to grant their demand. He released the man who had been thrown into prison for insurrection and murder, the one they asked for, and surrendered Jesus to their will.

(LUKE 23:23–25)

Pontius Pilate was the big cheese in Judea. He reported directly to the emperor in Rome. Pilate made all the decisions about prisoners, crimes, and laws in Judea. The Jews brought Jesus to Pilate hoping that Pilate would kill Jesus. But Pilate was a smart man. He investigated Jesus and found nothing wrong. The Jews still wanted Jesus dead, and they did not give up. They pressured Pilate for so long that he finally gave in. Pilate let them kill Jesus.

Pilate's situation was extreme, but pressure from a crowd (known as peer pressure) is hard for anyone to resist. Even fearsome rulers can cave in to a crazy crowd of demanding people. As you get older, you'll face peer pressure. In fact you probably already have, like when several kids gang up on someone else and push you to join in. When you are the only one saying "no," it will be tough. But if you stick to your beliefs about right and wrong, you may give someone else the courage to say no too. Plus, that kind of strength comes from God. He'll help you resist peer pressure.

Prayer

Jesus, I don't want to get pulled into doing the wrong thing or hurting others because of peer pressure. Help me see when I need to walk away or stand up for what's right.

Cleaning Up the Inside

Then the Lord said to him, "Now then, you Pharisees clean the outside of the cup and dish, but inside you are full of greed and wickedness. You foolish people! Did not the one who made the outside make the inside also?

(LUKE 11:39–41)

Your mom tells you to go make your bed so your cousin can sleep there when she visits. You run to your room, throw a beautiful purple quilt and pretty pillows over the bed. Then you notice all your dirty socks and shoes on the floor. You grab them quickly, toss them under the quilt, and smooth the quilt back down.

Think your mom would buy it? Probably not. There's no way your cousin wants to sleep on dirty laundry and smelly shoes.

The Pharisees, who were religious leaders, were doing the same kind of thing. "Hey, we wear the right church clothes. We memorized all the Scriptures," they said. But Jesus wasn't fooled. On the outside, the Pharisees looked like they were God followers. Looking on the inside, Jesus saw their hearts were full of dirty laundry. They didn't love God. They certainly didn't love others. And they weren't following God's ways of being kind, humble, and grateful.

Jesus cares about what's inside you, not how you look on the outside or what you pretend to be to others. If there is cleaning to be done inside, he wants to do it. Will you let him?

Prayer

Jesus, I know there are thoughts and feelings inside me that I haven't let you clean up. Even if I pretend to be perfect, you know who I really am. I need you to clean out the junk inside me, so that others will see your work.

Stubborn As an Ox

For I knew how stubborn you were; your neck muscles were iron, your forehead was bronze.

(ISAIAH 48:4)

Make your arms as stiff as possible down at your sides. Clench your fists if it helps, and press your arms into the sides of your body. Now ask a sibling, friend, or parent to try to move your arms or bend your elbows. It will be tough for them! Now try the opposite. Be flexible and loose, and then see how easy it is for the other person to bend and move your arms in any direction.

Stubbornness is like tightening all your muscles at once to create an unbendable body. But stubbornness is inside you. God has lots of experience with stubborn people. The Israelites—and everyone before and after them—threw tantrums when they didn't want to follow God or do what's right. It's like they clenched their fists, teeth, legs, and backs so that God couldn't move them. Oh, he could still move them, but he would warn them first to give them the chance to loosen up.

What do you feel stubborn about? Chores, homework, attending church? Go ahead and clench every muscle in your body (and stomp your feet even!) to get out the stubbornness. Then let it go. Loosen up, and be flexible to God's will.

Prayer

God, there are some things that I just don't want to do. When it comes to important stuff, though, like serving you and obeying authority, help me to stay loose and bendable.

Back on Track

Teach me your way, L<small>ORD</small>, that I may rely on your faithfulness; give me an undivided heart, that I may fear your name.

(PSALM 86:11)

Lots of things fight for our attention: TV, friends, sports, fashion. The things we like best can pull us away from God. A divided heart is undecided about what is most important. For example, you watch a show that doesn't honor God, but the action is exciting or your favorite celebrity is in it—your heart is divided. Or you join some friends when they pick on a kid who is an easy target, but you apologize to that kid later—your heart is divided.

The only way to have an undivided heart is to choose what is most important before anything else. Spend time learning more about God. Ask him to help you stand for good and to avoid evil. You can even ask him to grow your love for him. That is a prayer he loves to answer!

No one gets it right all the time. If we did, we wouldn't need God. Some days you'll be pulled in two directions. It's okay. God is waiting, and it's never too late to turn your whole heart back to him.

Prayer

Give me an undivided heart, God. A lot of things fight for my attention, and some of them aren't good, but I want to keep my heart focused on you.

Lock It Down

The mouths of fools are their undoing, and their lips are a snare to their very lives. The words of a gossip are like choice morsels; they go down to the inmost parts.

(PROVERBS 18:7–8)

Gossip. Everybody does it—boys and girls, kids and adults. If you're honest, you have to admit to doing your share, and the reason is pretty obvious. Talking about others behind their backs can feel fun and makes you feel important.

When that new girl moved in down the street, you couldn't wait to talk about her to your friends. When you see a classmate hanging with the sketchy group at the mall, you're tempted to tell your friends. When it comes to juicy tidbits, watch out! Even before you know if what you heard about someone is true, you are tempted to tell someone else.

You may feel powerful broadcasting "breaking news" about someone, but gossip is a sign of weakness. The Bible says that gossip is what fools do. It takes advantage of another person without them knowing it. Gossip spreads rumors that can really wound people or even kill their reputation.

As tempting as it may be to share a "choice morsel" of information, just swallow it and keep it to yourself. And when you catch your friends telling tales, ask them how they would feel if someone were talking about them.

Prayer

Lord, I need to learn to be careful of passing on gossip or starting it. Forgive me for spreading rumors. Remind me to speak kind words about people at school and church.

Owning Up

So [the man] said to [Jacob], "What is your name?"
And he said, "Jacob." He said, "Your name shall no
longer be Jacob, but Israel; for you have striven with
God and with men and have prevailed."
(GENESIS 32:27–28, NASB)

While Jacob was alone one night, God wrestled with him until daybreak. Then God asked his name. He wasn't asking because he didn't know. It was to get Jacob to acknowledge his character by stating his name. His name meant "cheater" or "schemer" in Hebrew. And Jacob was definitely a sketchy guy.

Jacob remembered the heartache he had caused his brother Esau and his father Isaac by cheating Esau out of his father's blessing. So when he identified himself as "Jacob," he was admitting his flaws and weaknesses.

This is an important part of how God's changes us. First, we have to own up to our faults, sins, and mistakes. God will not go to work on our problems until we admit that we have a problem. We need to say, "Lord, I'm in a mess. I admit I made it." Then God can go to work.

For Jacob, this life-changing experience transformed him into a new person, and he became known as "Israel," the man who the entire nation of Israel was later named after. After that experience, Jacob was never the same again.

Prayer

God, it's amazing how Jacob's experience transformed him into the important figure Israel. But I bet it was hard to admit his mistakes. I'm hesitant to own up to my sins sometimes, but I know I must in order to ask for forgiveness.

Sorry Enough?

Remember, Lord, what has happened to us; look, and see our disgrace. Our inheritance has been turned over to strangers, our homes to foreigners.

(LAMENTATIONS 5:1–2)

Your mom comes around the corner and catches you throwing rocks at the dog next door. "I'm sorry," you quickly say, hoping you won't get into too much trouble.

Saying you're sorry is enough in some situations. But not with God. God talks a lot about repentance. It's much bigger than an apology or confession.

When the Israelites realized just how bad the consequences were for their sin and how badly they had treated God, that's when they *repented*. They turned away from their sin. They turned toward God. They asked him to restore their relationship and their lives. They had missed him, and they missed the blessed life they had.

With God, save the "I'm sorry." Instead, turn your heart toward him and away from sin. Then you can have a conversation about your relationship and how to get it back on track.

Prayer

Lord, please help me to be so sorry for my sin that I stop. I don't want to cut myself off from your goodness.

No Excuses

*But if we confess our sins to God, he can always be
trusted to forgive us and take our sins away.*

(1 JOHN 1:9, CEV)

Have you ever noticed how easy it is to make excuses for our problems? We can be experts at blaming other people and may say something like:

"It's not my fault, you know."
"He started it."
"My parents caused it."
"My teacher didn't explain it."

Why do we act this way? Because it's hard to admit when we've messed up, and it can be scary to ask for help.

God asks for confession. Why? To let him know what's going on? No, he already knows that. When we tell God we have sinned, it is no surprise to him. He knew it all along. We confess because it humbles us. The good news is that once we do, God gives us all his resources and power to change us.

If we don't confess, we will just have the same problem again and again. If we don't learn the lesson now, we will have to learn it later. God is going to teach it to us one way or the other. But if we humble ourselves and confess, he takes over and cleans us up.

Prayer

God, thank you for loving me even though I sin. When I confess my sins and the times I've messed up, correct me and show me places in my life I can do better.

Remember What?

Then he adds: "Their sins and lawless acts I will remember no more." And where these have been forgiven, sacrifice for sin is no longer necessary.

(HEBREWS 10:17–18)

God forgets. Oh, he doesn't forget us or forget what he has to do every day. But he forgets our sins. Our mistakes. Our bad choices. The minute we come to him and ask for forgiveness, he wipes the slate clean. He forgets.

That's fantastic!

And hard to imagine.

When our friends do something to hurt us, we remember. We remember when a teammate makes a bad play. We also remember our own stuff, like when we lied or cheated or got in trouble with our parents.

It's harder for us to forget what we've done or what others have done to us.

God knows that we won't forget, but he doesn't want us to hold on to bad feelings, hate, or resentment. If someone asks for our forgiveness, we need to offer forgiveness and be done with it, even if we need to ask God to help us with that choice every day. God doesn't hold on to the bad stuff we do, and he doesn't want us to hold on to it either.

Prayer

Lord, help me not to hold on to the bad choices I've made or the hurt from others. I want to forget the things that you forget.

When You're Tempted

How can a young person stay on the path of purity?
By living according to your word. I seek you with all
my heart; do not let me stray from your commands.

(PSALM 119:9–10)

Everybody struggles with temptation. Because we are descendants of Adam, we entered this world with desires that are triggered by sin. Some people are tempted to misbehave. Some are tempted to cheat on schoolwork. Others are tempted to shoplift; and still others hide the truth.

God tells us that temptation will come our way. But temptation will always land us in hot water. Even if we know it is wrong to give in to temptation, how do we keep from messing up?

The key to standing up to temptation is seeking the Lord with all our hearts. That means putting him first. It means thinking about him. It also means talking to him. And when you talk to the Lord, be totally honest with him. Admit to him when you are feeling weak or tempted and why.

The fact that you are reading this today is proof you are taking time to be strong against the things that tempt you. Reading God's Word and thinking about what you read allows the Holy Spirit to give you power to remain pure. Why not memorize today's verse?

Prayer

Lord, I want to honor you with my life. Build my strength to resist temptations that come my way and to be completely honest with you about them.

God Sees More

Jacob named the place Peniel (God's Face) because, he said, "I saw God face-to-face and lived to tell the story!"

(GENESIS 32:30, MSG)

Jacob had come face-to-face with God, and it changed his life.

When Jacob began to cooperate, God started working, and the first thing he did was give Jacob a new name, a new identity. God changed Jacob from a cheater and schemer to a good man with the name "Israel," a "prince of God." God knew Jacob's potential; he saw through Jacob's attempt to be a tough guy. God saw all of Jacob's weaknesses, but he also saw beneath the surface: "That's not the real you, Jacob. You're actually an Israel. You are a prince." God saw the prince in Jacob and changed him into that kind of guy.

When we've had a personal encounter with God, we can no longer be the same. The good news is this: beneath all those things that you do not like about yourself, God sees an Israel. He sees the prince or princess. He sees what you can become. He sees your potential, and he wants to change you from a Jacob to an Israel. Let God do his changing.

Prayer

God, you see me as your valued child. You want the best for me if I repent. Would you help me grow and become a better follower of Christ?

Motives of the Heart

All a person's ways seem pure to them, but motives are weighed by the LORD.

(PROVERBS 16:2)

Most of us like to think we are good: "I listen to my parents; I do well in school; I look out for my friends. So I must be a good person!"

God looks at the heart. He knows whether we are being nice out of love or just to get people to like us. He knows if we're trying to show off or if we really want to work hard at school. He loves us even when we do good things for selfish reasons, and he uses those good deeds.

But how do you know if your motives are right? Ask yourself how disappointed you are when someone doesn't return a favor or applaud you for a job well done. When you are bummed because you didn't get something in return for your good deed, that means selfish motives were likely behind it all.

God wants to change our hearts so that his motives guide us rather than our own. If we ask him to show us what's really in our heart, he will point us toward good actions for the best reasons—his.

Prayer

Lord, look at my heart. I want to do the right thing for the right reasons. Will you please help me?

Let It Go

"All these I have kept," the young man said. "What do I still lack?" Jesus answered, "If you want to be perfect, go, sell your possessions and give to the poor, and you will have treasure in heaven. Then come, follow me."

(MATTHEW 19:20–21)

This guy talking to Jesus thought he was in. He had followed every rule since he was a little boy. He was excited, thinking he was as good as gold with Jesus. Then Jesus tells him that he needs to give away all of his stuff. The young man probably thought, "Seriously?" He could hardly believe it. He turned and walked away. He felt like Jesus was asking too much.

But was Jesus really asking too much? No. Jesus knew this guy loved money and stuff more than he loved God and that love of money was going to get this guy in trouble. That's the way it works. Any time we love something more than Jesus, we end up in trouble. This guy was just too scared to let go. He liked his stuff and couldn't live without it.

Jesus knows our hearts. He knows if we've put something ahead of him, whether it's looking good, a movie star crush, making the team, or fitting in with our friends. When those things get ahead of God, things get messy. So out of love, Jesus will ask us to set them down and keep him first.

Prayer

Lord, I don't want anything to get in the way of my relationship with you. Show me if I've put something ahead of you.

Serving God, Serving Others

Mission Possible

Moses said to the LORD, "Pardon your servant, Lord. I have never been eloquent, neither in the past nor since you have spoken to your servant. I am slow of speech and tongue." The LORD said to him, "Who gave human beings their mouths? . . . I will help you speak and will teach you what to say."

(EXODUS 4:10–12)

The Israelites had been slaves for a very long time—would you believe four hundred years? God had an outrageous plan to set his people free. Moses was going to be God's messenger to the king of Egypt. What God expected Moses to do was pretty scary. For Moses, it seemed like a "mission impossible." After all, from the time he was a little kid, Moses stuttered. It was hard enough talking to his family, let alone speaking in public or communicating with the king. The Lord assured Moses he would help him.

You know what you're good at. Sports? Reading? Organizing? Computers? You also know what doesn't come easy for you. Math? Language arts? Sports? Speaking up in class? Everybody has strengths and weaknesses. Just because a chore, subject, or activity doesn't come easy doesn't mean you can skip it. At times you'll just have to do it. But like God helped Moses accomplish God's mission, he will help you when you face hard assignments.

Prayer

Lord, I want to be your person at school. I want to be someone you can count on. When doing the right thing doesn't come easy, please give me the courage and help to do it anyway.

Doing Your Part

Then have them make a sanctuary for me, and I will dwell among them. Make this tabernacle and all its furnishings exactly like the pattern I will show you.

(EXODUS 25:8–9)

Do you love getting your hands dirty to build something or to create a stunning piece of artwork? A go-cart, a painting collage, a fort tucked deep in the woods? The guys in Exodus must have been bursting with excitement. Sure, they had built lots of things before—but this was the most incredible project they would ever get to do. God had given them the plans to build *his* house, *his* tabernacle.

Now that's a cool job.

Everyone pitched in with silver, gold, bronze, wood, and even yarn. People brought leather, stones, gems, and even spices, oil, and incense. They had everything they needed. And God laid out exactly how it was supposed to come together. Everybody just had to do their part.

Today every person who serves God has a job to do for him. It may not be building a cathedral, but we all have something to offer that will help reveal God to the world. No one is left out. Not one gift or talent is overlooked when God has a project to do on Earth.

Prayer

Lord, I want to be part of your modern-day construction crew—building your plans on Earth. Will you show me my part?

Original Beauty

Bezalel made the ark of acacia wood . . . He overlaid it with pure gold, both inside and out, and made a gold molding around it. He cast four gold rings for it and fastened them to its four feet, with two rings on one side and two rings on the other.

(EXODUS 37:1–3)

Bezalel did not have the prettiest or coolest name. But he knew how to make beautiful creations with his hands. He was like the best jeweler combined with the best carpenter—a master artist. God chose Bezalel to make a special ark. Bezalel spent days working with gold to get just the right glimmer.

Why did God care if the ark looked brilliant? God loves all things beautiful. When he created the world, he made the people, the animals, the plants, the gems, the lakes. He made many beautiful things. He's an amazing artist himself. And he wants you to find and admire beauty. Part of God's beautiful world is that he gave people abilities to create beautiful things like jewelry, houses, paintings, and clothes. It's okay to enjoy them. Just remember that the beauty originated with God, and use your own creations to offer something beautiful back to him.

Prayer

Lord, sometimes it seems that certain kids are better-looking or more gifted than me. Will you show me what is beautiful about me and how I can create beautiful things for you?

Inventors Welcome

*In Jerusalem [Uzziah] made devices invented for use
on the towers and on the corner defenses so that
soldiers could shoot arrows and hurl large stones
from the walls. His fame spread far and wide, for he
was greatly helped until he became powerful.*

(2 CHRONICLES 26:15)

Did you know that some inventions were made during Bible times? For that matter, do you stop to think about the inventions you use every day? Think of all the inventions that make your day go smoothly: bowls for breakfast cereal. Forks and knives for dinner. A hot water heater and faucet to clean up. A toilet so you don't have to go in the backyard with your dog. Creative minds come up with useful and ingenious ideas that improve the way we live.

Invention has been around for ages. God created humans with creative minds. And some people get to use their creativity to invent tools, instruments, vehicles, music, and language. Uzziah, a king and an inventor, made new military tools so his armies could beat everyone else. At the time, he was cutting edge in military and engineering technology.

Though you don't go around thanking God for the invention of the toilet, boy would you miss it if it broke! So take time today to thank God for all the inventions you use that make life easier.

Prayer

Lord, thank you for creativity and inventions. There are so many tools that I use every day without a thought for who invented it. But I know you are behind all those creations.

Open Up Your Gifts!

It is the same and only Holy Spirit who gives all these gifts and powers, deciding which each one of us should have.

(1 CORINTHIANS 12:11, TLB)

God gives spiritual gifts to every member of his family. You can't earn your spiritual gifts or deserve them—that's why they are called gifts! Neither do you get to choose which gifts you'd like to have; God determines the type of gifts you get. These are special God-empowered abilities for serving him that are given only to Christians. They include things like wisdom, teaching, faith, healing, special languages, prophecy, preaching, and discernment.

God loves variety, and he wants us to be special, so no single gift is given to everyone, and no one person gets all the gifts. If you had them all, you wouldn't need anyone else. That would defeat one of God's purposes—to teach us to love and depend on each other.

The Bible says, "The Holy Spirit displays God's power through each of us as a means of helping the entire church" (1 Corinthians 12:7, TLB). If others don't use their gifts, you get cheated. And if you don't use your gifts, they get cheated. So God wants you to discover and develop your spiritual gifts. An unopened gift is worthless. Ask him to show you which gifts are yours.

Prayer

Lord, it's easy to wish I had other people's gifts. Reveal to me the gifts you've given me, and show me ways I can use them for your purpose.

The Perfect Age

People were bringing little children to Jesus for him to place his hands on them, but the disciples rebuked them. When Jesus saw this, he was indignant. He said to them, "Let the little children come to me, and do not hinder them, for the kingdom of God belongs to such as these."

(MARK 10:13–14)

What's your age? Nine, ten, twelve years old? Sometimes you may wish you were older or younger. Or it may seem like high school students are more important than you are because you are young. Or you may think that adults have more influence with God. Guess what? God loves children as much as the oldest grandma. How old you are doesn't matter to him.

That doesn't mean that you don't have to respect adults or obey them. But it does mean that God can use you now. You don't have to wait to grow older. You don't have to wait until you are smarter. You don't have to wait to be stronger. When Jesus was in town, he told the children to visit him. When adults got mad about that, Jesus told them to knock it off. He got ticked. "Let them come to me," he said.

Jesus didn't play favorites, and he certainly didn't make anyone feel unimportant. You still need to respect those who are older than you (Jesus did say to honor your mom and dad and those in authority), but you can expect that Jesus will welcome a conversation with you or a visit whenever you need him.

Prayer

Lord, thanks for treating me as special, no matter how old I am. How can I serve you now instead of waiting until I'm older?

Don't Mess with Crazy

John wore clothing made of camel's hair, with a leather belt around his waist, and he ate locusts and wild honey. And this was his message: "After me comes the one more powerful than I, the straps of whose sandals I am not worthy to stoop down and untie."

(MARK 1:6–7)

Ever wonder why God chooses some crazy people to do his work? There's John the Baptist, running around in the wilderness, hair sticking out in every direction. He's draped in dirty camel fur and eats handfuls of locusts that he's dipping into honey.

God could have used anyone to pave the way for Jesus. Any Hollywood movie director would have encouraged the full red carpet treatment, major media coverage, and lights that "bring out your good side." Even back then, Jesus certainly could have used the celebrities of his day, like a strapping young Pharisee or an especially holy old rabbi. But no. Jesus chose locust-eating, sticky, stinky John the Baptist.

And John the Baptist was exactly who Jesus wanted. Jesus loved John and even allowed John to baptize him before Jesus kicked off his public ministry.

Don't underestimate how God will work in you or in those around you. God is all about going the unlikely route, using the outlandish or unique to bring about his purposes. Don't ever think you have to become someone different to live for Jesus. If a guy who chomps locusts for lunch can serve God, you're destined to play a part.

Prayer

Lord, thank you that I don't have to be like anyone else to serve you with all my heart. I want to be the person you created me to be—nothing more, nothing less.

Naturally You

He chose David his servant and took him from the sheep pens; from tending the sheep he brought him to be the shepherd of his people Jacob, of Israel his inheritance.

(PSALM 78:70–71)

Did you know Abraham Lincoln worked in a general store and a post office long before he became president? NFL Super Bowl quarterback Kurt Warner also worked at a grocery store. Former Secretary of State Condoleezza Rice was a pastor's kid. King David started out as a shepherd.

You wouldn't think of kings, presidents, and celebrities working in normal, everyday places and doing common jobs. But rarely does anyone become great by starting out great. Greatness starts with dedication and hard work right now.

Abraham Lincoln learned how to overcome failure. Condoleezza Rice studied Russian and wound up working for the president and with Russian diplomats. David learned to be quick to respond and how to fight against all kinds of attacks. It's appealing to want to be a big-name actor, athlete, or leader. But God wants you to focus on using the gifts and skills he's given to you right now, at your age. In God's world, he doesn't look for people in great places. He looks for them in the fields, the grocery stores, the playgrounds. Aim to be good at what comes naturally to you. Then you'll be ready when God picks you for a great role someday.

Prayer

God, it would be awesome to be famous or at least make lots of money. But fame and fortune don't last; only you are everlasting. Keep my eyes on you and what you've given me to do right now.

Gift-Worthy

King Solomon was greater in riches and wisdom than all the other kings of the earth. All the kings of the earth sought audience with Solomon to hear the wisdom God had put in his heart.

(2 CHRONICLES 9:22–23)

Would you let the naughty neighbor kid pet your new kitten? Not a chance! You've seen him try to scare big cats and pull the tails of brute dogs. Only a fool would turn over the kitty to that kid.

God feels the same. He doesn't want to give stuff to people who will misuse or waste his gifts. That's why he gave Solomon such great wealth. Solomon didn't ask God for money or victory over his enemies or the biggest stable of horses. Solomon asked God for wisdom—the smarts to make good and right decisions. With that kind of a king leading Israel, God knew he could give Solomon lots of gold and power and horses and servants. Solomon would handle those gifts with wisdom. He shared his gifts with his people. He helped them make decisions. He told everyone who came to him about God's ways. Solomon was trustworthy.

What does God want to give you? Are you ready to use his gifts with care?

Prayer

God, your wisdom is better than being a fool and misusing your gifts. Will you give me the smarts to value what you value?

Are You a Servant?

*We should help people whenever we can, especially
if they are followers of the Lord.*

(GALATIANS 6:10, CEV)

John Wesley was an incredible servant of God. His motto was "Do all the good you can, by all the means you can, in all the ways you can, in all the places you can, at all the times you can, to all the people you can, as long as you ever can."

Real servants pay attention to needs. Servants are always on the lookout for ways to help others. When they see a need, they seize the moment to meet it. When God puts someone in need right in front of you, he is giving you an opportunity. But often we miss many occasions for serving because we aren't paying attention to others.

God says the needs of his global Church are to be top priority. Remind yourself at the start of every day that you are God's servant. Then start looking for small tasks that no one else wants to do. Do these little things as if they were great things, because God is watching. Servants are happy for the opportunity to practice serving.

Prayer

God, open my eyes to small things I can do to serve others. I want to pay better attention to these things, too. Can you guide me to opportunities to serve you?

Heartbeats

*Watch over your heart with all diligence, for from it
flow the springs of life.*

(PROVERBS 4:23, NASB)

Physically, each of us has a unique heartbeat. Just as we
each have unique thumbprints, eye prints, and voice prints, our
hearts beat in slightly different patterns. It's amazing that out of
all the billions of people who have ever lived, no one has had a
heartbeat exactly like yours.

The Bible uses the term "heart" to describe the bundle of
desires, hopes, interests, dreams, and likes you have. Your heart
represents what you love to do and what you care about most.
We still use the word in this way when we say, "I love you with all
my heart." Your heart reveals the real you. Your heart determines
why you say the things you do, why you feel the way you do, and
why you act the way you do.

God has given each of us a unique emotional "heartbeat."
It races when we think about the subjects, activities, or circumstances that interest us. We naturally care about some things
and not about others. People rarely excel at tasks they don't
enjoy doing or feel passionate about. God wants you to use your
natural interests as clues to how you will best serve God and
others. What's your heart beating for?

Prayer

Wow, God, you've made each of us so unique! Will you show
me ways to use my unique "heartbeat" to serve you and others?

Ready to Serve

Be dressed ready for service and keep your lamps burning, like servants waiting for their master to return from a wedding banquet, so that when he comes and knocks they can immediately open the door for him.

(LUKE 12:35–36)

Say your best friend calls to invite you to rock climb or go to karate with her. Would you go in your pajamas? No way. You'd ask your mom or dad to help you find the right clothes and gear. You'd need a harness, climbing shoes, and ropes to climb the rocks. For karate, you'd need some safety pads and water (it's a tough workout!).

You know that certain activities require preparation and the right equipment. Living for Jesus also requires you to be ready. Jesus said that he will come back to Earth one day to take all his followers to Heaven. He didn't tell anyone when that would be. But he said, "Be ready." Being ready means waking up each day and asking God to lead you. He may have a job for you to do that day, or he may need you to help someone out. Each time you are ready to do something for God, it lets others know about him. Then hopefully, they will want to follow Jesus too and be excited for his return to Earth—whenever that may be.

Prayer

Jesus, what does it really mean to be ready for your return to Earth? That's hard to understand, because no one living today has ever seen you. I want to be ready for you, whatever you ask of me. Please show me how to do that.

Running Your Race

*Therefore, since we are surrounded by such a great
cloud of witnesses, let us throw off everything that
hinders and the sin that so easily entangles. And let
us run with perseverance the race marked out for us.*

(HEBREWS 12:1)

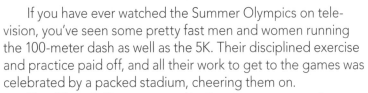

If you have ever watched the Summer Olympics on television, you've seen some pretty fast men and women running
the 100-meter dash as well as the 5K. Their disciplined exercise
and practice paid off, and all their work to get to the games was
celebrated by a packed stadium, cheering them on.

The Olympic Games started in Greece many centuries ago.
So when the writer of Hebrews says that being a Christian is
like running a race, the Hebrews knew exactly what he meant.
Christianity is more like a marathon than a dash, because faith
requires endurance. Unlike a flat asphalt track, the road of life
includes hills, dips, and puddles that can trip us up.

Did you notice the race Christians are called to run is unique
for each person? No one is called to run the exact same race. It's
not a race to beat others or stay ahead of the pack. God has a
running plan for each person, so don't compare yours to others.
Your running plan will require discipline, effort, and sweat. That's
why we are invited to look into the stadium and take courage
from those who have already finished their race.

Prayer

Lord, remind me of the medal stand that awaits those who finish
their race. Help me focus on Jesus as I plug away, one day at a
time.

Hopes and Dreams

Hope deferred makes the heart sick, but a longing fulfilled is a tree of life.

(PROVERBS 13:12)

What are your dreams? Do you want to sing your heart out on Broadway? Write the next great novel? Now, think about the simple day-to-day things. Maybe you want to do well in school, have a few good buddies, and get along with your sister. Any one of those things is a hope, a dream. And when something we wish for doesn't happen, it can be tough.

God understands that it's frustrating when you don't make the team, do poorly in guitar lessons, or get a D on a school paper. Oh, not that he will come down and give you a big ol' bear hug, but God might use a friend to cheer you up. He might create a blazing sunset or have your dog sit close by your side.

At times like these, re-evaluate your hopes. Are they set on God first? God cares about your hopes and dreams, but not everything you wish for is a dream from him. If you keep your heart set on something that is out of your reach and God has not confirmed that he is part of it, your heart can become quite sad. Instead, give your hopes over to God. Ask him to turn them into reality or change your heart's focus.

Prayer

Lord, you know my hopes and dreams. You know the ones I've had to put off, and you understand how frustrating that can be. Redirect my heart if you have something else in mind. Thank you for caring about me.

Millions of Skills

I've filled him with the Spirit of God, giving him skill and know-how and expertise in every kind of craft to create designs and work in gold, silver, and bronze; to cut and set gemstones; to carve wood—he's an all-around craftsman.

(EXODUS 31:3–5, MSG)

Your brain can store 100 trillion facts. Your mind can handle 15,000 decisions a second. Your nose can smell up to 10,000 different odors. Your touch can detect an item 1/25,000th of an inch thick. You are an amazing creation of God.

Your abilities are the natural talents you were born with. Some kids have a natural ability with words—they came out of the womb talking. Others have natural athletic abilities. Still others are good at math or music or mechanics.

Every ability can be used for God's glory. The Bible is filled with examples of different abilities that God uses for his glory. Here are just a few of those mentioned in Scripture: artistic ability, architectural ability, administering, baking, boat making, candy making, debating, designing, embalming, embroidering, engraving, farming, fishing, gardening, leading, managing, masonry, making music, making weapons, needlework, painting, planting, philosophizing, machinability, inventing, carpentry, sailing, selling, being a soldier, tailoring, teaching, writing literature and poetry.

God has a place in his family where your specialties can shine.

Prayer

Thank you for making me (and everyone else) so special and for giving me so many talents, Lord. Help me to use these talents for your glory. Help me to please you and use them for your purposes alone.

Part of the Team

The Son of Man will send out his angels, and they will weed out of his kingdom everything that causes sin and all who do evil . . . Then the righteous will shine like the sun in the kingdom of their Father. Whoever has ears, let them hear.

(MATTHEW 13:41, 43)

Following Jesus is tougher than we think. It's not like following our favorite sports team or cheering on the hero from an adventure movie. When we say "yes" to Jesus, it's not a sideline type of thing.

Sometimes the challenge is all about the little things: listening to Mom and Dad, helping out a classmate when he's stuck on a tough math problem, or being nice to siblings. Other times God will call you to bigger actions: sticking up for someone younger or weaker, giving away something you really like to someone who needs it, or even standing against your friends when they want to do something wrong.

Thankfully, in those high-pressure decisions, you're not alone. Jesus, God's Son, is always there for you. And your Christian friends and family are on the same team too.

Jesus asks us to follow him and tells us it won't be easy, but he promises that it *will* be worth it. We will shine like the sun in God's Kingdom. And being part of his plan is way better than cheering an exciting sports game from the sideline or watching a thrilling movie. Because bottom line? Jesus wins. And as we take action with him, we win too.

Prayer

Lord, thank you for inviting me to be part of your action plan here on Earth. Help me to do my part. Together we win!

Caring for the Weak

Blessed are those who have regard for the weak; the LORD delivers them in times of trouble.

(PSALM 41:1)

When you hear the term "special needs," who comes to mind? That kid in the wheelchair you see in the hall at school? A neighbor who has a blue disability sign hanging from the mirror in his car? That lady who comes to church with her guide dog? Maybe you think of someone in your family who has autism or Down syndrome.

The Lord is very protective of kids and grown-ups who deal with these kinds of problems. He understands how tough it is for them to get by. That's why the Lord promises to bless us when we help out those who are weak or handicapped. He watches us when we go out of our way to be kind. He hears when we stop others from making fun of someone with a disability.

One of the ways the Lord blesses those who look out for the weak is to take care of us when we are weak. Did you get that? You may not have a physical or mental disability, but you will feel overwhelmed and weak many times in your life. And at times like that, the Lord will give you the strength and the people you need to make it through that tough situation.

So, whom will you befriend today?

Prayer

Lord, give me a tender heart for those people I see who have special needs. I want to love them and treat them well.

Something That Lasts

Good will come to those who are generous and lend freely, who conduct their affairs with justice. Surely the righteous will never be shaken; they will be remembered forever.

(PSALM 112:5–6)

—◆◆—

Who won the Super Bowl MVP two years ago? Who took home the Oscar for Best Actor or Special Effects five years ago? Unless you have a memory like an infinite thumb drive, you probably don't know.

Everyone wants to be remembered. Some people try to achieve this legacy through becoming famous. They think if their name is all over TV, radio, and the Internet, they will be happy. Yet all it takes is one look at some actors and pro athletes to see that they're anything but happy!

Other people try the route of wealth, assuming that more money means more peace. If that were true, then wealthy people would never get divorced, commit crimes, or turn to alcohol or drugs. But we know that's not true.

So if it's not fame or fortune, what's the secret to leaving your mark on this world? The Bible says it's quite simple: be righteous and generous. It's great to work hard at a sport, instrument, talent, or school subject. None of those things, however, will give you a lasting legacy. But spending your life giving to and serving others? Now that will. And God will always remember it.

Prayer

Giving generously and living rightly doesn't come naturally, God. But that's how you treat me; you never withhold anything. Please show me how to do the same to make a difference in this world.

Weakness Expected

Keep falsehood and lies far from me; give me neither poverty nor riches, but give me only my daily bread. Otherwise, I may have too much and disown you and say, "Who is the LORD?" Or I may become poor and steal, and so dishonor the name of my God.

(PROVERBS 30:8–9)

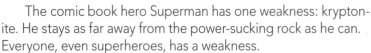

The comic book hero Superman has one weakness: kryptonite. He stays as far away from the power-sucking rock as he can. Everyone, even superheroes, has a weakness.

The writer of Proverbs knew his weakness was money. If he had too much or too little, it would get in the way of following God's ways. So he prayed about it, asking God to protect him from that weakness.

Do you know what your weakness is? If you do, how far away do you stay from it? You may like the thrill of having and hearing secrets. You may have a really strong desire to make lots of money one day and hoard your allowance. You may like bending the truth to get your way or persuade others to follow your ideas.

If you don't know your weakness, it's okay. As you get older, you'll discover it. When you do, get God on your side as soon as possible to help you fight it. You don't want your "kryptonite" to take you down.

Prayer

Lord, I'm not sure what my weakness is. Will you show me how to be on guard against the things that will hurt me or you?

Serve First

Then James and John, the sons of Zebedee, came to him. "Teacher," they said, "we want you to do for us whatever we ask." "What do you want me to do for you?" he asked. They replied, "Let one of us sit at your right and the other at your left in your glory."

(MARK 10:35–37)

Talk about being bold. That's exactly what these two sons of Zebedee were. They were obnoxious! They actually asked Jesus if they could have special privileges when they went to Heaven. James and John had one selfish goal: they wanted to be great.

Can you imagine saying that to Jesus? When the other disciples discovered what the brothers had asked Jesus, they came unglued. They were angry. And Jesus wasn't too happy either. But rather than get mad at them, Jesus decided to explain what real greatness means.

As far as Jesus is concerned, being awesome is not about asking for special favors but asking for ways to serve. Look for ways to be helpful. Choose to do what nobody else wants to. Being great in God's eyes isn't about sitting on thrones in palaces (or in Heaven). It's about caring for other people.

What about caring for your brother or your sister? What about your mom and dad? What can you do that would help them today?

Prayer

Lord, as much as I want to be important, I want to be great in your eyes most of all. Forgive me when I try to grab the best for myself.

Love What You Do

*Do not turn aside from following the L*ORD*, but serve the L*ORD *with all your heart.*

(1 SAMUEL 12:20, ESV)

How do you know when you are serving God from your heart?

Some things turn you on and capture your attention while others turn you off or bore you to tears. These reveal the nature of your heart. Listening to what's in your heart can point to the ways God intends for you serve him.

The first sign is enthusiasm. When you are doing what you love to do, no one has to motivate or challenge or check up on you. You do it for the fun or love of it. You don't need rewards or applause. On the other hand, when you don't have a heart for what you're doing, you are easily discouraged.

The second sign of serving God from your heart is that you're also effective. Whenever you do what God wired you to love doing, you get good at it. If you don't care about a task, you probably won't excel at it. As you grow up, you'll learn more about the ways God has wired you. Let him guide your heart, and your heart will guide your life.

Prayer

God, you want me to serve you with all my heart. Reveal to me who you created me to be. Show me places where I can serve you effectively and enthusiastically.

Roadblocks

As soon as the copy of the letter of King Artaxerxes was read to Rehum and Shimshai the secretary and their associates, they went immediately to the Jews in Jerusalem and compelled them by force to stop. Thus the work on the house of God in Jerusalem came to a standstill until the second year of the reign of Darius king of Persia.

(EZRA 4:23–24)

Building a church is no walk in the park. Try adding a bunch of rabble-rousers who really don't like you.

Zerubbabel and his band of ragtag construction workers faced this problem when they rebuilt God's temple. Their enemies, worried about the Jews gaining power, immediately got to work on "Operation Temple Trash." In fact, the temple sat unfinished for another eighteen years!

Does that mean Zerubbabel failed? No way! God saw his effort and passion for rebuilding the temple, and that pleased him.

When we do something awesome for God, it scares God's enemies. The Devil doesn't want us full of God's power, so he does anything to stop us. But it is temporary.

That temple eventually did get finished, but it wouldn't have happened without Zerubbabel's efforts. If your big plans to change the world for Christ hit a roadblock, don't worry. It may seem like God isn't ahead at halftime, but he always wins the game.

Prayer

Lord, I have trouble understanding why I don't always succeed when I'm doing something for you. Give me patience, perseverance, and faith as I wait for your green light.

Admit It

For he will deliver the needy who cry out, the
afflicted who have no one to help. He will take pity
on the weak and the needy and save the needy from
death.

(PSALM 72:12–13)

Wimps get made fun of. Poor kids get teased. Those who fail a class face snickers from classmates. Weak or sick kids are pushed around. If you've ever felt like a wimp, a loser, poor, weak, sick, or a failure, it's no fun to be the butt of other kids' mistreatment. Everyone wants to be strong and smart and healthy. But God is on the side of those who are feeling down and out.

God is kind to those who are hurting, small, and helpless. He loves them and cares for them because they need help. Though God loves everyone, often those who are strong think they don't need God—or anyone else for that matter. So God leaves them be and turns to those who aren't afraid to admit their needs. If you feel strong, let God shine through you to others and offer your help.

The cool thing is that God always helps those who aren't afraid to admit their needs. He is the strongest, most powerful friend you can have. God's care is more valuable and long-lasting than the teasing or joking from others. Some day when you are sick or weak, God will send others to meet your needs too.

Prayer

God, I want to be strong and healthy, but I see how it would be easy to look down on those who are not. Give me kindness and compassion toward others to help when I'm needed.

Get Wisdom

Get wisdom, get understanding . . . The beginning of wisdom is this: Get wisdom. Though it cost all you have, get understanding.

(PROVERBS 4:5A, 7)

Get it? Are you sure you got it? The writer of Proverbs seems pretty serious about making sure you get wisdom. He says it over and over . . . and over and over. He didn't mean it just for the old people, like grandparents. He tells a kid that wisdom is for him too. But where do you get it?

You can't run down to the store for wisdom, and you can't ask your parents to buy it online. You can't even trade lunch for a bite-size piece of wisdom.

Wisdom is the thing that helps you handle tough situations and relationships. Wisdom tells you when to bite your tongue. Or when to share your opinion with someone you disagree with. Or how to be patient with the annoying kid next door. Or how to be smart with your allowance.

Wisdom comes first by understanding. Understanding comes by paying attention to teachers, to friends, to parents, and to God's ways. After you pay attention long enough, the light bulb will go on in your head. "Aha!" you'll say. "Now I understand." That's when wisdom starts to take hold. That's when you've got it. Get it?

Prayer

God, it seems awfully important to be wise even while I'm still pretty young. Since wisdom comes from paying attention, show me how to watch and learn from others. Thank you!

The Right Kind of Attention

I'm not trying to win the approval of people, but of God. If pleasing people were my goal, I would not be Christ's servant.

(GALATIANS 1:10, NLT)

Ever notice some kids love being the center of attention? But that's not the kind of attention that matters. God's attention goes to those who act like servants.

Servants maintain a low profile. Instead of acting to impress and dressing for success, they serve one another. If recognized for their service, they humbly accept it, but they stay focused on their work.

Paul exposed a kind of service that appears to be spiritual but is really just a put-on, a show, an act. He called it "eye service" (Ephesians 6:6, Colossians 3:22), serving just to impress people with how spiritual we are. The Pharisees during Jesus' time did this and turned helping others, giving, and even prayer into a performance. Jesus warned to stay away from that kind of attitude.

Servants don't serve for the approval or applause of others. They live for an audience of One. The story of Joseph in Genesis is a great example. He didn't draw attention to himself but quietly served Potiphar, then his jailer, then Pharaoh's baker and wine taster, and God blessed that attitude. When Pharaoh promoted him to prominence, Joseph still maintained a servant's heart.

Prayer

Lord, it's easy to crave attention or praise for the nice things I do. But that's not what you call servants to be. When I get a big head about showing people how giving I am, turn my attitude back to being a humble servant.

Scientifically and Miraculously Designed

You made all the delicate, inner parts of my body and knit them together in my mother's womb. Thank you for making me so wonderfully complex! It is amazing to think about.

(PSALM 139:13–14, TLB)

Each one of us is truly unique. Our DNA molecules can unite in an infinite number of ways—the number is 10 to the 2,400,000,000th power. That number is the likelihood that you'd ever find somebody just like you. If you were to write out that number with each zero being one inch wide, you'd need a strip of paper 37,000 miles long!

Your uniqueness is a scientific fact of life. There never has been, and never will be, anybody exactly like you.

Obviously, God loves variety—just look around! He created each of us with a unique combination of personality traits. God made shy people and bold talkers. He made people who love early mornings and those who love late nights. He made some people "thinkers" and others "feelers." Some people work best by themselves while others work better with a team.

God uses all types of personalities and DNAs. Never question how unique you are. It's scientifically proven!

Prayer

God, not only have you made my personality unique, but my DNA is specially made for me! Sometimes I don't think I'm special, so emphasize to me how detailed I am created.

Too Big for Your Britches

*Pride goes before destruction, a haughty spirit before
a fall. Better to be lowly in spirit along with the
oppressed than to share plunder with the proud.*

(PROVERBS 16:18–19)

*Want to stand out in a crowd?
Don't be arrogant and proud.
Prideful people often fall.
Being humble's best of all.*

That little poem packs a punch. Like the words from
Proverbs, it reminds us that humility pays off in the end.

We all know guys who act like hotshots and girls who act
like divas—maybe you've acted like that yourself. The way they
parade or strut through the halls or on the playground, you'd
think they were royalty. Speaking of royalty, King Saul in the
Bible is an example of what happens when you get too big for
your royal britches.

The prophet Samuel told him what God expected, but Saul
didn't obey. He wrongly thought he could do what he wanted.
And what happened? Well, God knocked him off his high horse
and removed him from his throne.

There may be short-term payoffs to hanging with those
puffed-up self-proclaimed princes or princesses, but the long-
term consequences are not worth it. Better to have an honest
look at yourself and admit you really don't know it all. After all,
God knows the truth. Most of your friends do too. And they like
you even though you aren't perfect.

Prayer

Lord, forgive me when I pretend to be more important than I
really am. I'm glad you love me even though I'm not perfect.

Is Your Head Bigger Than Your Heart?

"You have done a foolish thing," Samuel said. "You have not kept the command the Lord your God gave you; if you had, he would have established your kingdom over Israel for all time."

(1 SAMUEL 13:13)

Saul was tired of waiting. Samuel was supposed to come take care of the offering, but he hadn't shown up. People were starting to leave, so Saul decided to take charge. "What's the big deal?" he probably thought. Saul figured he could take care of the offering just as well as Samuel could. He gathered everything together and took care of business.

Then Samuel walked up.

"What have you done?" Samuel asked.

Saul was guilty. He had been way too impatient and taken over Samuel's God-given job like it was no big deal.

God had given Saul success in some areas, so Saul thought he could do whatever he wanted. He thought too much of himself. The same thing can happen to us. Maybe God gives us success in sports, so we start acting like a know-it-all in the locker room. Or he gives us the chance to be a leader in the classroom, and we start acting like king of the world. It's easy to let stuff go to our head when God opens a door like that.

To keep from getting puffed up like Saul, we need to remember where all our success comes from and keep our eyes on the Lord.

Prayer

God, thank you for giving me skills and strengths. Help me to remember where they come from and not to let success go to my head.

Fashion Statement

In the same way, you who are younger, submit yourselves to your elders. All of you, clothe yourselves with humility toward one another, because, "God opposes the proud but shows favor to the humble."

(1 PETER 5:5)

Have you heard of the latest "clothing brand"? It's actually not that new; it's been available for thousands of years. The mall doesn't carry it; neither does Walmart. You can't get these clothes online, and this brand can't be worn alone.

The brand is humility. You get dressed like normal in the morning—shirt, pants, shoes. Then you throw on another layer, like a long coat, of humility.

Like wearing the right color for your skin tone, the humble brand enhances your appearance. This brand lets you show off your own style and goes with everything you already own. The only thing it clashes with is pride and selfishness. Even when you're wearing the humble brand, pride and selfishness may slip out from time to time.

Many people don't have the guts to wear the humble brand. They'd rather not cover up everything else. That's why this brand is exclusive. It's only for those who have a connection to the designer—the Holy Spirit. Want in?

Prayer

God, your brand is exclusive for good reason: humility is tough to wear. But it will outlast any other fashion. Please clothe me in it every day.

Notable Pray-er

Now Jabez called on the God of Israel, saying, "Oh that You would bless me indeed and enlarge my border, and that Your hand might be with me, and that You would keep me from harm that it may not pain me!" And God granted him what he requested.

(1 CHRONICLES 4:10, NASB)

Jabez is known for a short prayer, but his request shows a lot about taking requests to God. Jabez asked for more land, but he also asked for God's presence in his life. Jabez realized that if he got more land, it meant he would have more responsibility. He would have greater demands and more pressure. He would really need God's help, so he requested that God be with him. Whenever you ask for God's presence in your life, you can be sure he will answer.

Jabez also prayed for God's protection. Why did he do that? In those days, the more land you had, the more influence you had, and the better known you were. And that made you a bigger target.

It is still like that today: the more successful you are, the more critics you have. The closer you grow to the Lord and the stronger you become as a Christian, the more the Devil will harass you, because he doesn't want you to grow. But you can be sure, as Jabez was, that with God's blessing, he also gives his presence and protection.

Prayer

God, I'm glad I can count on you being with me. When I don't think I can handle something by myself, will you show me you're with me?

Use It or Lose It

God has given each of you a gift from his great variety of spiritual gifts. Use them well to serve one another.

(1 PETER 4:10, NLT)

God has given you some spiritual abilities, talents, and gifts. He has made an investment in you. He wants and expects to see you use what he's given to you. If you do not use the talents you have been given, other people are losing out because you are not contributing what God has uniquely equipped you to provide.

If you want to become more faithful, use your talents. You might say, "Well, I'm not talented like that person. I can't sing the way she can." Faithfulness does not depend on what you do not have or cannot do. Faithfulness depends on what you do with what you have. You are not responsible for singing solos for God if he didn't give you that gift. But you are responsible for using the gifts and talents God has given.

Life is largely made up of little things. Be faithful in the little things. The little things, such as reading God's Word and praying, produce big results. We cannot all be brilliant, but we can all be faithful. And faithfulness is what counts with God!

Prayer

God, I want to be more faithful, not just in the big things but in the little things, too. It doesn't feel like the little things make that much of a difference. But I know you will do big things if I'm faithful to you.

Looking in the Mirror Too Much

When Haman entered, the king asked him, "What should be done for the man the king delights to honor?" Now Haman thought to himself, "Who is there that the king would rather honor than me?"

(ESTHER 6:6)

"Mirror, mirror, on the wall, who's the fairest of them all?" Modern kids know these words come from the fairy tale "Snow White." But rewind several thousand years, and Haman, the arrogant bad guy from the book of Esther, might have said the same thing.

The Bible doesn't mention any magic mirrors, but Haman definitely had power and prestige. He also had another "p" on his list: pride. And it landed him in the hot seat!

Here's the deal: Mordecai, the secret uncle of Queen Esther, once uncovered a royal murder plot. When Xerxes found out Mordecai had never been thanked, the king asked Haman for reward suggestions. Haman thought the reward was for him. But of course we know Xerxes was talking about Haman's archenemy Mordecai! The king's sidekick was so blinded by his love for himself that he couldn't see the accomplishments of others.

The same thing can happen to us. It's good to be confident and proud of yourself, but pride goes beyond that. Pride says, "You are better than everyone."

Yet that's not what God teaches us. Instead, be like Jesus and celebrate the work of your friends, family, and classmates. And stay away from talking mirrors!

Prayer

Lord, have I ever thought I was the most important? I'm sorry for that prideful attitude. Teach me to see myself and others as equals, all loved by you and in need of mercy.

Are You Forgetting Someone?

It took Solomon thirteen years, however, to complete the construction of his palace.

(1 KINGS 7:1)

It took eleven years for Solomon to finish the temple and thirteen years to finish his own palace. Hmmm. Eleven years to build God's house and thirteen to build Solomon's own? Makes you wonder, doesn't it? God had given Solomon wisdom, and people traveled from all over to spend time with him. He must have been feeling good about himself. Maybe he thought that he deserved a palace that took thirteen years to build.

Solomon wasn't alone; we tend to do the same thing. God will give us a blessing or a talent, people start noticing, and we start feeling proud. "I am pretty good," we think to ourselves. "Oh yes—not bad at all!"

If we're not careful, pretty soon we'll be taking all the credit and leaving God out. The quickest way to fight that kind of pride is to always thank God for everything. Thank him for our blessings. Thank him for our talents. Thank him for our successes. Keeping our eyes on him will help us keep our eyes off of ourselves.

Prayer

Lord, it's easy to start thinking more of myself than I should. Help me to remember that everything I have and all that I am is because of you.

True Offerings

*Jesus . . . watched the crowd putting their money
into the temple treasury. Many rich people threw in
large amounts. But a poor widow came and put in
two very small copper coins, worth only a few cents.
Calling his disciples to him, Jesus said, "Truly I tell
you, this poor widow has put more into the treasury
than all the others."*

(MARK 12:41–43)

Flashy robes, jingling coins, a big show. The rich people
were throwing in their coins, letting them drop with a loud clang.
"Notice me!" "Look how generous I am!" Then a widow came up
to the offering and dropped in two tiny copper coins. No jingle,
just two small clinks. Maybe she lowered her head as the rich folks
glanced at each other. "That's it?" they probably wondered.

But Jesus knew the truth. He knew that while the rich people
were giving a small portion of all they had, the widow was giving
all she had.

Jesus pointed her out. He wanted her to know—he wanted
us to know—that there is no gift unseen. Even if what we bring
seems smaller than what others bring, God doesn't see it that way.

When you pour out kindness to a loner, when you give
allowance money to buy someone lunch, when you help out
your teacher instead of going to recess, you are offering what
you have, and Jesus sees. He notices. He points you out to the
others in Heaven. "See her? Others give what they have left over.
But she gave all that she had."

Prayer

Lord, I'm not sure what I can give to you, but I want to gladly
give an offering that will make you happy. Will you please show
me what that is?

The Gift of the Present

Be very careful, then, how you live—not as unwise but as wise, making the most of every opportunity, because the days are evil.

(EPHESIANS 5:15–16)

Someone once said, "Yesterday is the past. Tomorrow is the future. Today is a gift. That's why it's called *the present.*"

That's more than just a play on words. Today is God's gift to you. It's wrapped up with a bow. It even has your name on it! But you have a choice. Will you leave it on the table, or will you unwrap the present and enjoy it?

You will never get today back again. God wants you to make wise choices and live your day as though it is a gift. (The fact that you are reading your Bible today is a good start.)

So just like you would start using a gift as soon as you open it and show it off, talk to the Lord about this day. What is planned for today? What will you be facing? Ask him to help you enjoy it, use wisdom, stay away from bad influences, and stand up for what is good.

At the end of the day, think back on what you did. God may have sent you a blessing or a challenge. Were you able to see them for what they were and let him guide you through them?

Prayer

God, thank you for today and the gifts you have given me. Please give me wisdom and show me how I can be a blessing to others.

Ego Check

For the sake of Christ, then, I am content with weaknesses, insults, hardships, persecutions, and calamities. For when I am weak, then I am strong.

(2 CORINTHIANS 12:10, ESV)

Be content with your weaknesses? Huh? At first this doesn't make sense. We don't want to be weak! But when we accept our weaknesses, it's an expression of faith in the goodness of God. It says, "God, I believe you love me and know what's best for me."

Paul gives us several reasons to be content with our inborn weaknesses. First, they cause us to depend on God. Referring to his own weaknesses, which God refused to take away, Paul said he was happy about them because he had to trust God more (2 Corinthians 12:9). Paul also knew he wouldn't get a big head. So our weaknesses also prevent arrogance. They keep us humble.

God often attaches a major weakness to a major strength to keep our egos in check. A limitation can keep us from going too fast and running ahead of God.

Prayer

God, it's weird to admit my limitations. But it's cool that you can use my strengths and weaknesses. I'm grateful I can depend on you.

The Boy King

In the seventh year of Jehu, Joash became king, and he reigned in Jerusalem forty years. His mother's name was Zibiah; she was from Beersheba. Joash did what was right in the eyes of the Lord all the years Jehoiada the priest instructed him.

(2 KINGS 12:1–2)

Think back to when you were seven years old. What was a normal day like for you? You probably did a little bit of homework, played outside for an hour or two, maybe logged on to the computer or game center. Ate dinner with your family.

Did you know any seven-year-olds (then or now) who spent their time pondering the depths of the Bible and how to become president some day?

Joash wasn't a typical seven-year-old. He spent the first part of his life in hiding and hanging out with a bunch of priests. Learning God's ways and how to serve him was the daily norm. Then when he was seven, he was chosen to be king—well, he was rightly king by birth anyway, but the priests thought they better make Joash king sooner rather than later. And you know what? All that time spent in hiding with the godly guys paid off. Joash took over the country and became a good king who did what was right.

Even though Joash was not the norm, if he could become wise, then age doesn't matter. God wants children who will follow his ways now. Would you be ready to step up to the throne?

Prayer

God, I can't imagine becoming the leader of a country at my age. But I do want to follow your ways in everything I do.

Directed By a Dream

*After Paul had seen the vision, we got ready at once
to leave for Macedonia, concluding that God had
called us to preach the gospel to them.*

(ACTS 16:10)

Have you ever had a weird dream? One where you chase
down a bear or hang off a cliff above a roaring river? We've all
had dreams that make us shake our heads and wonder, "Where
did that come from?"

Paul had a dream that a man from Macedonia was begging
him to come over and help. Paul and his friends figured they
should go check it out. Maybe along the way they wondered if
Paul's dream was just because he ate some bad food or got too
hot while he was sleeping.

God will sometimes prompt you with a feeling to do something, but how do you know if the feeling is from God? The best
thing to do is talk to some godly adults and then start to take
some steps. God has a neat way of letting you know if you're on
the right path. He gives a sense of peace to keep going. But if
it seems wackier by the moment, then ask God to point you in
the right direction. God will never ask you to do something that
doesn't line up with his Word. And the Holy Spirit will always
direct you when you need it.

Prayer

Lord, I want to do whatever you ask me to do. Please point
me in the right direction and help me to pay attention to your
confirmations!

Award-Winning

God is not unjust; he will not forget your work and the love you have shown him as you have helped his people and continue to help them.

(HEBREWS 6:10)

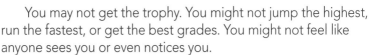

You may not get the trophy. You might not jump the highest, run the fastest, or get the best grades. You might not feel like anyone sees you or even notices you.

But God does. He sees. He notices. Even when it seems like everyone else overlooks you, God doesn't. He sees when you take out the trash for your mom. He sees when you study into the night. He sees when you stand up for your sister.

And even though you may not have a trophy on your shelf that says, "Best garbage-taker-outer," God has a trophy in his heart for you. Because every time you do something kind or good (whether anyone else notices or not), God takes note. You show that you love him every time you love someone else. You serve him every time you work hard. And that is no small thing.

Prayer

God, thank you for noticing me. Thank you for seeing what no one else seems to see. I love you.

It's All the Same

Surely the lowborn are but a breath, the highborn are but a lie. If weighed on a balance, they are nothing; together they are only a breath. . . . Though your riches increase, do not set your heart on them.

(PSALM 62:9–10B)

The poet of Psalm 62 sure didn't seem to like people. He calls the poor basically nothing and the rich a big fat lie. Well, the poet was actually being poetic. He wasn't insulting people. He was pointing out that what you are born with or without doesn't make you more or less valuable than anyone else. You have lots of money—doesn't matter to God. Only have one pair of shoes—no worries. The kid down the street has the best toys and goes on the coolest trips every year—not much different than the King of the Universe.

You see, God created every person. He puts some people into poor places and some into rich. But he loves them all the same. For some reason, though, humans like to look up to rich, famous people. And we don't think those who are poorer than us are worth our time. No matter if you're a "have" or "have-not," everyone has a heart, feelings, and value. So before you look down on people because they are poor, consider how everyone would look if you were roughing it on a wilderness trip. Everyone would be on equal ground. When you can see past the stuff—or lack of it—you'll see the creation of God.

Prayer

Lord, it's hard to look past the money or things that someone else has or doesn't have. Please help me to treat all people with respect, no matter their earthly status.

Worth It?

You must be on your guard. You will be handed over to the local councils and flogged in the synagogues. On account of me you will stand before governors and kings as witnesses to them.

(MARK 13:9)

❧

Weigh the consequences: stay up late tonight to watch the movie you've been waiting for but lose out on going to your best friend's sleepover this weekend. Eat a warm chocolate chip cookie before dinner but lose out on ice cream cake after dinner. Join the youth group choir instead of singing in children's church but you'll only be a backup singer. These decisions might not be too hard for you. Raise the stakes, and you'd have to think harder.

The disciples had to weigh the odds. And the odds were high: follow Jesus and risk being beaten and attacked but get to speak in front of the political leaders on Jesus' behalf. A beating is much harder to accept than waiting in the pews for your turn to sing in the choir or giving up one dessert for another.

Jesus didn't want the disciples to be surprised by the risks of following him. He was straight with his followers: this will be hard. The rewards will be miraculous, but it may cost you a lot. If you faced those risks today for following Jesus, would you still choose him? That's a tough question. Only the strongest faith will take the risk.

Prayer

Lord, I don't know if my faith is strong enough to take risks for you. Please build my faith and show me your awesome power, so I won't think twice about serving you in the face of major risks.

Wilderness Camp

And the child grew and became strong in spirit; and he lived in the wilderness until he appeared publicly to Israel.

(LUKE 1:80)

Do you like camping or hiking? You might love camping all summer long and wish your parents would let you set up a tent in the backyard. John the Baptist did something like that. His family lived near the wilderness, an area of rugged rocky hills. John stayed in the wilderness even when he started his preaching ministry. He ate bugs and wild honey. He dressed in simple clothes. He probably even slept outside. But the wilderness is where God prepared John to become a prophet. John spent his time studying and preparing for ministry.

Occasionally, God asks his followers to serve him in extreme conditions, like in the wilderness or in the desert or in a poor, rundown country. This kind of call from God usually begins early in life, just like with John the Baptist. He was used to wilderness living and finding his own food.

What is God doing in your life today to prepare you for later? It's okay if you don't know. But if he sends your family to the wilderness, God may have a special calling for you one day to preach to those in the wilderness. They may not hear about God any other way.

Prayer

Wow, God. Those were extreme conditions that John the Baptist lived in. Am I cut out for a special ministry like that? I need your preparation for whatever calling you have for me.

Ordinary Is Extraordinary!

But God has chosen the foolish things of the world to shame the wise, and God has chosen the weak things of the world to shame the things which are strong.

(1 CORINTHIANS 1:27, NASB)

God has never only cared about super strong people. In fact, he loves people who are weak and who admit it. Everyone has weaknesses. In fact, you have a bundle of weaknesses too. Do you ever admit that? Not usually! Instead we usually excuse, hide, or deny our weaknesses.

Guess what—God deliberately allowed weaknesses in your life so he can use them. You may have thought God only wants to use your strengths, but he wants to use your weaknesses for his glory too. In fact being "poor in spirit" is the number one attitude Jesus blesses (Matthew 5:3).

The Bible is filled with examples of how God loves to use ordinary people with regular weaknesses to do extraordinary things. That's encouraging news!

Prayer

God, I'm glad I don't have to hide anything from you, including my weaknesses. Thank you for loving me and my struggles.

Hoping for Change

*To keep me from becoming proud, I was given a
thorn in my flesh, a messenger from Satan to torment
me . . . Three different times I begged the Lord to
take it away. Each time he said, "My grace is all you
need. My power works best in weakness."*

(2 CORINTHIANS 12:7B–9A, NLT)

What is the one thing you would most like to change about
your life? Maybe it's a habit. Maybe it's a weakness. Maybe it's
a difficulty. Maybe it's something that has gotten you into more
trouble than you could have imagined. Maybe you are in a situation that bugs you.

It's hard to say, "God, I have a weakness. I have a problem."
But until you do, things will just stay the same. And you'll still be
annoyed, frustrated, or cranky.

Do you really want God to change your life? He will—in his
own way. And when he does the changing, it will become permanent. All he requires is your cooperation. So have you been
limiting God by making excuses, blaming other people, or being
stubborn? When you're ready to cooperate, he'll take charge,
and then you can relax and let him do his work.

Prayer

God, only you can help me change. But change is scary and
takes work. When change gets hard, remind me of your purpose
for me and give me the motivation to change.

Weak and Proud of It

But he said to me, "My grace is sufficient for you, for my power is made perfect in weakness." Therefore I will boast all the more gladly about my weaknesses, so that Christ's power may rest on me.

(2 CORINTHIANS 12:9)

Did you know there is a World's Strongest Man contest? Competitors heft logs, roll cars end over end, bend metal pipes, and hoist giant stones trying to out-muscle each other. For these men, weakness is not an option.

Paul felt the exact opposite. He wrote about embracing your weakness. Huh? Paul sure wasn't trying to win the World's Weakest Man title. Instead, he learned what seems like a backwards part of Christianity: even though we face some really hard issues, we experience more strength when we concentrate solely on God—not ourselves.

We are no different than Paul. We just have to realize that we can do anything once we figure out that we can do *nothing* without God. God might allow us to experience a tough situation, like he did with Paul—like an injury, sickness, or struggle at school, to build our spiritual muscles. But we must let God's strength take over our weakness.

Prayer

God, feeling weak stinks, but I know your grace is enough for me. Help me see problems as muscle-building exercises. May your power be made perfect in my weakness.

Imperfect for God

"Neither this man nor his parents sinned," said Jesus, "but this happened so that the works of God might be displayed in him."

(JOHN 9:3)

What characteristics have you inherited from your parents? Maybe you have your father's ears or mom's eyes. Our parents even pass on quirky habits, like how both you and your dad stick out your tongues while shooting free throws.

In Jesus' time, many people believed parents passed down more than looks. They thought the mom's and dad's sins caused diseases and disabilities in their children. So if a baby was born deaf, it meant the parents had done something really bad and God was punishing the child.

Such was the case in John 9. Jesus and his disciples saw a man who had been blind all his life. His disciples ask, "Whose fault is it that this man was born blind?"

Jesus' answer in John 9:3 blew their minds. He then made some mud with his spit and dirt and rubbed it on the man's eyes (tell that to your mom when she says no spitting!). The blind man could soon see.

Because of sin, we live in an imperfect world. That means people get sick, bodies and brains have flaws, and accidents happen. It does not mean that you or your family did something wrong to deserve it. Just like the blind man, our imperfections give God an opportunity to demonstrate his power.

Prayer

Jesus, sometimes I want to blame you or others for problems I've had for years. Please give me faith to believe that you can take care of them.

Tough as Nails

But I will make you as unyielding and hardened as they are. I will make your forehead like the hardest stone, harder than flint. Do not be afraid of them or terrified by them, though they are a rebellious people.

(EZEKIEL 3:8–9)

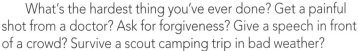

What's the hardest thing you've ever done? Get a painful shot from a doctor? Ask for forgiveness? Give a speech in front of a crowd? Survive a scout camping trip in bad weather?

Sometimes God may ask us to do hard things that may not seem fair. But if God's people don't tackle the hard jobs, who will do them?

God told Ezekiel that he had a really tough job to do. God likened it to being stuck by thistles and thorns again and again—how terrible! Or like sitting on a scorpion—ouch! Ezekiel's job was going to be very uncomfortable.

Guess how God prepared Ezekiel. God made Ezekiel as tough as nails. God turned Ezekiel into something like an impenetrable super agent. Ezekiel could take the rebellion of the Israelites. He could withstand their threats and attempts to hurt him. Ezekiel was transformed to survive the toughest assignment.

So, be encouraged. Whatever hardships or tough jobs you face, expect God to give you what you need to handle it.

Prayer

God, please prepare me to do what you ask of me, no matter how hard it is.

Ask a Lot

Now glory be to God, who by his mighty power at work within us is able to do far more than we would ever dare to ask or even dream of—infinitely beyond our highest prayers, desires, thoughts, or hopes.

(EPHESIANS 3:20, TLB)

What do you ask God for when you pray? God dares you to ask for big requests. This means that you cannot out-ask God. You cannot out-dream God. If you could stretch your imagination to the greatest limits, God can go beyond even that. In Exodus, God parted the Red Sea. In the book of Daniel, he stopped the furnace fires from burning Shadrach, Meshach, and Abednego. In the gospel of Luke, he healed the sick, cast out demons, and raised the dead.

God says, "Trust me. Bring any request to me. I can do it."

What do you want God to do in your life? Heal an injury or sickness? Ask him. Help you with a problem at school? Ask him. Save your family? Ask him. You can always trust that he will answer.

Prayer

God, it's amazing that I can pray to you about anything! Help me to be bold in my prayers because you will always listen.

A Little for a Lot

Jesus then took the loaves, gave thanks, and distributed to those who were seated as much as they wanted. He did the same with the fish. When they had all had enough to eat, he said to his disciples, "Gather the pieces that are left over. Let nothing be wasted." So they gathered them and filled twelve baskets with the pieces of the five barley loaves left over by those who had eaten.

(JOHN 6:11–13)

"Lunch is on me!" Jesus said. The disciples were a bit confused. All they saw was one kid's little lunch. In an instant, Jesus didn't just take care of lunch; he also treated everyone to a feast. Everyone ate as much fish and bread (think hamburgers and French fries today) as they wanted. The food just kept coming. They had so much they had to bring home the leftovers.

God is a big God. His supplies are endless. So when God takes care of a need, he loves to give more than we ask for. He loves to be generous with blessings. He is not stingy. He gives more than what we need. Sometimes, though, we can get confused about what we actually need. We want things and demand that God give us what we want. But he knows best and will take care of us better than we could ourselves.

Prayer

Jesus, you know the needs my family has right now. We really need you to provide for us in a big way. I believe you are big enough and will give us what we need. Thank you.

Feeling Forgotten

How long, L<small>ORD</small>? Will you forget me forever? How long will you hide your face from me?

(PSALM 13:1)

Have you ever asked your mom or dad to help you with a craft or a recipe or a project, but they say to wait because they are busy? You wait. But after a few minutes, you go back. You don't want to be forgotten. Even if they haven't forgotten, you might worry that they will.

The same thing might happen when you pray. You ask God for help. Then you wait. Then you wonder why you are waiting so long. King David felt like that. After he'd been waiting a while, he'd go back to God to ask if God had forgotten about him. God hadn't, but God didn't mind that David asked.

It's okay to tell God what you want and when you want it. It's even okay to ask him if he has forgotten about you. The cool thing, though, is that God never forgets about you or your prayers. He remembers exactly who you are, where you live, how you fix your hair, what games you play, your favorite colors. If you feel forgotten, maybe you haven't talked to God in a while. Or he may have a different answer than the one you asked him for. Tell him how you're feeling, then read a story in the Bible about times when God reminded other people that he never forgot them, like Hagar (Genesis 16:9–13) or Hannah (1 Samuel 1:12–20).

Prayer

God, even though the Bible tells me you won't forget me, sometimes I feel like others do or that you might. Will you remind me that you are always close to me?

You Tracking?

*I am sending you Huram-Abi, a man of great skill . . .
He is trained to work in gold and silver, bronze and
iron, stone and wood, and with purple and blue and
crimson yarn and fine linen. He is experienced in all
kinds of engraving and can execute any design given
to him.*

(2 CHRONICLES 2:13–14A)

King Solomon faced so many choices with his building project. He constructed a temple (like a church) using materials like stone, wood, and precious metals. And he needed someone really talented to help him finish the job.

So Solomon hired a man named Huram-Abi, who could do wonders with metals, rocks, wood, and fabrics. Those skills made Huram-Abi the rock star of ancient Jewish design and construction. And because the temple would glorify God, Huram-Abi was definitely needed to make it the best-looking building in the world.

How about you? What are you good at? Maybe working with metal and wood like Huram-Abi is not your thing. But maybe you rock at fixing bikes, drawing, teaching little kids, or helping with computers. Guess what? God loves that!

You don't have to be singing hymns or reading your Bible to praise God. Like Huram-Abi, you can use your growing talents to help others and make God smile—even if it's building Lego cities.

Prayer

Lord, I really love doing what I'm good at. But I hadn't thought about it as more than just fun. Will you show me how and when to use my abilities to serve you?

Mid-Combat Picnic

Even though I walk through the darkest valley, I will fear no evil, for you are with me; your rod and your staff, they comfort me. You prepare a table before me in the presence of my enemies. You anoint my head with oil; my cup overflows.

(PSALM 23:4–5)

Imagine you're having a snowball fight with the neighbors. Your mission: to secretly take over their super-cool snow fort. Peering around the corner of the house, you see several players armed with icy ammo. What's your next move?

Probably the *last* thing you'd do is casually spread an old blanket, and plop down for a snack. Yet that's exactly how David viewed his relationship with God.

As a rich and powerful king, David had many political enemies. He also was the head of a nutty family; his own son, for example, tried to kill him and take over the country. That's enough to stress anyone out!

David's relationship with God provided some much-need relief. Because David spent time in prayer, worship, and reading God's Word, he could receive strength and security from the most powerful being in the universe.

You can be like David. Ask for strength and comfort from the Lord. He gladly gives us relief and peace anytime at all. Are you surrounded by your enemies? Don't fear. Instead, sit down with God for a mid-snowball fight picnic.

Prayer

Lord, thank you for reminding me you are always available, even in the middle of a tough situation. Help me to focus on you instead of my problems, and give me your peace.

Touchdown Faith

Jabez was more honorable than his brothers, and his mother named him Jabez saying, "Because I bore him with pain."

(1 CHRONICLES 4:9, NASB)

What's more important than being talented, having strong abilities, or a great education? Faith—believing that God will work through you. I've met many super-talented people who are sitting on the sidelines while ordinary people with faith are making the touchdowns. They believe God, so he uses them. Like Jabez, they are just ordinary people with extraordinary faith.

Jabez apparently had some type of handicap or disability. In the Hebrew language Jabez means *painful*. Jabez caused his mother so much grief during childbirth that she named him Painful. How would you like to be named Painful? "Here comes Painful," or "There's old Painful over there." He may have been unwanted and unloved. His name constantly reminded him that even his birth caused grief. But Jabez's faith kept him going. He believed God would help him with his goals and his dreams.

Prayer

God, I want to be someone you use to do extraordinary things. Please guide my life, because I know you have greater plans for me than I can imagine.

PURPOSE 6

You Were Made for a Mission

Pass It On

> He told them, "The secret of the kingdom of God
> has been given to you. But to those on the outside
> everything is said in parables . . . Then Jesus said to
> them, "Don't you understand this parable? How then
> will you understand any parable?"
>
> (MARK 4:11, 13)

What's your favorite way to learn? Maybe you memorized your multiplication tables through a rap song, learned about chemical reactions by mixing baking soda and vinegar, or remembered all fifty state capitals by watching a movie. Some people like to read or see information. Others prefer to hear it or use their hands and body to learn.

In Jesus' time, many people couldn't read. They didn't have TV, Internet, iPhones, or even public libraries in each town. So they learned through sermons at the local temple.

Jesus, however, knew the best way to make a point was through a good story. So, instead of just saying people accept God's Word in different ways, Jesus told a story about a farmer planting seeds (Mark 4:1–20). The crowd, full of farmers, got it. Jesus didn't care about impressing the crowd; his goal was to use ideas that everyone could understand.

If Jesus lived in a different time, he would have told different stories. He will do anything to help people understand their need for God's forgiveness, love, and guidance.

Are you willing to share God's life-saving message in a way that your friends, family, teachers, and coaches will understand?

Prayer

Jesus, I'm glad you care about helping me understand the Bible. Please help me do the same for others at school, home, church, and in my neighborhood.

Lasting Legacy

The king stood by his pillar and renewed the covenant in the presence of the LORD—to follow the LORD and keep his commands, statutes and decrees with all his heart and all his soul, and to obey the words of the covenant written in this book.

(2 CHRONICLES 34:31)

What is your family known for? Maybe your family all play musical instruments, go to the same college, or have red hair. Or perhaps people with your last name are famous for being athletic, big eaters, or celebrating strange holidays.

Our families pass down certain characteristics, habits, and values. That's called a legacy. But did you know your family can leave a spiritual legacy?

Eight-year-old King Josiah's relatives left him with a tough spiritual legacy; both his dad and grandpa were known for their evil ways. Around sixteen, however, something clicked in Josiah's heart, and he started learning everything he could about God. By twenty-six, he decided to repair the rundown temple. During the rebuilding, someone found the Scriptures and read them to the king. Josiah held a marathon Bible-reading session, challenging everyone to commit to God.

Some people come from a long line of church-going, Bible-reading Jesus-followers. Others, are the first (and sometimes the only) followers of God in their family. If that's you, take heart. God can use you to form a new spiritual legacy—one of love, selflessness, compassion, and obedience to Christ.

Prayer

Jesus, make me like Josiah, inspiring my relatives toward a relationship with you through my words, actions, and attitudes.

Special Mission

They brought the boy to Eli, and [Hannah] said to him, "Pardon me, my lord . . . I prayed for this child, and the LORD has granted me what I asked of him. So now I give him to the LORD. For his whole life he will be given over to the LORD." And he worshiped the LORD there.

(1 SAMUEL 1: 25–28)

Samuel was one of the bravest boys in the Bible. Because Samuel was a miracle from God, his mom dedicated Samuel's life to God's special task force. Samuel had gone to live at the tabernacle under the high command of Eli, the priest of the whole country. As soon as he arrived, Samuel started his training for God. Even though he left home, Samuel wasn't afraid to be in a new place. When he was about your age, Samuel accepted a big mission from God. One day he too would become a priest.

Can you imagine going off on a mission for God when you turn twelve? God may not send you to another country, but he doesn't care how old you are. He uses all kinds of people and all ages to bring his messages to the world. Are you ready for his assignment? Maybe you too will have a mission like Samuel when you are young. Get ready.

Prayer

Dear God, I don't know if I'm ready for a big mission. Will you prepare me to do whatever you ask me to do? I want to accept your mission.

Don't Keep It Secret

God uses us to persuade men and women to drop their differences and enter into God's work of making things right between them. We're speaking for Christ himself now: Become friends with God; he's already a friend with you.

(2 CORINTHIANS 5:20, MSG)

If your friend or mom had cancer and you knew the cure, it would be a crime to keep that lifesaving information a secret. Even worse would be to keep secret the way to forgiveness, purpose, peace, and eternal life. Jesus died for our sins, invites us into his family, gives us his Spirit, and makes us his agents in the world. What a privilege! We have the greatest news in the world, and sharing it is the greatest kindness you can show to anyone.

Our mission is important for eternity—more important than any achievement or goal we will reach during our life on Earth. Nothing else we do will ever matter as much as helping people find a relationship with God.

God wants you to share the Good News where you are. As a student, friend, son, or daughter, continually look for people who you can share the Gospel with. Start praying, "God, who have you put in my life for me to tell about Jesus?"

Prayer

God, I want to tell other people about your love. Please give me the courage to do that. Show me someone in my life who especially needs to hear the Good News.

Creeping In

Do not fret because of those who are evil or be envious of those who do wrong.

(PSALM 37:1)

Don't be envious? That's easier said than done. Sometimes the feeling just sneaks up. We see another kid who is nasty or mean, and she gets away with it. Nothing bad seems to happen. She's happy. She seems to have all the fun or the popularity. Meanwhile it feels like we're stuck following a whole lot of rules that don't feel fun.

Sooner or later, envy sneaks up on us. But we have to remember a few things. First, the bad choices other kids make may *seem* fun in the moment, but they usually don't work out in the long run. Second, God doesn't want us to worry about others doing wrong. He'll take care of them in time. Plus, he isn't looking to rob us of fun. Anything he asks us to do, he asks for a good reason. God is just like a smart mom who would stop her child from running out in front of a big truck; he sets up rules so that we won't get run over by the messy things in life.

So next time envy creeps up, remind yourself that God is looking out for you. Forget about those who are doing wrong and getting away with it. It won't last.

Prayer

Lord, sometimes I want to do things that other kids are doing even though I know they are wrong. But I don't want to hurt myself in the long run. Help me to make choices that will please you. I believe you have good things ahead for me.

Witnesses Needed

The news of your faith in God is out. We don't even have to say anything anymore—you're the message!

(1 THESSALONIANS 1:8, MSG)

God wants to speak to the world through you. Yep, you. When you believe in Jesus Christ, you also become God's messenger.

You may feel you don't have anything to share, but that's not true. The Devil would love it if you kept quiet. But God chose you to speak out for him. This is called witnessing. In a courtroom, a witness isn't expected to argue the case, prove the truth, or press for a verdict; that is the job of attorneys. Witnesses just report what happened to them or what they saw.

So what has God done for you? You need to learn how to share your life message. It has four parts:

- Your testimony: the story of how you began a relationship with Jesus or why he's important to you
- Your life lessons: the most important lessons God has taught you
- Your godly passions: the topics or activities God shaped you to care about most
- The Good News: the message of salvation

Simply share your experiences about the Lord. Then let him make the case.

Prayer

God, you have done so much for me. Help me share the story of your love with others.

Stand Firm

The wicked are overthrown and are no more, but the house of the righteous stands firm.
(PROVERBS 12:7)

Have you ever played King of the Hill—the game where you fight your way to the top of a pile of dirt, snow, or rocks? When you get to the highest point, you defend your turf and send everyone flying back down.

Though that game is fun, it's definitely not fun when your whole life feels like a giant, never-ending round of King of the Hill. In their rush to be the coolest, have the most friends, earn straight A's, or make the best team, people often shove and push others to keep them down. Can you relate?

Maybe your teammates talk trash about you or the school bully posts something horrible on the Internet about your best friend. Whatever the case, watching the bad guys have all the fun while nice guys finish last gets old after a while!

The writer of Proverbs 12 knew how that felt. But he also knew that God is in control—even over people who don't follow him. God sees when people become king (or queen!) of the hill through mistreating others. Most important, as a justice-loving God, he won't let the wicked get away with everything forever. If you stick with Jesus (the real King!), you will outlast the bad guys—no pushing or shoving required.

Prayer

God, being on top looks great, but I know it's temporary. I want to "stand firm" like the righteous and do the right thing. Help me pray for—not envy—those who stomp on others.

Ready to Answer

Solomon answered all her questions; nothing was too hard for the king to explain to her.

(1 KINGS 10:3)

If you sold a million records, won a gold medal, cured cancer, or explored Mars, you would be famous or rich or both. Now imagine if you accomplished that entire list. Your popularity would skyrocket, and your bank account would explode!

Welcome to King Solomon's life. He was royal from birth, wealthy beyond imagination, incredibly intelligent, and the wisest man around. To top it off, Solomon and God were very close. Life was pretty sweet.

So sweet, in fact, that other royals wanted to know his secret. The queen of Sheba (an area probably around Ethiopia) came to check out Solomon's kingdom. Everything she saw and heard greatly impressed her. So she jumped at the chance to pick Solomon's brain.

Just like the queen of Sheba, people still have questions about life. They want to know why there is so much pain in the world, where God is, and how they can know him. Maybe we're not modern-day princes or Einsteins, but like Solomon, we are representatives of Jesus.

Will you be prepared to answer your friends' questions when they come to you? You don't have to know everything; after all, you are still learning about God yourself. Just remember to pray for wisdom and point people toward God, who can answer every question.

Prayer

God, I don't have all the answers, but you do. Please teach me to be ready like Solomon when my friends and family come to me with life's questions, so you get the credit and glory, not me.

Your Choices Matter

Manasseh was twelve years old when he became king, and he reigned in Jerusalem fifty-five years. His mother's name was Hephzibah. He did evil in the eyes of the LORD, following the detestable practice of the nations the LORD had driven out before the Israelites. He rebuilt the high places his father Hezekiah had destroyed; he also erected altars to Baal and made an Asherah pole, as Ahab king of Israel had done. He bowed down to all the starry hosts and worshiped them.

(2 KINGS 21:1–3)

Want to be president? You've got a few years to go; the US Constitution says you have to be at least thirty-five to run the country. In the Bible, there were no age requirements. When a king died, his oldest son took over, no matter how old he was.

That's how Manasseh became king of Judah at twelve. His father Hezekiah had faithfully followed God, but when he died, Manasseh failed to continue his dad's legacy. The young king was seriously wicked.

As Manasseh demonstrates, the choices we make even when we're young have a huge impact. Manasseh's decisions from age twelve on led to the ruin of an entire country.

You're probably not a king, but like Manasseh, you do have power. Every day you can choose to glorify God and show his love to others, or you can lead your family, friends, and teammates away from him. Which will you pick?

Prayer

At my age, God, it seems like nothing I do makes a difference. But I know that's untrue. Help me remember that my choices matter.

No Comparisons

We won't dare compare ourselves with those who think so much of themselves. But they are foolish to compare themselves with themselves.

(2 CORINTHIANS 10:12, CEV)

Can you think of a time when you compared your looks to a friend or a sibling? We grow up comparing everything: appearance, grades, athletics, and other talents. But God says such comparisons are foolish.

Why is it foolish to compare yourself with others? Because you are incomparable! So is everyone else. God made each of us "one of a kind." Besides, comparing leads to pride or jealousy. You can always find someone you think you're better than—this is called pride. And you will always find people who you think are doing better than you—an easy setup for envy. It doesn't matter who's better off. It matters that you are doing what God created you to do. Are you making the most of what you've been given?

God doesn't judge you for talents you don't have or for opportunities you didn't get. He evaluates your faithfulness by how you lived with what he gave you. So are you going to break the habit of comparing yourself to others?

Prayer

God, you made me wonderfully unique, and you made everyone else wonderfully unique! Help me appreciate other people's strengths without comparing myself to them.

Walk the Talk

You, then, who teach others, do you not teach yourself? You who preach against stealing, do you steal?

(ROMANS 2:21)

If your neighbor talked on and on about the cool new pair of shoes she got but you never saw her wear them, at some point, you'd say, "Show me the fabulous shoes!" Come to find out, her mom owns the shoes, but your friend has no idea how to walk in platform heels—plus, her mom won't let her! She talked big but had no walk.

Talk the talk or walk the walk? Which one do you do? Claiming you are a follower of Jesus is easy. Following what Jesus taught takes a lot more. God wants his daughters and sons to put feet to their faith. He wants you to practice what you believe. If you only have the talk, your actions will show the truth.

For instance, if you cheat or lie but say you believe the Bible's command about honesty, it won't take long before someone notices the difference. God wants you to be a kid who hears his Word and lives by it. Start walking around with his help; soon enough your steps will show exactly whose talk you believe.

Prayer

Lord, I don't want to pretend to know you. I want to live according to your ways so that everyone knows it.

Unlikely Missionary

Then he said: "The God of our ancestors has chosen you to know his will and to see the Righteous One and to hear words from his mouth. You will be his witness to all people of what you have seen and heard."

(ACTS 22:14–15)

Talk about a change of heart. Paul's conversion to Christ is mind-boggling—from a Christian hater to a Christian hero. Paul used to hunt down Christians to put them in jail or kill them. Then Paul becomes the one person hunted down by Jesus himself. Jesus tells Paul that he has been chosen to know God's will and to see and hear him.

But Paul wasn't the only one Jesus chose. Jesus has chosen all of us to know and experience the very same thing. By reading the Bible, we have access to God's words, and we get to know his Son too.

The other important message Jesus shares with Paul is that he will be a witness to others of how God has changed his life. What an important assignment—telling others about his meeting with God. Paul did that very thing. He traveled for hundreds of miles and many years sharing God's story of salvation from his own experience.

The Lord has given us the same assignment. We are his witnesses too. We simply tell what we have experienced and learned about God. Then God takes it from there.

Prayer

Lord, thanks for choosing me to know your will and to let others in on your plans for the world. It's exciting to be your ambassador.

Right Compassion

*This is why I weep and my eyes overflow with tears.
No one is near to comfort me, no one to restore my
spirit. My children are destitute because the enemy
has prevailed . . . Streams of tears flow from my eyes,
for your law is not obeyed.*

(LAMENTATIONS 1:16; PSALM 119:136)

Jeremiah knew what was coming: God's judgment was going to destroy Israel, because they kept spitting in his face with their sin. At times Jeremiah was angry and frustrated. But mostly he was sad. He was sad that his people weren't following God's rules. He knew it was going to turn very bad in the end.

As you grow in God, you learn right from wrong and what pleases him. The tricky thing is letting love and grace grow with you. As you get better at recognizing truth and living right, self-righteousness wants to step in. Self-righteousness is a haughty attitude about doing good. It's an I'm-better-than-you view of others. It sees doing right as the ultimate goal rather than loving God and others.

Jeremiah was alone in doing right. He was a solo God-follower. But instead of being proud about it, it made him very sad. He saw people hurting themselves and their country. He watched them destroy all the goodness God had given them. It broke his heart. While he did pass along judgments from God, Jeremiah just wanted his people to stop ruining their lives, because he loved them like God loved them.

Prayer

God, it's easy to judge others when they do something wrong or mess up. Sometimes it doesn't make me sad. Instead, I feel good about myself. I need you to give me love and grace for others so I don't get too full of my right living.

Messengers Needed

Your vine is cut down, it is burned with fire; at your rebuke your people perish . . . Revive us, and we will call on your name.

(PSALM 80:16, 18)

The Israelites were God's chosen people, but that doesn't mean they were his favorites. Instead, Israel served as an object lesson to show God's love and salvation plan for mankind. But they didn't always obey God. Nope! Israel was filled with normal people who made mistakes, including turning away from the Lord and his ways.

The writer Asaph recounted this back-and-forth history in Psalm 80. First, God freed his people from the Egyptians and brought them into Canaan, the Promised Land. When they trusted God and obeyed his laws, they were strong and powerful. When they decided to ditch God, he let them face the consequences.

But Asaph had hope. He knew that no matter how many times people stray, if they ask for forgiveness, God will gladly grant it. Instead of detesting his cranky and rebellious children, God loves every country and all the people in them.

No matter where you live, your nation needs God—just like Israel did. You can be a messenger of God's truth. How? By praying over your country and its leaders, building your own relationship with Jesus, and showing God's love.

Prayer

God, like Israel, my country sometimes ditches you. Please forgive us. Let me be someone who is true to your ways and shows others who you are.

Timeless

This is the interpretation, Your Majesty, and this is the decree the Most High has issued against my lord the king: You will be driven away from people and will live with the wild animals; you will eat grass like the ox and be drenched with the dew of heaven.

(DANIEL 4:24–25A)

There once was this king who had a crazy dream, so he called in the dream interpreter. The dream interpreter told the king exactly what the dream meant—and it wasn't good news. Would you want to be the one telling bad news to a king?

Daniel did. He was so wise that even telling the harsh truth wasn't a risk for him. He carefully delivered the truth so that even the king wouldn't get upset. Basically Daniel said, "This may be bad news, but I can give you good advice that will help you continue to prosper" (see Daniel 4:27). That doesn't sound so bad.

Often we want to shy away from telling the truth about tough topics such as the idea that sin separates us from God or that God's Son Jesus Christ is the only way to Heaven or that there is right and wrong. But God's wisdom—the kind that he gave Daniel—will help us deliver the truth in the right way at the right time. Why not use Daniel's words when the time comes?

Prayer

God, I need your wisdom to speak truth and to speak it well. I don't know if I am bold enough to do that. You'll have to speak through me like you did with Daniel.

The Tenth Commandment

I observed that the basic motive for success is the driving force of envy and jealousy! But this, too, is foolishness, chasing the wind.

(ECCLESIASTES 4:4, TLB)

Every time you wish you were someone else, have what they have, or do what they do, it's like you're saying, "God, you made a huge mistake with me! You could have done better. You could have made me like that person, but you didn't! Why did you mess up with me? If I were God, I would have made me more like that person!"

Jealousy is an insult to God. It's actually a form of spiritual rebellion based on ignorance and pride. It assumes that you have a better plan for your life than your Creator does. Do you really believe that?

Jealousy is such a destructive attitude that God outlawed it in the Ten Commandments: "You shall not covet." Coveting is another word for jealousy or envy. God absolutely prohibits us from envying what others have, how they look, what they accomplish, and who they are, because he knows the damage envy does. When you notice envy creeping into your heart, turn your mind toward God's goodness and love. He knows what's best for you.

Prayer

God, you love me so much. You made me exactly the way you want me to be. The next time I get jealous, help me focus on that instead of the things I don't have.

Divine Courage

We had previously suffered and been treated outrageously in Philippi, as you know, but with the help of our God we dared to tell you his gospel in the face of strong opposition.

(1 THESSALONIANS 2:2)

Talking about Jesus can be tough. Friends look at us funny. Teachers think we're silly. Paul knew all about that. But people didn't just look at him funny; they also tortured Paul. Put him in prison. Starved him.

Yet Paul still dared to continue sharing God's message. Paul was scared. He was worried about what might happen. But with God's help, he was determined to tell the people about Jesus.

It's okay if you're nervous about telling friends about Jesus. It's okay if you get scared to share your faith. Being scared or nervous isn't wrong. Paul felt those things too. He asked God for help, and God gave him courage. And sometimes God told him it was time to leave. God will give you courage too and show you when the time is right.

Ask God to help you talk about Jesus. Ask him for just the right words. And when the time comes, you'll know. You'll be brave and bold.

Dare to tell.

Prayer

Lord, I want to talk about you. I want my friends, my teachers, and my family to know you. Help me to be strong and courageous.

No Sides

I am obligated both to Greeks and non-Greeks, both to the wise and the foolish. That is why I am so eager to preach the gospel also to you who are in Rome.

(ROMANS 1:14–15)

When you are out and about, who is nicest to you? Who gives you the evil eye or insults you? Do you ever treat others that way? Maybe the smart kid makes you angry, so you spin on your heel away from her every time she passes by. Maybe you are jealous of the rich guy, so you never ask him to join your team (even though he is nice enough). It's easy to pick sides and hang out only with people who are like us or make us feel good.

For a long time, the missionary Paul was so against certain people that he did everything he could to hurt and kill them. But when Paul met Jesus Christ, Paul changed. (He even changed his name, which was a good move, since he had such a bad reputation!) Paul started loving everyone. He was so excited about God that he wanted to talk with everyone and break down all the barriers. Who cared if the Gentiles and Jews weren't supposed to mix! Paul was going to do it anyway. He saw himself as a servant of God with a message for everyone.

Could you be like Paul? With God's help, you can. Picking sides doesn't matter much when you see people in need of God. You'll want everyone to hear about what's most important: God's love with no barriers.

Prayer

Lord, I just don't get some people. They are too different or strange. But you love them, and so should I. Forgive me for choosing sides and leaving people out.

To Speak or Not to Speak?

*Some of the Jews were persuaded and joined Paul
and Silas, as did a large number of God-fearing
Greeks and quite a few prominent women. But other
Jews were jealous; so they rounded up some bad
characters from the marketplace, formed a mob and
started a riot in the city.*

(ACTS 17:4–5A)

Do you speak your mind or hold your tongue? Jump in with your opinion or wait to see what others say? When it comes to faith, church, and God, talking about them may not seem easy. If you are bold, you'll have no problem telling others what you believe. But you may get upset when you aren't able to win others to your side. If you are shy, you won't let out a peep unless someone really wants to know about your faith. Neither way is right or wrong.

Paul, the bold guy who followed Christ, demonstrated that either way, you'll always see a variety of responses. He was unafraid to talk about his faith, but he also knew when it was time to shut his mouth. He knew he wasn't the one who would convince others about God. God would have to do work in their hearts. And if Paul's boldness or quietness helped, then he was ready to do his part, silently or loudly.

Prayer

Lord, you are amazing and worth talking about, but it's not always easy to share you with others. Please give me boldness when I need it and silence when it's not the right time to speak.

Okay with You

Daniel replied, "No wise man, enchanter, magician or diviner can explain to the king the mystery he has asked about, but there is a God in heaven who reveals mysteries."

(DANIEL 2:27–28A)

Scientists can help us understand a lot. They have the knowledge (and means) to explain why nature behaves the way it does. But they can't explain everything. For example, the exact beginning of the universe baffles them. They can only guess. Some things remain a mystery, and only God can explain such things (if he wants to).

That's exactly what Daniel was attempting to tell the king. Although Daniel had a reputation for being able to interpret dreams, he was quick to credit the Lord for his ability. He knew he was only an average guy and didn't want to steal God's glory.

It's easy to be intimidated by those who are smarter than you. When you compare yourself to others, you will always find someone who is more capable. But the comparison game is pointless. A smarter use of time is to thank God for the gifts you have and express gratitude that he knows more than the person with the highest IQ.

Don't put yourself down. Instead, look up!

Prayer

Lord, I may not know a lot about some things, but I know this much: you know it all, and you know me. Thank you.

Who Are You Watching?

Envy can eat you up.

(PROVERBS 14:30B, CEV)

How often do you notice what other kids have or wear? We are fascinated with how others look, act, talk, and live. There is nothing wrong with this. God wired us to be interested in others. But here's a caution: noticing others becomes a problem if you start envying what they have.

Since technology allows us to see how everyone else is living all the time, envy may be the most common reason people miss God's unique plan for their lives. Envy is a trap. You will find it in every age group and ethnic group around the world.

"Why does she get to live in that house?"

"Why did he get that award?"

"Why can't I be that attractive, that smart, or that famous?"

Envy distracts you, because all you can see is what you don't have. Envy sidetracks you from God's unique plan for you. You can miss your purpose and lose your joy at the same time. Instead, focus on what you do have. Thank God for the limitless variety of people he chose to create instead of making all of us exactly alike.

Prayer

God, I admit that I get jealous sometimes. Teach me how to love those people instead of envy them. Help me to be grateful for all the good things you have put in my life.

Spill It

Now there were some Greeks among those who went up to worship at the festival. They came to Philip, who was from Bethsaida in Galilee, with a request. "Sir," they said, "we would like to see Jesus."

(JOHN 12:20–21)

Greece is a long way from Israel. But the Greeks mentioned in John 12 had made the lengthy trip to be at a Jewish festival in Jerusalem. They were curious enough about what the Jews believed about God to go to their festival. So it's safe to assume they were spiritually thirsty. Somehow they had heard about Jesus. When they found out that Philip knew Jesus personally, they asked him if he could arrange for them to meet Jesus.

If you are serious about your relationship with Jesus, it probably isn't a secret. It is quite possible that kids at your school know you go to church on Sundays and to youth group. That's a good thing! If they ask you to introduce them to Jesus, well, that's an even better thing.

With that in mind, start thinking about what you would say to someone who asks you about the Lord. You could start with something simple. Maybe you could invite that person to church.

Philip went to his friend Andrew because Philip wasn't quite sure what to say to the Greeks. Start asking the Lord to make some of your classmates curious about your faith and for wisdom about where you should go for answers you don't know.

Prayer

Jesus, I am serious about you, but I don't always know what to say about my faith or who you are. Please give me the right words at the right time.

He Sees It All

Seated in a window was a young man named Eutychus, who was sinking into a deep sleep as Paul talked on and on. When he was sound asleep, he fell to the ground from the third story and was picked up dead. Paul went down, threw himself on the young man and put his arms around him. "Don't be alarmed," he said. "He's alive!"

(ACTS 20:9–10)

Eutychus, a young man from a coastal town called Troas, was listening to Paul preach. But he started getting drowsy. As Paul kept talking, Eutychus felt sleepier and sleepier. Finally, around midnight, Eutychus completely fell asleep.

He hadn't picked the best snoozing spot, though—a third-story window ledge. Poor Eutychus fell out the window to his death. Paul the Killer Preacher ran downstairs, put his arms around Eutychus' dead body, and brought him back to life with God's power!

As our Creator, God intimately knows our bodies. He knows how many calories we need, how much water we should drink, and how many hours of sleep our brains require. So when Eutychus fell asleep—doing what he was designed to do—God wasn't angry.

Instead, the Lord looked at Eutychus' heart. He saw the way the young man listened to Paul talking about Jesus and how he stayed even when he could have gone home.

Prayer

God, when I am tempted to "prove" my Christianity to others, stop me. I don't want to rack up points with others—I want you to be my best friend.

Joy Forever

I tell you, there is rejoicing in the presence of the angels of God over one sinner who repents.

(LUKE 15:10)

Many Christians will say, "I've lost my joy." But when you ask them, "When was the last time you told someone about Jesus Christ?" they usually answer, "A long time ago." Joy comes from developing an attitude of gratitude and sharing our knowledge of the Good News. Your greatest joy will come when you commit your life to Christ, and your second greatest joy will be to introduce others to him.

Imagine the scene in Heaven: someone you told about Jesus comes over to you and says, "I want to thank you. I am here because you cared enough to share Jesus with me." Now that will be a reason for joy. But that joy begins here on Earth when you bring others into the family of God.

The apostle Paul said, "My heart's desire and my prayer to God for them is for their salvation" (Romans 10:1, NASB). Ask God to give you a burden like that. It will lead to true joy.

Prayer

Jesus, I admit that I don't always feel like talking to other kids about you. Give me a heart full of love for those who have not yet found you.

Missionary Mindset

I have become all things to all people so that by all possible means I might save some.

(1 CORINTHIANS 9:22B)

Imagine going to a remote part of the world as a missionary. The people who live in that far-away nation speak a different language. They also eat food that is unfamiliar to you. Chances are the clothes they wear are unlike yours. What they do for fun is quite different than what you are used to doing.

That's what Paul discovered as he traveled far from Jerusalem. Although he was Jewish, God had called Paul to be a missionary to non-Jews in places where life seemed strange. But Paul was quick to understand an important but simple truth: if he was going to tell people about Jesus, he needed to explain the Good News in ways foreign people would understand. He needed to dress like them and show an interest in things they were interested in. Even though such "ways" weren't really natural for him, he became like them in order to win them to God.

God calls every one of his followers to be a missionary to some degree, such as in your neighborhood and school. Most likely, the people he wants you to befriend speak your language. But they have interests and hobbies that are different than yours. Spend time with them to learn how to become part of their world. Then you can invite them into your world to see how Jesus is part of it.

Prayer

Lord, it's scary and exciting to think of myself as a missionary like Paul in the Bible. How can I be a good one to my friends and neighbors?

Keeping God in the Neighborhood

Son of man, if a country sins against me by being unfaithful and I stretch out my hand against it to cut off its food supply and send famine upon it and kill its people and their animals, even if these three men— Noah, Daniel and Job—were in it, they could save only themselves by their righteousness, declares the Sovereign Lord.

(EZEKIEL 14:13–14)

Noah, Daniel, and Job—three of the most godly men ever. Two of them have books named after them in the Bible. All three of them were godly examples back then and today. God says they were righteous—that means they lived right—and God was impressed.

So if these guys prayed on your behalf or asked God to spare your life, you can bet that God would consider their request. But this time in Ezekiel, God said not even the most godly, righteous people could save Israel from destruction. Because there were none! The Israelites had become extremely evil and anti-God.

Our country needs right-living people. Our example of living a good and godly life keeps God present in our neighborhoods. Our words can point others to his love and grace. As long as there are righteous people, God will hear our prayers and continue to offer his grace to the ungodly around us.

Prayer

Lord, may I be a light to people around me. Let them see your love and goodness through me.

Poisonous Thoughts

*As they danced, they sang: "Saul has slain his
thousands, and David his tens of thousands." Saul
was very angry; this refrain displeased him greatly.
"They have credited David with tens of thousands,"
he thought, "but me with only thousands. What more
can he get but the kingdom?"*

(1 SAMUEL 18:7–8)

Everyone cheers when a player hits a home run or scores a
goal. But you boo or moan when a player's fly ball gets caught or
a shooter misses the net. Even if two players hit the same ball the
same distance, no one cheers for the player who is tagged out.

Have you ever been the player who strikes out? It's not much
fun when no one cheers for you. King Saul was a strong fighter
and soldier, but he sure didn't like it when David did better than
he did. Jealousy killed the friendship between Saul and David—
literally. Saul actually tried to kill David several times because
Saul was so jealous of him.

It seems a common thing for girls and boys to get jealous
of other kids. Do you find yourself stewing over someone else's
victory? Do you find it difficult to be happy for friends who do
better than you? Watch out for the poison of jealousy. It ruins
teams and ends friendships.

Prayer

Lord, it's hard when others do better than I do, especially if I
was at the top. Will you help me rejoice with my teammates and
friends and truly be happy when they do well?

Kind Example

Isaac was forty years old when he married Rebekah daughter of Bethuel the Aramean from Paddan Aram and sister of Laban the Aramean.

(GENESIS 25:20)

Rebekah was a brave woman. She helped strangers. She agreed to marry a man she'd never met. She moved away from home when she was young. That took guts! She was generous, sharing what she had with others who needed help. She was hospitable, inviting visitors from long trips to her home and feeding them and their animals. She was gracious and acted properly when she first met Isaac, who would become her husband. After they married, they didn't stay in one town, so she had to be comfortable packing up and moving a lot.

Rebekah is an example of someone who trusted God and treated others kindly. You can be that kind of person too. It doesn't matter what your personality is or where you live. When you treat others with kindness, other kids will want to be around you. Behaving well and being hospitable sends a message that you think other people are important and you notice them— which is how God sees them. When you are known as kind, you actually show what God is like. That's the kind of kid God blesses for honoring him.

Prayer

God, what kind of person do you want me to be? How can I treat others better and show them your love?

Don't Give Up on the Bad Guys

Have you noticed how Ahab has humbled himself before me? Because he has humbled himself, I will not bring this disaster in his day, but I will bring it on his house in the days of his son.

(1 KINGS 21:29)

As king and queen of Samaria, Ahab and Jezebel were spoiled rotten. So when Ahab saw a vineyard close to his palace, he wanted it. One problem: the vineyard owner, Naboth, said "no." Eventually, with Ahab's approval, Queen Jezebel had Naboth stoned to death.

It was just one more episode of "The Sinful Life of King Ahab." In fact, the Bible says, "There was never anyone like Ahab, who sold himself to do evil in the eyes of the LORD," and that he constantly behaved in the most terrible way (1 Kings 21:25, 26). So when the evil king actually listened to the prophet Elijah's warning to shape up or ship out, it must have been pretty shocking!

We all know girls and boys like Ahab; they hurt others, take what's not theirs, and then brag about their meanness. Often these people have intimidated others for years, so we think they will never change.

But as Ahab demonstrated, they can. Like Elijah, we don't have to be their best friend, but we can help steer them toward God through our prayers, words, and actions. Don't give up on the Ahabs and Jezebels in your life.

Prayer

God, I wish the mean kids in my life would just disappear. But you created those kids and want them to become part of your family, just like I am. Help me guide them to you with my prayers, words, and behaviors.

Squashing Prejudice

He did not discriminate between us and them, for he purified their hearts by faith.

(ACTS 15:9)

Are you prejudiced? If you never think twice about the color of someone's skin, great! But treating people differently because of their skin color is not the only way to be prejudiced. Feeling like you are better than others is also a form of prejudice. You may think that neighbor kid who is homeschooled doesn't measure up to your Bible quiz skills. Or you can't believe how the family down the block dresses for church. It's easy to treat that individual or group as an outcast—even at church.

That's what was going on in the early Church. Paul had been sharing about Jesus with non-Jewish people all over the place. Amazingly, they were accepting Jesus as their Savior. But the Jewish Christians weren't so happy. They had a problem seeing the Gentiles as equal to themselves. As far as the Jewish believers were concerned, non-Jews were second-class citizens in the Kingdom of God. That kind of thinking drove Paul crazy.

The kid who goes to a Korean church probably doesn't worship exactly the way you do. But if he has asked Jesus into his heart by faith, he is part of the family of God. Your job is to treat him with respect and friendliness. After all, in the family of God, he is your brother.

Prayer

Lord, I'm guilty of thinking I'm better than those who don't think the way I do. I'm sorry. Help me to be a friend to everyone who is your friend.

Envy Rots the Bones

A heart at peace gives life to the body, but envy rots the bones.

(PROVERBS 14:30)

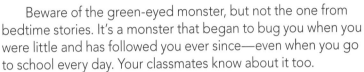

Beware of the green-eyed monster, but not the one from bedtime stories. It's a monster that began to bug you when you were little and has followed you ever since—even when you go to school every day. Your classmates know about it too.

Do you know its name? Give up? The green-eyed monster is envy. Envy is a monster because it can eat you up from the inside out. Envy convinces you that if you have what someone else has, you'll be happier than you are now. That other person's smart phone. The neighbor's TV. A classmate's swimming pool. If only you had _____ (fill in the blank) . . .

The truth is simple: the happiest people are those who are content with what they have. The Bible uses the phrase "a heart at peace." Peace happens when you lock out envy. As long you are jealous of another person's possessions, the monster will "rot your bones" and make you really miserable. Shut the door on the green-eyed monster by thanking the Lord for what he's given you.

Prayer

Lord, I reluctantly admit it: I'm guilty of envy. Help me defeat this monster so that I can be at peace inside.

DAY 355

Oops, Did I Think That?

There is neither Jew nor Gentile, neither slave nor free, nor is there male and female, for you are all one in Christ Jesus.

(GALATIANS 3:28)

When Jesus was a little boy growing up in Nazareth, the men in town prayed a prayer that went like this: "Lord, I thank you that you didn't create me a Gentile, a dog, or a woman." Can you imagine being a girl back then? You and the family pet would have received equal treatment. Most men were not that nice toward women, and some unfortunate individuals were slaves—that's just the way they did things.

But when Jesus died on the cross and then defeated death, he redefined the rules. Even though Jewish society still followed the old way, in the Church things were different. Jews and non-Jews were viewed as equal. So were men and women. Slaves and masters were on level ground before God. Long before Abraham Lincoln set American slaves free, Jesus offered freedom to everyone.

Although God views people as equal, we don't always act as though it's true. This happened in the Old Testament, and it still happens today. Kids who are different at school are still made fun of. Kids with special needs aren't always treated with the same respect as gifted ones. Neither are those from different cultures. Will you spread freedom and respect by helping Galatians 3:28 become a reality where you live?

Prayer

Lord, please forgive me for acting as though I'm better than others. I want you to use me to make changes for the better in my school.

Tuning In

To answer before listening—that is folly and shame.
(PROVERBS 18:13)

What's the most important thing a surgeon should know before entering the operating room? What body part he's operating on! Can you imagine if he wasn't paying attention to the nurse's instructions? He might amputate the wrong leg or remove tonsils instead of an appendix.

Or consider a soldier. Before he heads into battle, his commanders deliver strict instructions about the enemy and battlefield. But if the private interrupts, "Nope, I got this!" as he guns onto the battlefield, he might only know half the story, like that the war ended yesterday.

Listening is obviously important when you're a doctor or soldier. But what about the rest of us?

When we dominate conversations, always chiming in with our opinion, we're telling the other person they're not worth listening to. Of course, some people are shy and quiet, while others have a more outgoing, talkative personality. That's okay. But you should be just as eager to hear what your friend has to say as you are to talk.

We're meant to listen more than we speak. Otherwise, we become arrogant know-it-alls. When we treat people respectfully—looking them in the eye, smiling, and paying attention—we reflect Jesus. After all, doesn't he listen to us?

Prayer

Lord, may my words be wise, encouraging, and bring you praise. Teach me to listen to others like you listen to me.

Take Care

If you see your fellow Israelite's ox or sheep straying, do not ignore it but be sure to take it back to its owner . . . Do the same if you find their donkey or cloak or anything else they have lost. Do not ignore it.

(DEUTERONOMY 22:1, 3)

You're at the park when you find a smart phone. You know you should locate its owner or give it to an adult before someone steals it, but you're late to play basketball. "Oh well," you think, walking away. "It's the owner's fault for leaving such a sweet phone!"

The Israelites dealt with something similar. No, they didn't have cell phones or GPS (just think of how much time they could have saved in the desert if they had!). Back then, people didn't have cash like we do; they had animals. So when a cow roamed too far, the owner lost money and maybe his ability to feed his family. That's why God commanded his children to take care of each other's stuff and return lost items.

That lesson is just as relevant today. Something as simple as helping people when they lose things (or animals!) demonstrates an unselfish, Christ-like attitude. So when you find money on the ground in a store, a lost phone, or a missing game, turn it in or try to return it. After all, if you lost something, what would you want the finder to do?

Prayer

Sometimes doing the right thing takes time, God. I don't always feel like doing it. Please give me a caring, selfless attitude like yours and the desire to treat others how I want to be treated.

The Golden Rule

"Love your neighbor as yourself." Love does no harm to a neighbor. Therefore love is the fulfillment of the law.

(ROMANS 13:9B–10)

Gold is beautiful and very valuable. Who wouldn't want something made of real gold? The Golden Rule is also valuable, like gold: do unto others what you want them to do to you. That's the kind of gold God likes. He wants you to treat others the way you want to be treated. The reason is pretty clear: everybody matters to the Lord. He loves them as much as he loves you.

Here's a little assignment for today that we'll call "mining for gold." Write down five things you would love for your friends or family to do for you. Surprise you with a trip to get ice cream, perhaps. Send a link to a song they think you'll like. Maybe ask you to go to the movies for the afternoon. Then come up with your own list. Use it as a reminder for practicing the "golden rule," and do those things for others.

Prayer

Lord, I want to look for gold today. I want to treat others the way I like being treated. Will you help me?

Christ Will Return

Then the angel took the censer, filled it with fire from the altar, and hurled it on the earth; and there came peals of thunder, rumblings, flashes of lightning and an earthquake.

(REVELATION 8:5)

"I would have died from embarrassment," your older sister says about finding a piece of egg stuck in her hair before she got school. You wouldn't call 9–1–1 thinking she's going to die. It's just an expression of how awful she would feel.

Many things in the book of Revelation are expressions or illustrations of things that will happen when Jesus comes back to Earth. The prophecies include many images that seem scary or frightening. The man writing about them had never seen these things before, so he described them with words and pictures that would make sense to the people who would read his book. When John saw fire or beasts or blood, we don't know exactly what he was describing, such as which words were literal and which ones were expressions.

Though we may not be able to interpret all that John saw in Revelation, when Christ comes again, it will be a glorious day for all people who follow God's ways. And it will be judgment time for those who reject God. Either way, these prophecies are not meant to scare us but to help us understand how important it is to tell others about Jesus Christ.

Prayer

God, I don't think I can understand a lot of what's in Revelation, but I don't want to be scared of the end of the world. What I do understand is that you will come back to take me and all believers to Heaven with you. Thank you for that promise.

Change the World

Speak up for those who cannot speak for themselves, for the rights of all who are destitute. Speak up and judge fairly; defend the rights of the poor and needy.

(PROVERBS 31:8–9)

Unselfishness + godly wisdom = unstoppable world changer.

Yep, you read that right. So just stop being selfish, get the mind of God, and you will change the world. Easy, right?

Okay, so the selfishness thing might not be so simple. After all, what kid likes sharing toys, food, clothes, or a room? But here's a trick: think about how possessive you are of your things. Now, funnel that same reaction into passion for those who don't have many things of their own. Get possessive for them. They deserve to be cared for.

Now, onto the godly wisdom part. God says he gives wisdom generously—lots and lots—to anyone who asks (James 1:5). So start asking. Then ask for help from your parents or church teachers to study the books of wisdom: Job, Proverbs, and Ecclesiastes. They will give you tips on how to defend and speak up for others in a way that persuades people to help them.

You know how to start. Now get on your way to changing the world for God.

Prayer

Lord, am I really capable of being a world-changer for you? It seems like such a big job. I am willing and ready, though, if you want to use me.

Eternal Records

You yourselves are our letter, written on our hearts, known and read by everyone. You show that you are a letter from Christ, the result of our ministry, written not with ink but with the Spirit of the living God, not on tablets of stone but on tablets of human hearts.

(2 CORINTHIANS 3:2–3)

Sports and statistics go together like peanut butter and jelly. Thanks to behind-the-scenes stats keepers, we know that Mia Hamm scored 158 international goals—more than any other player, male or female, in the history of US soccer. Wayne Gretsky, NHL's "The Great One," has been the only hockey player to score more than two hundred points in one season. And Babe Ruth slugged 714 home runs over his nearly twenty-one-year baseball career.

Whenever professional athletes play, their every movement goes into the record books. But did you know that Christ-followers have their own set of "statistics" and "record books"?

You can't see these numbers inscribed on a trophy or displayed on a website. Instead of physical data, Christians have people. When we live to glorify God, people notice. They see that we are different in a good way.

Of course, Christianity isn't a contest; it's not about how many people we take to church or witness to. But the lives we touch are far more lasting than a set of sports figures. People who we introduce to Jesus are eternal, while records are temporary.

Prayer

Lord, sometimes I forget that leading others to you should be my top goal. Will you help write my life "not with ink but with the Spirit of the living God"?

Nobody's Perfect

*Asa did what was right in the eyes of the LORD,
as his father David had done . . . Although he did
not remove the high places, Asa's heart was fully
committed to the LORD all his life.*

(1 KINGS 15:11, 14)

If there were a "World's Greatest Christian" contest, there are a few people who might take the top spot. Some of them are missionaries, others are preachers, and still others are everyday people in our communities who minister to others selflessly.

Obviously, there is no "Best Christian" contest—although you wouldn't know it by the stuck-up way some churchgoers act. We all sin—even the most honored saint! Yet imperfect people please our perfect God.

Take King Asa. He was dedicated to God all his life. Yet he wasn't perfect; he never destroyed areas where people worshipped and sacrificed to false gods. So how could God still be happy with Asa? Isn't he happy only when you do things right and don't sin?

The Lord knows you inside and out, and he knows that you are sinful. He knows you cannot be perfect. He doesn't hate (or even dislike) you when you blow it. Love doesn't end when you make mistakes.

Of course, it breaks God's heart when you disobey his commands, but like King Asa, you can still be known as a girl or guy after God's own heart. Make that your goal. Perfection is never possible anyway.

Prayer

Lord, I'm glad serving you doesn't require perfection, because I would fail! Help me be "fully committed" to you like Asa, focusing on our relationship instead of keeping track of my sins.

Thankful for Good News

Let the redeemed of the LORD tell their story—those he redeemed from the hand of the foe, those he gathered from the lands, from east and west, from north and south.

(PSALM 107:2–3)

Getting a new baby brother or sister, going on a trip, earning an A, enjoying a birthday party—most kids would agree these things are good news. They make you happy or excited. Good news, no matter how small, is what's worth sharing. You don't want to keep it to yourself. What fun would that be?

In many psalms, the writers urged people to announce good news. That's quite different from the approach of newscasters today. They usually report on all the bad things happening in the world—shootings, tsunamis, fires. So it's easy to focus on all the negatives.

Follow the example of the psalmists. The Israelites had a lot to tell about everything God had done for them, like saving them from enemies, delivering them from slavery, providing rain for food, and blessing their families with health. "Pass it on!" they encouraged. "Let others know about the goodness of God."

Brighten the world with some of the positives in your life. What good news can you pass on today?

Prayer

Lord, there are so many good things in my life, but it's easy to focus on the negative stuff. Thank you for all the wonderful blessings you've given me. Help me to share them with others today and every day.

Focus on the Giver

*This is what the LORD says: "Let not the wise boast
of their wisdom or the strong boast of their strength
or the rich boast of their riches, but let the one
who boasts boast about this: that they have the
understanding to know me, that I am the LORD."*

(JEREMIAH 9:23–24A)

Who do you admire? An amazing guitarist? A speed skater?
An actor who does all kinds of stunts? A highly decorated military officer? A genius computer game developer?

We admire people who have wonderful talents from the
Lord and who use them in wonderful ways, like their smarts,
musical talent, speed, or money. No one can deny that the
best of the best are enviable when they use their gifts for the
glory of God.

Everyone admires special gifts and skills. But those things
don't belong to the person who possesses them. God is the
owner and grantor of talents, skills, and abilities. He gives differently to each person for his own purposes.

Instead of being in awe of the person you admire, let it be
a reminder of how amazing God is. Rather than focusing on
the person, focus on God's gift to them. Others will probably
admire you some day for something wonderful you do. When
you receive praise, remember that your talent is a gift from God.
Point others to him, and thank him for what he's given you.

Prayer

Lord, thank you that you've given special skills that will help or
benefit others now or in the future. Remind me of your gifts and
to point others to you.

Shout It Out!

Praise God in his sanctuary; praise him in his mighty heavens.

(PSALM 150:1B)

You've learned about God's awesome power. You've read about his amazing love. You know of his victorious justice. The Bible has told you how he saves the sick, the dying, and the hurting. He protects his children. He provided his own son, Jesus Christ, to die for your sins. And he wants you to live with him in paradise.

That's worth singing about.

That's worth shouting about.

If you are poetic or creative, write a song about God. If you like lists, jot down some of the details about God that you've learned from reading this book.

Thank him for the goodness in your life and even for the things you don't understand. Put your trust in him to direct you all your days. No one will care for you like God will. He is the almighty Creator who made you and loves you forever. Praise him!

Prayer

God, I praise you for your wonderful creations, marvelous love, and awesome power. Thank you for bringing me into your family.

Why So Many Translations?

This book contains more than 350 quotations from the Scripture. I have intentionally varied the Bible translations used for two important reasons. First, no matter how wonderful a translation is, it has limitations. The Bible was originally written using 11,280 Hebrew, Aramaic, and Greek words, but the typical English translation uses only around 6,000 words. It is always helpful to compare translations of the Bible since nuances and shades of meaning of different words and phrases can be easily missed.

Second, and even more important, is the fact that we often miss the full impact or meaning of familiar Bible verses, not because of poor translating, but simply because they become so familiar! We think we know the message of a verse because we have read or heard it so many times. Then we find it quoted in a book, we skim over it, and miss the full meaning. Therefore, I have occasionally used paraphrases on purpose, in order to help you see God's truth in new, fresh ways. English-speaking people should thank God that we have so many different versions of the Bible to use when reading Scripture and devotions.

Also, since the verse divisions and numbers were not included in the Bible until 1560 AD, I haven't always quoted entire verses in a devotion, but rather focused on the phrase that was most appropriate for the message. I got this idea right from Jesus and how he and the apostles quoted the Old Testament. They often simply quoted a phrase to make a point while teaching.

CEV *Contemporary English Version* (New York: American Bible Society, 1995)

ESV *English Standard Version* (Carol Stream, IL: Crossway, 2001)

MSG *The Message* (Colorado Springs: NavPress, 2002)

NASB *New American Standard Bible* (La Habra, CA: The Lockman Foundation, 1995)

NCV *New Century Version* (Nashville, TN: Thomas Nelson, 2005)

NIV *New International Version* (Colorado Springs: Biblica, Inc.®, 2011)

NLT *New Living Translation* (Carol Stream, IL: Tyndale House Foundation, 2013)

TEV *Today's English Version* (New York: American Bible Society, 1992)

TLB *The Living Bible* (Carol Stream, IL: Tyndale House Foundation, 1971)

The Purpose Driven Life

What On Earth Am I Here For?

Rick Warren

Over 10 years ago, Rick Warren wrote *The Purpose Driven Life*, which became the bestselling hardback non-fiction book in history, and is the second most-translated book in the world, after the Bible. PDL has inspired and changed tens of millions of lives ... more than any modern book.

Rick has updated and expanded the book with new chapters on the greatest barriers to living your purpose, plus 42 video introductions to each chapter theme, and 42 additional audio messages that go deeper into each chapter.

Available in stores and online!